D0891544

THE DARK PEOPLE OF BOURKE

The Dark People of Bourke

A study of planned social change

MAX KAMIEN

Looking at a man with the naked eye, he is an individual. Looking at him with a microscope, he is a biological specimen. Looking at him from the long view, he becomes a unit of society, bound into its culture with bolts of steel. The doctor needs all three perspectives to do justice to his great mission.

CHASE, 1965:101

AUSTRALIAN INSTITUTE OF ABORIGINAL STUDIES CANBERRA

HUMANITIES PRESS INC.
New Jersey, U.S.A.
1978

AIAS new series no. 1

National Library of Australia card number and ISBN 0 85575 074 X (hard cover)
0 85575 080 4 (soft cover)

USA edition ISBN 0 391 00947 8 (hard cover)
0 391 00949 4 (soft cover)

Printed in Australia by The Dominion Press, Melbourne, Vic.
10.78.3000

*This book is dedicated to the late Wally Byers,
field officer and friend. He taught me much. It is
also dedicated to the Dark People of Bourke with
affection, admiration and hope.*

The late Wally Byers, photographed by Mrs Pat Cameron, in Bourke in 1976.

Foreword

Max Kamien's book speaks for itself. But since he has invited me to write a foreword I have the chance to mention one or two matters which it is not usual for most authors to emphasise.

I was privileged to witness the compilation of the data from which this book has resulted, tackled step by step during the three years that Dr Kamien was involved with the Human Ecology of the Arid Zone Project in the far west of New South Wales. Dr Kamien, as a physician and psychiatrist, systematically examined most of the major health and adjustment problems of a part-Aboriginal community within an established white community. The results will be of great value to all who need a quantitative measure of health and adjustment problems in these marginal societies. So much is obvious.

Of at least equal value with Dr Kamien's clinical activity, and this meticulous recording of the health status, was his work in primary prevention. He was concerned with the lowering of stressful situations and the augmenting of resources. The basic equation of his work is Symptoms $=$ Stresses *divided by* Resources. His intervention might change this equation by altering any of its three components.

After an initial period of testing, Dr Kamien made good friends among the *Murrie* community, and as he amusingly describes, among the *Gub* community as well. It was the way he endured this 'ordeal' that made me recognise the calibre of the man, and I am sure this will not escape the reader.

The community which evolved seemed to resolve many of its customary disagreements and suspicions, and worked together to stimulate self-help and social integration. Coteries of people formed: an advancement association, clubs of various kinds, a housing co-operative, adult education, and the like.

Dr Kamien's role as change agent was to invite this community to define its needs, and then respond as to how these needs might be realised. He wanted to be a resource person rather than a leader. Of course, it is inevitable for a medical practitioner to be cast by any community in a leadership role in certain matters, and Dr Kamien did not shrink from this.

Things happened. Changes occurred. Most of them were beneficial. Some are self-perpetuating. Others need consolidation. Still others occurred which the author neither anticipated nor would have endorsed.

Publication of this book will enable it to reach a wide reading public and I commend this timely act because, so far as Australia is concerned, the project represents a fairly radical innovation in health care.

Since many Aboriginal and part-Aboriginal communities have reached crisis proportions—and possibly worse—the model of a resident doctor as an agent of social change must be carefully considered. It is hoped that the availability of Dr Kamien's experience will bring this intervention model to the attention of other comparably stressed communities, to our administrators and to the Australian public in general.

John Cawte
(former) Director,
Human Ecology of the
Arid Zone Project,
University of New South Wales

Contents

Plates

Figures

xi

Acknowledgements

There are many people to thank for their help in carrying out the work described in this book. First and foremost is Professor John Cawte, the Director of the Human Ecology of the Arid Zone Project, who provided me with the opportunity of embarking on this project as well as introducing me to the concept of a doctor consciously acting as an agent of social change.

During the three years of this study I was supported by a research fellowship from the New South Wales Institute of Psychiatry. I am grateful to the Board of the Institute and especially to the Institute's Director, Dr Maurice Sainsbury, who recognised that the first allegiance of a change agent was to his client community.

Dr Sylvia Nobile and Miss Pam Rosevear of Vitamin Laboratories of Roche Products Pty Ltd, together with Dr Joan Woodhill, Chairman of the Division of Nutrition and Dietetics, Department of Medicine, Prince Henry Hospital Sydney and Mrs Pat Cameron helped me to collect and analyse the data on nutrition described in Chapter 4.

In Bourke, Mrs Pat Baker and Mr John Bissett, Matron and Chief Executive Officer of the Bourke District Hospital respectively, gave me personal assistance while the Board of the District Hospital made their facilities available to me.

Dr David Jones, the Chief Medical Statistician of the New South Wales Health Commission, gave me invaluable help in the design of the physical and psychological surveys and later in the processing of the collected data. Further assistance in the final processing and statistical analyses was readily given by Mr Brian Murphy and Mrs Rosalie Rendell of the Raine Unit of Medical Statistics, University of Western Australia.

The final preparation of this book was made easier by Mr Geoff Hall, who spent much time in helping me to clarify some of my more opaque and convoluted writings. Mrs Connie Mauger organised me and together with my secretary, Mrs Wendy Townsend, made the task of typing and preparing the final manuscript relatively easy.

Mr Harry Upenieks, the Director of the Department of Medical Illustrations at the University of Western Australia, processed the illustrations and photographs and Miss Wendy Millington of the Medical Library of Western Australia checked the accuracy of the references.

Mrs Shirley Andrew of the Australian Institute of Aboriginal Studies turned the typed manuscript into a book and I am grateful to her for the care and interest she displayed in this painstaking task.

Some of the material in this study has been printed previously and I gratefully acknowledge permission to reprint to the *Medical Journal of Australia*; the *Australian and New Zealand Journal of Medicine*; the *Australian Journal of Social Issues*; the *Australian and New Zealand Journal of Psychiatry*; and *Food Technology in Australia*.

I am indebted to Mr Bill Cameron, Research Secretary and Editor of the Bourke and District Historical Society, for help in locating source material and for permission to draw upon the large amount of local history he has incorporated into the five published volumes of the Society.

I should like to express a particular debt of gratitude to Mrs Pat Cameron, the Chief Medical Technologist at the Bourke District Hospital. She spent many hours of her own time in performing all of my laboratory investigations and without her help much of my baseline data could not have been collected. In addition she was a constant source of encouragement and ideas, and her own work and friendship with Aborigines and the interest of her children, Ian and Barbara, in Aboriginal affairs still contribute much to social change in the Bourke area.

Similar encouragement came from Mr Brian Ross, Vice Principal of the International Training Institute in Sydney. He helped me to explore and examine my role as a change agent and in doing so, contributed to the insights which I have expressed in Chapter 12.

Other interested whites are rarely mentioned by name in this book. Nevertheless their contribution to Aboriginal advancement in Bourke has been a major one. Mr and Mrs Trevor Buckman assisted in adult education; Reverend Don Duffy participated in the affairs of the Aboriginal Advancement Association and gave help in obtaining films on full-blood Aboriginal life; Mrs Esther Whitton, a teacher at the Bourke pre-school, was active with Aboriginal mothers. Mr John Luckens, Mr Bernie Coates, Ms Trees Westcott and Ms Julie Janson were also involved in the building programme and in a child play and acting centre. Mr Arthur Roy provided help to some Aboriginal sporting teams, as well as introducing a 'community development' approach to his job as an officer of the New South Wales Department of Child Welfare and Social Welfare (now N.S.W. Department of Youth and Community Services). Mr Stephen Joseph of the University of N.S.W. Abschol movement also helped with liaison between Bourke and Sydney, and Mr Bill Lucas, a Sydney architect, spent many hours in trying to help Aborigines to solve their housing problems. More important than all their activities, official and unofficial, was that all these people made themselves available to Aborigines.

It remains to express my indebtedness to the Aboriginal people of Bourke for their friendship and trust. Their elected field officers Mr Wally Byers and Pastor Bill Reid, provided me with help, insight, understanding and friendship which often sustained me in times of harassment.

Finally, I could not have completed this book without my wife Jacqueline's secretarial help in the preliminary typing and filing, and most of all for her continued forbearance of the daily and nightly travails that befall the wife of a doctor who also tries to be an agent of social change.

The author wishes to make the following acknowledgements for permission to use material previously printed in part elsewhere:

Chapter 3, *Medical Journal of Australia*, Special Supplement I, 1976:33-44.

Chapter 4, *Australian and New Zealand Journal of Medicine*, 1974, 4:126-37; 1975, 5:123-33; *Food Technology in Australia*, 1975, 27:93-103; *National Times*, 25 February 1974.

Chapters 5 and 6, *Medical Journal of Australia*, Special Supplement II, 1976, 6-16; 1975, 1:261-64, 291-98.

Chapter 8, *Australian Journal of Social Issues*, 1976, 11:187-200.

Chapters 9 and 11, *Medical Journal of Australia*, Special Supplement II, 1975:6-11; 1975, 1:19-21, 25-28.

Chapter 13, *Australian and New Zealand Journal of Psychiatry*, 1975, 9:15-20.

Introduction

Medical research has shown that Aborigines have by far the worst health of any section of Australian society. The ever-growing medical literature documenting this sickness and disease abounds in prescriptions for improving the situation. What is lacking are well documented exploratory programmes which have tested the reality or the distance from reality of some of these proposed remedies. This book describes and analyses one such action-oriented experiment. It is an account of my interaction as a white Australian doctor and a change agent, with a rural Aboriginal community.

Poor health is only one of the many problems of Australian Aborigines. To improve their health it is necessary to enhance their overall condition. It is my contention that a doctor who wishes to improve the health of Aborigines must concern himself with more than purely medical matters. He must be prepared to act as an agent of change and work towards improving those social and environmental factors which contribute to their ill health. This concept of the doctor's role is not new. It was advocated at the beginning of the nineteenth century by Johann Peter Frank who held chairs of medicine in Austria, Italy and Germany. In 1848 the famous German pathologist and politician Rudolph Virchow, in the first issue of his new journal *Medizinische Reform*, drew attention to the responsibility of physicians to support social reforms that 'would reconstruct society according to a pattern favourable to the health of man'. More recently some enlightened doctors including the medical profession's most famous political activist of recent times, Che Guevera, have again realised that many of the major health problems affecting people can be traced to social, psychological and environmental factors. They have started a growing cry around the world for doctors to be more radical in accepting social responsibility for some of the changing needs of people and communities (Guevera, 1969).

In Australia, only a few voices have been raised in advocating that doctors extend their traditional role. One of these doctors, Professor

John Cawte of the School of Psychiatry of New South Wales, has over the last ten years organised teams which have collected data from several different Aboriginal populations around Australia in an endeavour to understand the defensive and the adaptive responses to environmental stress which determine the behaviour of Aborigines (Cawte, 1972; 1974). One of these populations lived in the Bourke Shire of New South Wales and this was chosen as the experimental centre for the Human Ecology of the Arid Zone Project. The original aims of this project were to assess the effects of psychiatric intervention and community development on the mental health and psycho-social discomfort of both Aborigines and whites in the area (Cawte, 1968).

In March 1967, Mr Brian Ross, a social psychologist, became the first research worker to take up residence in Bourke. He was joined by Dr Otto Reichard, a psychiatrist with an interest in the epidemiology of mental illness. Gradually the Human Ecology of the Arid Zone Project expanded into a loose association of workers each contributing according to his interests and expertise. To mark his twentieth year in general practice in Bourke, Dr R. E. Coolican made a complete recording of illness episodes in patients who consulted him in the year 1968 (Coolican, 1973).

In September 1969 the School of Paediatrics of the University of New South Wales also became involved. Dr Barry Duffy and Professor John Beveridge began a survey of the growth and development of all children born in Bourke in the eighteen months prior to September 1969. Dr Barry Nurcombe, a child psychiatrist, and Mr Paul Moffitt, a clinical psychologist, started what is now a highly popular pre-school aimed at enriching the language of those children both black and white who were found to be in need (Nurcombe *et al.*, 1973).

In July 1970 I joined the Human Ecology of the Arid Zone Project and with my family took up residence in Bourke. Much of this book is about my role and my explorations as a change agent and as a doctor and since it is probable that the outcome of this project has depended as much upon the singer as upon the song, explanation is needed about who I am, what factors conditioned me to take an interest in Aborigines, and why I applied for this particular research position.

My parents were of Polish-Russian-Jewish origin and migrated to Australia in 1927. I was born in Perth, Western Australia in 1936. As a result of this migrant background I have always had an awareness of the insecurities and difficulties in minority groups. I first became aware of the plight of Australian Aborigines when I was sixteen years old. A small hostel for Aboriginal girls was opened in a fairly select Perth suburb in which I had a vacation job as a postman. Nearly all the people in that street signed a petition to have the hostel closed. I aggressively rose to the defence of the Aborigines and young as I was I became a very unpopular postman. After I had graduated in medicine my awareness about minority groups was reinforced through working with refugees in Korea, Nepal, Jordan and Israel. I specialised in psychiatry and general medicine before applying for a research fellowship in the Human Ecology of the Arid Zone Project. My chief motive at that time was to obtain experience in research work which I regarded as necessary to round off my general medical training.

The success of any doctor living in a remote area is often dependent on his wife's ability to adjust to her new surroundings. My wife accomplished this despite her upbringing as an urban dweller in the industrialised French city of Lille. Her parents were Jewish refugees from Poland and this undoubtedly resulted in the general empathy that she felt for Australian Aborigines.

My part in the Human Ecology of the Arid Zone Project had originally been to establish the first psychiatric epidemiology of black and white people in a sparsely populated area of Australia and to determine the modifications of psychiatric services needed for such regions. However, because of my growing awareness and interest in the general condition of Australian Aborigines, the Human Ecology of the Arid Zone Project became oriented more towards the broad application of social medicine to Bourke Aborigines than to a narrower social-psychiatric intervention with the total population of the far west of New South Wales.

Strategy

The short term aim of my work was to improve health. I proposed to accomplish this by working as a doctor and trying to influence and improve all those medical factors which contributed to the poor health of Bourke Aborigines. This included paying particular attention to cultural and organisational factors which were being neglected, and introducing needed services not previously available, such as family planning, nutritional help and health education.

The long term aim was to leave behind me a group of Aborigines with the knowledge, skill and self-confidence to continue the process of change towards a functioning self-regulating community able to organise its own affairs without the continued advice of white helpers. My strategy was to extend my established role as a doctor into the field of change agentry in order to help Aboriginal people fulfil some of their felt needs. This meant becoming involved in the development of the Aboriginal community by initiating political structures and assisting in political action, adult education and a variety of social and sporting endeavours.

The data presented in this book was obtained through a variety of methods. Nearly all the Aborigines in Bourke were interviewed on at least five occasions. Further information was obtained from key informants in both the Aboriginal and white communities and also through my becoming involved, experiencing, observing and discussing the events, and a variety of facets of the life of both whites and Aborigines in the town. It will become obvious to the reader of this book that I identified strongly with the Aboriginal people of Bourke. I became not so much a participant-observer as an involved observer. Further information was obtained from all the available records at the Bourke District Hospital, the Bourke Shire, and past issues of the local newspaper, the *Western Herald*. In addition I examined over 90% of the total Aboriginal population in October 1971 and on a variety of other occasions that arose in the course of my general practice services to them. All this material was entered onto information sheets and these were later processed with the aid of a computer.

This book consists of four main parts. The first part tells the history and describes the condition of Bourke Aborigines in 1971; the second part describes the process of community development; part three discusses those conditions which affect the present health, well-being and dignity of these people and part four describes my efforts to improve their physical and social condition through my role as an agent of social change.

Some definitions

There are some words which recur throughout this book which have several meanings even among those social scientists who work in similar disciplines. The usages which I have adopted are as follows: An Aborigine is a person of Aboriginal descent who identifies him or herself as an Aborigine. The Aboriginal community are all those people who identify themselves as Aborgines and who live in a designated geographical area, eg. the Bourke Aboriginal community. The white community are all those people who are not Aborigines. The total community were all those people black and white who lived in a designated geographical area.

The word 'ecology' is used more in its sociological than in its biological context. It is used specifically to refer to the relationships of human beings to each other, and to their cultural and physical environment. A change agent is a person who works with a client community or system in a deliberate effort to improve and to solve the problems which confront this community.

Two frequently appearing words in the recorded statements by Aborigines are 'Murrie' and 'Gub'. A 'Murrie' (sometimes spelt Murree) is the word for man in the Wiradjuri language. It is now widely used by New South Wales Aborigines as a collective term for all Aborigines. There is some dispute among Aborigines and white Aboriginologists as to the exact derivation of the word 'Gub'. Some Aborigines said that it came from 'government' and others that it came from 'garbage'. It is widely used by Aborigines throughout New South Wales as a collective term for whites. Like the white Australian vernacular 'bastard' its use covers a wide emotional spectrum, from hatred to affection.

Although my aim was to improve the health of the Aboriginal people with whom I worked, this account is not just a narrow, medical text of use to health personnel involved in the social and cross-cultural aspects of health care. A major part of this book is concerned with social change and my stumbling attempts together with the Bourke Aborigines to achieve it. As a result of my experience, I have reached the conclusion that government decree and intermittent government finance will not really solve the problems of Aborigines if this is not accompanied by a growth in the independent functioning of Aboriginal communities. It is my thesis that this will only occur if those who assist Aborigines at the grass-roots level, have a working knowledge of the principles of community development.

The reader may not agree with my conclusions and so the events which occurred in this detailed community case study are presented in such a way that the reader can make his or her own analyses of many of the situations I describe. In retrospect, I hope this book will be of interest to all who work with or on behalf of Aborigines including

Aboriginal workers themselves. By using many case studies and quoting Aborigines verbatim, I have intended that the reader should gain a feel for Aborigines as people. Consequently, it may also hold the attention of the general reader who is interested in Aboriginal affairs. In particular, my aim is to assist all Australians who are interested but who do not realise the magnitude of the task of aiding an Aboriginal community towards integration and self regulation.

Chapter 1
The people of Bourke Shire

A cardinal rule too often ignored by those who work with Aborigines is to understand their history, their environment and the way in which these have moulded their cultural beliefs and practices. No less important for a change agent of any kind is a similar understanding about the white culture whose attitudes and actions have such a profound effect on the life of Australian Aborigines.

Aborigines before white contact[1]

The tribes

Archaeological surveys and carbon dating of old camp sites have shown that Aborigines have occupied western New South Wales for at least thirty thousand years. Although there is considerable discrepancy amongst early Australian historians, contemporary anthropologists and elderly Aboriginal informants, it would appear that the tribe which lived around Bourke was the Ngjamba. To the north were the Marawari, the Gu:rnu and the Badjari, whose descendants now live at Weilmoringle and Enngonia. In the corner of north-western New South Wales around Tibooburra the Wanggumara (Wangumara) lived in close physical and social proximity with the Maljangaba. South-west of Bourke around what is now Wilcannia were the Ba:gundji. South to south-west of Bourke were the Wongaibon, north-east the Waljwan and eastward were the large nation tribe the Gamilaroi[2] (*see* Fig. 1).

1. This pen picture of life in the early days of European occupation is a conglomerate from Teulon, 1886; Curr, 1886; Dunbar, 1943; Sturt, 1833a and b; Mitchell. 1839; Beckett. 1958 and 1967; and the following Aboriginal informants who spent their youth in a tribal or semi-tribal situation—Mr George Harrison, the late Mr Jack O'Lantern, Mrs Granny Moysey, the late Mr George McDermott, his daughter Mrs Edith Edwards, and the late Mrs Lorna Dixon.

2. The spelling of tribal names follows the style used by the Australian Institute of Aboriginal Studies, Canberra.

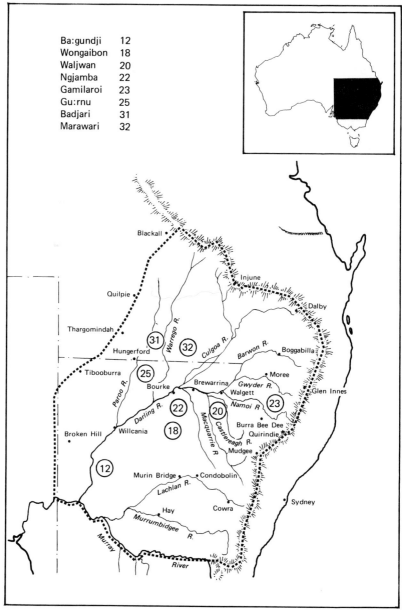

Ba:gundji	12
Wongaibon	18
Waljwan	20
Ngjamba	22
Gamilaroi	23
Gu:rnu	25
Badjari	31
Marawari	32

Figure 1 Tribal areas of Bourke and neighbouring districts (courtesy of the Australian Institute of Aboriginal Studies *after* Oates and Oates, 1970, p.162).

8

The Ngjamba men were about 5 ft 7 in [170 cm] tall. They had straight hair and none were bald. The men wore loin nets and both sexes used kangaroo skins to keep warm and as a mark of self-esteem. A feather head band, a nose-stick and a hair arm band were worn as ornaments. They sometimes covered their bodies with grease as a protection against insects.

The Ngjamba lived in well-made bark and grass shelters of a semi-permanent kind along both sides of the Darling River which they called Calle-watta. Each hut housed ten to fifteen people. They made bark canoes, trapped and speared fish, caught birds in nets and hunted kangaroo, emu, bilby (kangaroo rat) and goanna. Native trees provided wild orange (*Capparis mitchelli*), bush banana (*Leichhardtia australis*), bush lemon (*Canthium oleifolium*), gruie apple (*Owenia acidula*) and quandong (*Santalum acuminatum*). In times of drought the seed of the four-leaf clover, known as nardoo (*Marsilea quadrifolia*), was collected by the women and ground into a meal. Food was cooked over open coals or on hot stones in a small hole in the ground like an oven. There was a large trade in the addictive alkaloid pituri (*Duboisia hopwoodii*), whose leaves were dried, mixed with white ash from the bark of the cassia, made into a cake and chewed. When there was a shortage of pituri, the leaves of the river cooba tree (*Acacia stenophylla*) were used for what was recognised as a poor substitute.

The tribe was divided into four sections, each with its own totem. Polygamy was the privilege of the better warriors. Circumcision and subincision were not carried out and initiation in both sexes consisted of knocking out the upper right incisor and sometimes dividing the nasal septum. Disputes were settled by a conclave of the older men, the accent being on reconciliation. Severe infringement of the law was punished either through death by clubbing, or by banishment. There was a belief in two supernatural beings, Baimi and Deramulan, although it is possible that these were two names for the same deity.

Some historians recorded that infanticide of first born female children was practised, while others state it occurred only in times of increased fertility and shortage of food.

Warriors painted themselves with red ochre in times of action mostly over the stealing of women. Wars were brief, with little physical damage resulting and bitterness between adversaries was short lived. These civilised war practices were cited by the local historian Teulon (1886) as an indication of Aboriginal indolence.

Mourning

In times of mourning everyone covered themselves with white clay. The widow or widower wore a cap of clay over the top and back of the head and this was put on the grave after all the burial ceremonies had been completed (Plate 1). Teulon wrote that:

Nowhere, perhaps, may be met more face to face than at the funeral of a Black that touch which makes the whole world kin. The procession in twos and threes, for fellowship's sake, the hanging of heads, and the wringing of hands; the wailings in camp, en route, and at the grave's mouth, that come plainly from no hired lips; the carefully swathed body; the carefully swept holy ground containing it; the green leaves laid under it and over it. (1886:202)

The body was buried beside the river in a foetal position at the highest flood mark. (Plate 2.)

The historian Lindsay Black held the view that:

From what we can now find in connection with the customs of the Darling River Valley Aboriginals we know that they were a fine race and it indeed seems strange that those people who displaced them did not even enquire into their customs and habits. (1950:47)

One aspect of the ceremonial life of Bourke's original inhabitants is shown in Plate 3.

'Mystery Stones'

A particular feature of the Aborigines of the Darling River Valley was their use of a cylindrical stone artefact (Plate 4). These stones are fairly abundant around old campsites, but their former use is not known. The late Mrs Lorna Dixon and the late Mr George McDermott independently told me that the stones were called *murrioguggo* in Wanggumara and were used by their mothers to pound nardoo seed. A variety of other theories implicate the stones in relaying messages, making rain, avulsing teeth and recording messages. Black (1942) made the most extensive examination of the evidence available about the stones and concluded that they were 'mystery stones', which he called 'cylcons'. Assuming that the Aborigines have not hidden their significance from the white man, the lack of knowledge about these artefacts illustrates the degree of deculturation which they have undergone since European settlement.

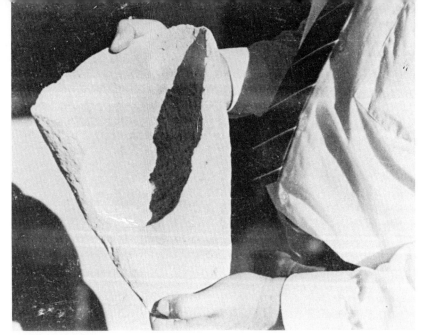

Plate 1   Widow's cap made from clay and worn until conclusion of burial ceremonies (photograph by courtesy of W. Cameron, Research Officer of the Bourke Historical Society).

Plate 2   Aboriginal burial site at Multagoona near Bourke.

Plate 3 Cave painting of a dancing man from Ngjamba ceremonial site at Mount Gundabooka illustrating one aspect of the rich ceremonial life of the original inhabitants of the Bourke Shire.

The Aborigines since white contact

The first recorded contact of the Ngjamba with the white man occurred in 1829 when Captain Charles Sturt was making the first of his expeditions into the interior of southern Australia. Sturt records that the Aborigines were docile and peaceful, cool and courageous. He advised succeeding explorers 'not to alarm their timidity, to exercise patience in intercourse with them, to treat them kindly, and to watch them with suspicion, especially at night' (1833a:179).

In 1835 Thomas Mitchell, then Surveyor-General of New South Wales, found the tribe to be quick and intelligent and by far the best conducted natives he had met on the Darling River. He expressed the hope that European settlement would not result in their destruction. Despite his sentiments his relationships with the Ngjamba were less cordial than Sturt's had been, and that is why he built Australia's only fort there. It was named Fort Bourke in honour of the seventh Governor of New South Wales, Sir Richard Bourke.

Both Sturt and Mitchell noted that many of the Aborigines were pock-marked. Sturt was able to elicit that a 'violent cutaneous disease had raged through the tribe and killed great numbers of them' (1833a:93). Mitchell felt he was seeing only the remains of a depopulated tribe. The pock-marks were smaller than those found in white men who had recovered from smallpox. James Souter, a convict who accompanied Mitchell as his medical assistant, thought the disease had been the 'confluent smallpox' (Mitchell, 1839:307). Although it is possible that this could have been the effects of chickenpox on a non-immune population, it is most probable that it was smallpox since several epidemics of smallpox had occurred in the first fifty years of white settlement and the disease could have been spread through inter-tribal contact (Bridges, 1970).

Other diseases were spread through white contact and on his second trip up the Darling, Sturt records that 'syphilis raged amongst them with fearful violence; many had lost their noses, and all the glandular parts were considerably affected' (1833b:125).

The arrival of the white man

The first official white settler was William Mayne, who paid for a licence to settle the west side of the Barwon River in 1841. By 1849 the whole of the Darling River from Bourke to Menindee in the south-west of New South Wales was being settled.

13

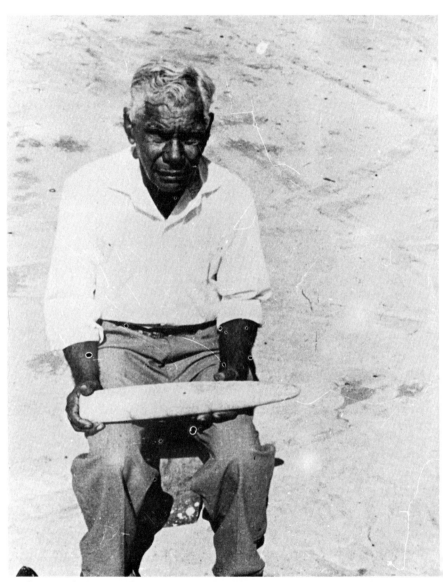

Plate 4 The late Mr Charlie Phillips with a 'Mystery Stone' (photograph by courtesy of W. Cameron, Research Officer of the Bourke Historical Society).

The coming of the white man and his stock marked the rapid demise of the Aborigines. In 1845 there were about 3000 in the vicinity of Bourke, by 1863 that number had dwindled to 1000 and by 1884 there were only 25 men, 35 women, 10 boys and 10 girls left. 'There had been a decrease to an extent scarcely short of annihilation (the majority of the remnant being decrepit in the extreme), owing in part to the diseases that accompany the white man; in part to whatever must be the result of putting "a piece of new garment upon an old"' (Teulon, 1886:186).

Massacre

At that time in history, it was inevitable that contact between two such totally different cultures both desiring the same land and the subsistence it offered, should result in bloody conflict. A few white settlers lost their lives at the hands of Aborigines. Almost as galling to the whites was the loss of their livestock. They retaliated with random killings and sometimes with systematic murders. Evidence of one such massacre is visible 20 km north of Brewarrina where skulls with bullet holes can still be found after it has rained. 'The wild blacks were that bad that all the cattlemen had to deal with them old and young on the Qantambone Plain and shot them. There was about 400 and that is how the creek got its name, Hospital Creek, there was only two piccaninnies left, a boy and a girl, the boy they took to Milroy (a large pastoral property) and he was still there when I went there in 1841, he died not long after, I am not quite sure but I think the girl was there too' (Kerrigan, about 1882).

The keeper of the 'pub' at Barringun, about 130 km north of Bourke on the Queensland border, the late Mr Jim Lack, had a letter by an old resident, written in 1884 telling of an ex-bushranger from Coonamble whose wife and family were killed by Aborigines and who was given an unofficial pardon and permission to shoot as many Aborigines as he liked. He used to erect a log shelter with holes in the walls and shoot Aborigines as they came in for water. The billabong near the town was known for some time as the Stinking Lagoon because of the large numbers of bodies that were placed there at any one time so that an approaching flood would remove them. It is little wonder that the Aboriginal view of a white man was synonymous with a gun and this is preserved by one of the names a revolver', still used to describe him.

By 1891, the Aborigines' Protection Board could find only sixteen full-blood and five half-caste Aborigines in the Bourke-Byrock district. In 1915 their census was one full-blood and two half-caste Aborigines.

The Aborigines since 1936

In 1935 about 80 to 100 people lived near Tibooburra, 320 km west of Bourke. They were the remnants of the Wanggumara tribe. The men worked on outlying properties and the mothers and children stayed in the town. Two residents of Bourke, Mrs Edith Edwards and the late Mrs Lorna Dixon, related how three large trucks arrived and gave the Aboriginal people two hours to collect their belongings and be taken to a 'mission' station near Brewarrina. 'No warning; just told to pack up a few belongings and get on the trucks. Worse than animals we got treated.' They attribute this to the work of a malevolent policeman who pressured the Aborigines Protection Board into shifting them. Anthropologist Jeremy Beckett also suggested (1958) that white agitation was responsible for the expulsion of the Aborigines from Tibooburra. Whatever the underlying reason, the powers for arbitrary movement of Aborigines were provided in a 1936 Amendment of the Aborigines Protection Act of 1910 (Long, 1970).

Both Mrs Dixon and Mrs Edwards recalled that many of the old people died in the first six months of residence on the station at Brewarrina. 'I lost a sister, me mother and father and an uncle, all in a year. That's when we got out.' Her people decided that they would walk back to Tibooburra. They got as far as Wanarring where they were blocked by a flooded river and they returned to Bourke.

Other Aborigines from a radius of about 500 km later moved into Bourke because of the work that was available with the opening of the meatworks. The remnants of the Ba:gundji came from Wilcannia, the Marawari from around the Paroo River, and from Peak Hill came those who knew they were descended from the Wiradjuri and the Wongaibon tribes. With the exception of five Aborigines who claim to be full-blood, all the other Aboriginal people now living in Bourke are part-caste and none are descended from the original Ngjamba. White blood entered their stock in the latter half of the last century and since then, with few exceptions, they have married amongst themselves and regard themselves as Aborigines.

Bourke Reserve

When they first went to Bourke the Aborigines camped either by the railway line, near the rubbish tip, or next to the river upstream from the town. In 1946 an area of 10.5 ha 1.5 km west of Bourke on what had been the Bourke Common was declared an Aboriginal Reserve under the jurisdiction of the Aborigines Welfare Board. Pressure was brought on all Aborigines by the Health Inspector to move to this area. In 1948 the Aboriginal population of Bourke was recorded as 55 persons.

A disintegrated society

A glance at the death register for the immediate post-war years gives an indication of the severe disintegration of their society in which the most common causes of death for women were childbirth, bashing and drinking methylated spirits.

Poor health was probably even more common than now and the two matriarchs quoted above (Mrs Edwards and Mrs Dixon) stated that 'when our babies were small they were everlasting with colds and sickness'. Other residents such as Mrs Violet Barden are ambivalent about those times:

In some ways things are better now. We're not old slave gins any more. In some ways things were better 25 years ago. Not so much grog. We used to gamble with dice and play cards. Lots of people used to work on stations. We used to live on the river bank. The mothers used to look after their kids better. They didn't neglect them to play bingo. We used to have dances on the clay pans or play rounders or something like that. The men didn't drink as much. Now they don't seem to be able to do without it. It's worse since the flagon[1] came out.

White settlement

As the black man declined the white man prospered. To do so he had to pit his wiles against unpredictable elements, isolation and a fearful awareness of his vulnerability to attack by hostile Aborigines whose culture he was little interested in, and did not understand. The ruthlessness which resulted in so much tragedy for the Aborigines was a trait without which the white man would not have survived. His relationship with other pastoralists was often also poor, due to the frequency of cattle stealing and to the resultant disputes (Heathcote 1965).

1. Large containers (2.25 l) of cheap wine or spirits.

17

Large properties sprang up, the biggest of which were *Dunlop* and *Toorale*, each of about one million acres, and *Winbar* with half a million acres. In 1888 *Dunlop* sheared 186 000 sheep.

In 1862 Surveyor Arthur laid down the town of Bourke at the request of the New South Wales Surveyor-General. The first steamer *The Gemini*, had arrived in Bourke in 1859 to open up river navigation from Goolwa in South Australia. As the pastoral properties prospered so did the port of Bourke. A telegraph was installed in 1873, a bridge across the Darling at north Bourke in 1883 and the railway line from Sydney was completed in 1885.

Despite a major flood in 1890, Bourke reached its zenith in 1892. There were 3145 people in the town and 6540 in the electorate of Darling. There were also 1 300 000 sheep producing 12 000 000 pounds weight of wool each year. A business directory at that time listed 200 businesses, 23 hotels and five banks. A block of land in the town cost £2500. Bourke had become the greatest stock centre in Australia and was known as the 'Chicago of the West'. There was a six acre market garden run by some Chinese and a brewery (Lindsay's) which won several prizes for its beer and ginger beer at an international competition in Melbourne. Bourke boasted about its new gaol which could hold 30 men and was said to be a perfect paradise in the scorching heat of summer.

There was a theatre, a library, a debating society and three weekly newspapers, two published in Bourke and one in Louth. The latter was 'remarkable for the frequency with which it changed owners and the small amount of reading matter (barring advertisements) which it gave to its subscribers' (*Town and Country Journal*, 5 July 1873).

The climb to the zenith was gradual, but the decline was rapid. By the end of a six-year drought in 1900 a Royal Commission had been called to assess the reasons for the depression and the general unprofitability of the pastoral industry in the Western Division of New South Wales. The eight factors they listed were: low rainfall; rabbits; overstocking; sandstorms; increase of non-edible scrubs; fall in prices in pastoral products; and areas too small for subsistence; other causes including high cost of transport. (Votes and Proceedings of the N.S.W. Legislative Assembly, 1901, vol. IV:136-9).

In the drought 1895 to 1900, *Toorale* lost 224 000 sheep and *Dunlop* 186 000. The decline of Bourke continued until 1931 when there were only a dozen businesses and it was possible to get bogged in the main

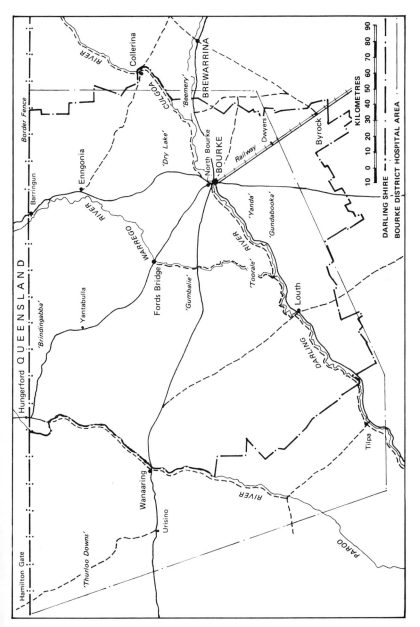

Figure 2 The Darling Shire showing the area served by Bourke District Hospital and the Darling-Murray Rivers system.

street. The population of the Darling Shire in 1933 had dropped from over 6500 to 1778. In the years since then, and particularly after World War II, Bourke has gradually recovered, due to better use of stock and land, taxation concessions and the extermination of the rabbit by myxomatosis. In 1938 a meat works was opened giving Bourke an industry and employment for about 200 people with seasonal employment for others. The town flourished during the wool boom of the early 1960s when wool sold for £1 per pound weight, but this was followed by another depression, the reasons for which, with the exception of the rabbits, differed little from those causes of the 1895–1900 recession. At present the economic future of the district is uncertain, with hope being held for tourism and a federal government policy of decentralisation.

Description of the Darling Shire

The physical setting

Bourke, the town in which this study was centred, takes its name from the fort built by the Surveyor-General Major Mitchell in 1835. It is situated on the Darling River at an elevation of 106 m above sea level at latitude 30°05′ and longitude 145°58′ (Fig. 2). The summers are hot and dry with occasional dust storms which darken the sky and choke up the lungs (Plate 5). The mean maximum temperature for January is 36.8°C with a mean minimum of 21°C and a mean mid-afternoon humidity of 24%. Bourke holds the high temperature record for New South Wales of 51.7°C (125°F), which occurred on 3 January 1909. Winter is mild like a fine English summer and the corresponding average figures are 17.8°C, 4.5°C and 48%. (*Official Year Book of the Commonwealth of Australia, 1968.*)

The annual rainfall is just under 300 mm a year spread over 44 days. However there are wide fluctuations in rainfall, and drought, which Sturt found can turn the inland into 'a heartless desert' that is an ever-threatening hazard to the economic well-being and general morale of the people of the area. Flooding is less of a threat although there have been eight major floods since 1890 (Plate 6).

Soil and vegetation

The alluvial grey clay loam is known locally as 'the black country'. It has a low tensile strength when wet, which makes it unsuitable for

Plate 5 Dust storm in Bourke.

Plate 6 Bourke under flood, 1971 showing the levee bank encircling the town cemetery and race course but not the Bourke Aboriginal Reserve.

Table 1 Age and sex distribution of Bourke Aborigines midway through
1971

	Males	Females	Total
Number of children			
under 1 year	14	16	30 ·
1– 4 years	61	53	114
5– 9 years	79	77	156
10–14 years	58	52	110
Number of adults			
15–19 years	32	36	68
20–29 years	44	52	96
30–39 years	37	32	69
40–49 years	19	23	42
over 50 years	24	21	45
Total	368	362	730

house or road foundations. Coolabah (*Eucalyptus coolabah*) and black
box (*Eucalyptus largiflorens*) trees are the most common. South of
Bourke there is a slightly acidic hard red soil formed from light clay to
clay loams. Mulga (*Acacia aneura*), bimble box or shiny leaf box
(*Eucalyptus populnea*) and budda (*Erimophilus mitchelli*) predominate.
To the north and west the red soil is softer and alkaline and supports
the gidgee tree (*Acacia cambagei*). Both gidgee and mulga are shrub
trees and the wood is still used by Aboriginal craftsmen to make
weapons and artefacts. There are many other species of plants, shrubs
and trees, some of which have value for man or for sheep. A heavy fall
of rain brings out a profusion of wildflowers and changes the colour of
the countryside from brown to green.

Population statistics

In June 1971 there were 4399 white people and 819 Aborigines in what
was then called the Darling Shire (the name was changed to the Bourke
Shire at the 1971 census). Of these, 3009 whites and 730 Aborigines[1]
lived in the town of Bourke itself. The age and sex distribution of the
Aborigines is shown in Table 1. A comparison of the age distribution

1. The population figures for whites are taken from the 1971 Census. The figures for
   Aborigines are based on my own census, in which I 'found' 121 people more than
   did the official census takers who have difficulty tracing all the Aborigines. This has
   also been noted in Victoria, where the 1966 Census recorded only 1790 Aborigines,
   although as many as 4432 were known to have had contact with government
   agencies (Tatz, 1970).

Table 2 Proportion of Aborigines and whites in the Bourke Shire and in New South Wales by age group[1]

Age Group	Bourke Shire		New South Wales	
	Aborigines[2]	Whites	Aborigines	Whites
under 15 years	56.7%	30.7%	48.7%	27.6%
15–65 years	41.8%	62.9%	49.1%	63.9%
over 65 years	1.5%	6.4%	2.2%	8.5%

1. Figures from the Commonwealth Bureau of Census and Statistics 1971.
2. The figures for Bourke Aborigines are based on my own census.

for whites and Aborigines in the shire and in New South Wales is shown in Table 2. The Aboriginal birth rate for the shire in the period 1964–1971 was 6.1%, as compared to 2.1% for the shire's whites over the same period. The Aboriginal rate of population increase per year was 4.2% and for whites 1.0%[1] (in fact the birth rate among the town Aborigines was 7.1%).

Government

Federal and state   In January 1971 there were 1850 people registered to vote in the Bourke sub-division of the Darling electorate, of whom only 37 were Aborigines.

At the 1972 federal elections the voting pattern was: Australian Labor Party 1120; Country Party 359; Liberal Party 301; Democratic Labor Party 74 (*Western Herald*, 8 August 1972). Most Aborigines claimed they voted for the Labor Party.

Local   In 1971 the Bourke Shire had an area of 4 346 154 ha with some 3500 km of road of which only about 200 km were bitumen sealed. The unimproved capital value in 1971 was $11 675 575. The shire was administered by a council elected every three years with four representatives from the town and eight from outlying ridings. Because of the low population density of these outer areas a grazier's vote carried five times the weight of a town person's vote.

The annual budget of the shire was about $1 000 000. The income sources were 15% from rates, 50% from federal and state government grants and the rest from loans.

Executive functions were carried out predominantly by a Shire Clerk, a District Engineer and a Health Surveyor. Although these men

1. This calculation is based on the formula used in the *Official Year Book of the Commonwealth of Australia, 1968*:132.

did not make policy, they could wield great influence with the Council. Council meetings were open to the public. The Council reserved the right to sit *in camera* but did so only when discussing something which might embarrass a ratepayer. This was usually only for non-payment of rates and the discussion would centre around his supposed financial state and whether he would not or could not pay. In the latter case the Council would make conditions as easy as possible in order to preserve the dignity of their fellow citizen.

The Council was very conscious of the history of Bourke and proud of its town. It was in my opinion a fair minded, responsible body whose members were only likely to show bias when their anxieties were aroused about the welfare of the town whose citizens they represented.

There were however a large group of people whom they did not represent. These were the Aborigines. Only 37 of the shire's 819 Aborigines were on the electoral role and they had never put up an Aboriginal candidate for the Shire Council. They had no political pressure group to represent their interests at either local, state or federal government level and they had no individual who had membership of any influential group. In 1971 only eight Aborigines knew the name of their State Member of Parliament (Mr J. Renshaw) and only one knew that of their Federal Member (Mr J. FitzPatrick).

Potential Aboriginal leaders received no encouragement, in fact were deterred by their community by being accused of trying to 'big note' themselves and being subjected to ridicule and rejection. Although two Aborigines claimed to be leaders, one on the basis of trade union experience and the other on the basis of his standing amongst the Reserve dwellers, the only real leadership was shown by Pastor Bill Reid, who exercised influence on those members of his church and basketball team, and who has organised a very popular talent quest on every 14 July since 1970 to mark National Aborigines' Day.

Employment

The prosperity of the district lies in cattle and sheep. Bourke has long prided itself as being the railhead with the greatest annual throughput of wool in the world. Normally more than 50 000 bales of wool are trucked from the railway station each year, coming from the 430 pastoral holdings in the north-west of New South Wales. In 1971 there were three large citrus orchards and recent American settlers have introduced cotton growing. The Bourke abattoir slaughters more than

250 000 sheep and 30 000 cattle annually for export to the United States of America and to Sweden and, at times of full production, over 400 people are employed.

The Shire Council, Department of Main Roads and the district hospital are the second largest employers of local people. In 1971 two soft drink factories and two shearing contractors employed about 24 men. Four banks, two public schools, the public works and police force were staffed by transient personnel, known locally as 'blow-ins', who were often responsible for bringing new ideas into the town and contributing to the maintenance of ailing organisations or to the resurrection of defunct ones.

There were fourteen retail food stores, three cafes, seven retail hardware or electrical appliance shops, five retail clothing stores, four woolbroking firms and two pharmacy shops. Together with ten garages, seven licensed hotels and three motels, these provided the bulk of the service work for the Bourke people. Self-employed people included ten cartage contractors, six taxi drivers, five hairdressers, four insurance agents, two builders and one welder and blacksmith.

In time of drought, flood or recession, the economy of the area was boosted by relief money grants from the federal government. Since 85% of this money had to be spent on wages and not on materials, most of the work done was road maintenance and improvement.

Aboriginal men were able to obtain permanent work in the Department of Main Roads, the Shire Council, the Railways and Post Office and 38 Aboriginal males (24% of the adult males) were so employed in 1971. Only nine of them could be classified as semi-skilled, the others being unskilled. All the other employable Aboriginal males obtained work when it was available on sheep stations and at the meat works. From 10–20% of the Bourke Aboriginal population would journey to Wee Waa or Mildura where whole families could obtain work cotton chipping or fruit picking for periods from four to eight weeks. About 20 women supplemented the family income by taking casual jobs as packers at the meat works or picking oranges in the local orchards.

In the main, Bourke is a working class town. In 1971 incomes for men in steady employment averaged between $3500 to $5000 per year. The middle of 1971 was a time of almost full employment for Aborigines with only fourteen men and eight women unemployed. The per capita Aboriginal income from all sources at this time was just over $8 per week.

Aboriginal men on the permanent staff of the shire, the Main Roads or meat works, had the same incomes as whites. Itinerant Aboriginal seasonal workers had incomes of about $2000 to $2500 per year and were unemployed for three to five months of the year. Some of the graziers, had made fortunes and kept them, others, through poor land, poor management or sheer bad luck, were considerably in debt to the woolbroking firms and banks.

Housing

White   In 1971 just over half the 800 houses in Bourke were owned by their occupants. About 200 houses were quite old, and some of these had been condemned by the shire building and health inspector, but were temporarily reprieved and still occupied. The large number of Housing Commission houses were 'modern' and adequate, but monotonously uniform in design. The population density for the white population was low—just under one person per room (Commonwealth Bureau of Census and Statistics 1971).

Aboriginal   There were 92 dwellings occupied by Aborigines in Bourke. Thirty-one of these were one-roomed shanty dwellings on the Bourke Reserve. With the exception of the few houses which were owned or being bought by their occupants, Aboriginal houses were distinguished by their lack of gardens, trees or flowers. Only four families kept either chickens, pigs, goats or sheep. Overcrowding was the rule with half the houses being less than 18.5 m² in area.

Accommodation was not cheap in Bourke and the cost of food included freight, making most items some 20% more expensive even than similar items in the more exclusive eastern suburbs of Sydney.

The Aborigines' lack of money was compounded by their poor use of what they had. Money was spent as fast as it was received. Few Aborigines took advantage of supermarket prices and bought goods at a much higher cost in the small shops that were open at night. Approximately a quarter of the weekly wages earned by men was spent on alcohol.

There was a ratio of one car to every four white people. Cars were owned by seventeen Aborigines, a ratio of one car to every 42 Aborigines (Commonwealth Bureau of Census and Statistics 1971). The six taxis in Bourke were supported almost entirely by the Aboriginal population.

A rough comparison of outlay between a white and an Aboriginal family of six to eight members based on a total income of $70 per week is shown in Table 3.

In reality the $70 of the Aboriginal man had to go further in providing food, cigarettes and alcohol for his extended family, and his relatives from other areas. He was by far the most poverty stricken of the inhabitants of Bourke. When times were hard he conserved money by cutting down on food and perhaps relying on friends to buy most of the alcohol which was a social and perhaps psychological necessity of Aboriginal male life. The only whites approaching the Aborigines' level of poverty were pensioners with no property or savings and alcoholics with large families. No Aborigine owned a business in Bourke, few Aborigines had bank accounts and only 12 of the 92 Aboriginal houses were either owned or being paid off by their occupants. Some credit was available to Aborigines from certain shops and one bank provided finance of up to $700 for those in regular employment. This was used to buy old, run-down cars, the life expectancy of which could be judged by the number of car bodies cluttering the areas of Bourke in which the Aboriginal people lived.

Aboriginal education and achievement

In 1971 there were 178 Aboriginal children enrolled at the Bourke Primary School and 36 Aboriginal children at the Catholic School. This was 28% of the total primary school enrolment in Bourke. The high school had 44 Aboriginal students, just under 15% of the secondary school enrolment. No Aboriginal adolescent had progressed beyond the

Table 3 Comparative expenditure by whites and Aborigines in Bourke, of an average weekly wage in 1971

	White	Aboriginal in town	Aboriginal on Reserve
Rent, electricity	14	12	
Food	30	20	20
Alcohol	7	12	15
Cinema	4	6	6
Taxis		2	8
Cigarettes	4	5	6
Gambling	4	6	10
Other	7	7	5
	$70	$70	$70

third form (approximately 15 years old) and nearly all the Aboriginal children were in occupational or general activities classes (ie. 'slow learner' classes)[1]. This situation paralleled that of the rest of New South Wales (New South Wales Teachers' Federation 1972).

Attendance at school improved in the years that I was in Bourke. This was mainly out of fear of the Child Welfare Officer. Even so there was always a score of school age children playing on the Reserve during school hours and on the days in which I did some survey work at the primary school four or five Aboriginal children would be missing from each class. Despite this, the greatest acculturating influence on Aborigines, especially females, was school. At the same time the education system had little apparent relevance in influencing any upward mobility in Aborigines' aspirations or living standards. One indication of this was that no Aboriginal child ever attended any of three vocational guidance days which took place in the three years that I was in Bourke.

Young Aboriginal adults had attended school for more years than the older people (*see* Table 4). However, even those who had attended school for more than six years had an education level of nominally third or fourth grade primary school. There was no Aborigine in the town with the School Certificate. Although 54% of the adult Aboriginal population claimed to be able to read enough to understand the local weekly newspaper, the *Western Herald*, it was doubtful if 5% of Aborigines had a full comprehension of any feature article. Books were totally absent from all but ten Aboriginal households. The most commonly found reading matter, in order of frequency, was comics, *True Romance* and the boxing magazine *The Ring*. In practical terms there were only four men and four women who could fill out an Income Tax Return without assistance.

Table 4   Number of full years spent at school by Bourke Aborigines

Years at school	Age group in 1971						Total		
	15–29		30–49		50+				
	M	F	M	F	M	F	M	F	Combined
Nil			6	2	9	6	15	8	23
1–3	4	5	19	7	9	4	32	16	48
4–6	41	23	16	16	5	4	62	43	105
7+	31	60	15	30	1	7	47	97	144

1. Education is compulsory in New South Wales for all children up to 15 years of age.

Religious organisation

White affiliation to different religious denominations was as follows: Roman Catholic 43%; Church of England 39%; Presbyterian 11%; Methodist 3%; others 4%. Forty per cent of the adult Aboriginal population claimed to be practising Christians and a further 35% occasionally attended church. The remaining 25%, mostly in the 15–29 year age group, never attended church. The religious denominations to which the Aborigines belonged were: Roman Catholic 65%; Church of England 16%; Presbyterian 10%; United Aboriginal Mission 7%; Methodist 1% and Brethren 1%.

Social organisation—formal

White

The white men and, to a lesser extent, the white women of Bourke were well catered for by a variety of sporting, social and service clubs, the most important in terms of membership and strength of support being the Returned Services League Club, the bowling club and the golf club. There were thirteen different sporting clubs in Bourke in 1971, although seven of these were in a dormant condition. The Country Women's Association and the Red Cross Society provided some outlet for the energies of a few of the women of Bourke. Service clubs, such as Rotary, Rotaract and Apex were very active and provided a considerable number of services and special events for the town. There was also a chapter of Freemasons and one of the Order of Buffaloes. The Parents' and Citizens' Association gave fluctuating support to the schools and attracted from six to thirty people to its meetings, depending on the issues to be discussed.

'Cultural' activities in Bourke were limited and spasmodic. The Dramatic Society organised one function a year in conjunction with the Arts Council of New South Wales. The Bourke Shire Band was more active and presented creditable performances at most town functions.

The young people of the town were limited to joining the Scouts or Girl Guides and participating in a Saturday morning sporting competition. The continuation of all these activities depended upon the availability of parents willing to organise them.

In general it could be said that all the strong and stable organisations in Bourke had the support of long-standing residents in the district, whereas the weak and moribund clubs relied for continued life on 'blow-ins'. Sometimes these itinerants hastened a club's demise by alienating the local people who had given some spasmodic support. Active members were at a premium in all the clubs and their names recurred again and again on the various executive committee honour boards. Their commitments took up almost every evening, sometimes causing difficulties in family life.

Aboriginal

In 1971 there were so few Aborigines in the clubs mentioned above that it was easy to count and document them. There were seven Aborigines in the Order of Buffaloes, one in the Returned Services League, one had been recently invited to join the Chamber of Commerce and two brothers were Scouts. In the sporting sphere, four Aborigines belonged to the Rugby League Football Club, two played cricket and the Aborigine in the Returned Services League also belonged to the bowling club. An Aboriginal team, 'The Astronauts', competed in the girls' basketball competition.

Social organisation—informal

Informal social life at all levels in Bourke centred around the exercise of 'bending the elbow', usually outside the home, in clubs or in the hotels, which were treated like clubs by their loyal patrons. The white men of the town rationalised their neglect of their women in this aspect of life by maintaining that the West was 'a man's world'.

There was some social contact between white and Aboriginal men in the public bars of the hotels. In most cases these men also worked together in labouring jobs for the shire or the Department of Main Roads. The Aborigines' favourite social activity was to play bingo with relatives and friends (see Plate 7). The games usually started in the early afternoon and continued until dark. Disputes over alleged cheating might break up the usual large school into several smaller ones until relations were smoothed over.

A single bingo card cost 20 cents and since people played four and five cards at once, it was not uncommon for individuals to lose between $30 and $40 in an afternoon. The constant call of bingo numbers in the Aborigines' own idiosyncratic way had a conditioning effect on toddlers, who would sit together in a ring calling out 'No [sic] one, no two, no three' etc.

31

Plate 7 A Bingo school.

Recreational facilities for Aboriginal children of all ages were almost non-existent in Bourke. The younger children spent much time in the town swimming pool in summer and playing on swings and see-saws in the park in winter. Teenagers tended to congregate around the fun parlour in the middle of the town, playing a juke box and pinball machines and occasional games of snooker.

Status

Descendants of the original white pioneers constituted the aristocracy of the area centred on Bourke, some of the families being represented in the seventh generation by children of pre-school age in 1971. These families had a powerful web of relationships throughout the north-west of New South Wales and it was unwise in Bourke to criticise any member of such a family to another person of similar ancestry, for they would surely be related, and proud of it. Those with only two or three generations of local ancestors were still aristocrats, but mere barons compared with the dukes of longer standing.

These people were generally found only on the periphery of Bourke's club life, if at all. Only in local government, and in the running of 'the sport of kings' did they make their presence felt. Of the twelve members of the Shire Council in 1971, only two were not from pioneer stock. The councillors included a father and three sons, a brother and sister and a man and his son-in-law.

Next in status to the pioneer families came Bourke's professional men—two doctors, two lawyers, two dentists, several clergymen and the school headmasters. However, this status was not conferred automatically, but involved an element of merit. For instance, a doctor who was obviously in Bourke simply to make his fortune in a short time would not enjoy the confidence of the local populace and was unlikely to be highly regarded. The clergy still enjoyed high status 'ex officio', but their standing could be further enhanced by participation in secular activity. Local businessmen and the managerial staff of the meat works and banks enjoyed a standing about the same as that of the professional men. Next, and also highly regarded, came skilled workers, such as shire or Department of Main Roads foremen. Even 'reffos'[1] in these positions were well regarded, provided they assimilated.

1. Vernacular for a European migrant. It stems from just before and after World War II when most of Australia's immigrants were refugees. It is still used as a term of derogation.

33

Near the bottom of the social ladder were the poor whites, people without family connections to soften their incompetence or with families too large to support, people with quirks of personality that made them non-competitive and people to whom chance had never dealt even a hopeful hand. Nevertheless, the humblest whites could always feel that there were other people even lower on Bourke's social ladder than themselves: the Aborigines.

Identity and prestige

Some Bourke Aborigines introjected the view that most white society had of them. They described themselves as the 'lowest of the low'. Some responded with what the anthropologist, Ruth Fink (1957:103), has described as 'an aggressive assertion of low status'. Their dress and unkempt appearance was an affirmation of their belonging to the Aboriginal Reserve. It was a uniform of defiance that some insisted on wearing, even when they knew that it was to their detriment, such as when they appeared in court.

A more common response, especially amongst women, was to exhibit shame over their poor housing, food and dress. Most Aborigines believed that success was beyond their control, and that long-range goals were futile. As one Aborigine said, 'We want things but we know we won't get anywhere before we start'. Some became despondent like one man who said, 'I drink because I've got nuthin else. I got no money, I can't write, never been to school. I can't get a job or keep one and what's the use I'll never get anywhere. A black man with one eye who can't even read out of the other. A fellow oughtn't to talk that way but maybe he'd be better off dead.' Many Aborigines were sensitive, quarrelsome and became uncontrolled and violent after drink. They could also become suspicious and impulsive.

Fewer than ten families could be described as white oriented in that they showed a desire to assimilate with whites. This upward mobility was not seen as rejection by other Aborigines unless the people concerned severed their connections with the Reserve and with other Aborigines. The caste barrier between white oriented and Aboriginal oriented Aborigines observed in Brewarrina by Fink in 1957 was not evident in Bourke, with the exception of three families. Nevertheless, some Bourke Aborigines with white aspirations showed an ingratiating attitude towards whites and a desire to receive salutations of

34

recognition from them. For such Aborigines, the pinnacle of social achievement was to be invited for a cup of tea in a white house.

Aboriginal men often expressed their desire for prestige through boasting to their children, relatives or to white visitors from outside Bourke about their capacity for work. ('I built this road myself. The whole seven miles of it.') Amongst themselves, Aboriginal men sought prestige by telling how 'I told the big gub a few things. I really spoke up to that big gub.' A less common form of prestige-seeking was the strict adherence to a form of religious observance thought to be regarded as virtuous by the white population. Aborigines with money and cars enjoyed prestige amongst their people only so long as they were willing to share these with their extended families.

Aboriginal identity and status was also maintained through the strength of the family. Despite the frequency of interparental disagreements sparked off by alcohol or sexual jealousy, liaisons between couples were relatively stable. Two parent families were more the norm than had been the case with the older Aborigines (see Table 5). Formal marriage ceremonies were relatively rare and the most common form of relationship was a stable de facto one. The functional group was the extended family with the oldest woman wielding the most influence. Brothers, sisters and cousins tended to congregate in family groups living in close proximity.

Intra-family disputes were far less common than inter-family ones and consanguinous ties were usually more important than those of marriage. The family unit provided security for Aborigines in that they would never see a family member go hungry or without a place to sleep.

Children were particularly proud of their siblings and their cousins and introduced them to strangers in the same manner that a white child would do when drawing attention to a coveted possession.

Table 5 Family background of Bourke Aborigines

Family background	15–29 years		30–49 years		50+ years		Total
	M	F	M	F	M	F	
One parent	29	26	22	13	10	9	109
Two parents	38	53	31	30	11	10	173
Uncle	3	6	3	7	2	1	22
Adopted	4			3			7
Institution	2	3		2	1	1	9

Family reunions were significant occasions and a great deal of money would often be spent to transport whole families to another town to celebrate an event such as the birthday of a brother. Some trips were more than 500 km and families would start saving up to six months ahead in order to pay the taxi fare. Family members who were frequently inebriated would become almost teetotal in order to contribute their share. There was a unity and integration in the extended family that showed itself in a generosity of spirit for the problems and the troubles of other family members. About half of the Aborigines who had drifted into Bourke in the previous 20 years had done so because they had relatives in the town and the other half because they thought they could find work there. More than two-thirds of the adults regarded Bourke as their home and stated quite categorically that they had no desire to live anywhere else.

The remnants of Aboriginal culture

Identity was also maintained through the preservation of the remnants of their Aboriginal culture. It was generally believed that nothing of tribal origin remained (Nurcombe, 1970; Coolican, 1973). Further west from Bourke, Beckett (1958:47) found that Aborigines under the age of forty could not speak their tribal language, and to hear it made them feel 'shamed'. However, on close contact with the Bourke community it became apparent that they were still trying to preserve what they had left of their Aboriginal tradition. All Aboriginal adults and most children knew to what totem they belonged, and still referred to it by the Aboriginal name, eg. Emu: Gulbri; Yabbie: Wailabukly. Most still refused to eat their totem. Morris Edwards stated that 'eating your own totem would be like eating your own flesh. That is our religion and we wouldn't do that. We all know our meat and we teach the kids. Percy [aged 4], he knows.' Most Aboriginal males above the age of thirty still claimed to know where the sacred areas and initiation trees were situated. They claimed to have been taught the ritual of how to approach these areas and how to leave them.

Following a drinking session one man now in his thirties told me how his 'almost full-blood' father had taken him to a bora ground[1] to initiate him when he was thirteen years old. He was frightened and had run

---

1. A sacred site where the initiation of young men and other ceremonies were performed.

36

away. This incident had deeply influenced his future life and he expressed this by saying 'so you see I'm not a proper man'.

There was still a great belief in spirits and ghosts and in the evil that could befall one if one's faeces should fall into the hands of an enemy and be subjected to a bad curse[1]. Bourke Aborigines held a belief in 'maternal impression', similar to that reported in various other societies. This is the belief that 'visual, auditory or tactile contact by the pregnant women with various environmental objects will produce corresponding stigmata in the infant' (Pearn and Pavlin, 1971:1123). Aboriginal women in Bourke rationalised the cause of birth marks by saying that a snake or a spider must have crawled over the pregnant mother's abdomen and left its shape on the baby.

Even young Aborigines exhibited fear of the *min min* lights, ie. refractive images due to heat conditions which appear as lights darting across the sky and which, Aborigines say, lead people morally astray. There was still a fear of places in which a person had died and the wailing and sobbing at funerals were in accord with the description of Aboriginal funerals by the earliest white historians. One man had a wooden hand which had apparently been used for holding the pointing bone. Although he was a staunch practising Christian, he refused to show this to a white man because the full-blood Aborigine who gave it to him predicted dire happenings should he do so. A few Aborigines who knew of his possession refused to go anywhere near this man's house.

Many Aborigines over the age of thirty still spoke several hundred words of their language and when travelling to the area from which they originated lapsed into a vernacular difficult for me to understand. They claimed that it was English but one man stated that it was mixed up with about 500 words of his old language. In Bourke there were six fairly fluent speakers of Aboriginal languages and four of them spoke Wanggumara.

All of this knowledge was treated with some secrecy and had been concealed from white people. A similar set of circumstances has been described by the anthropologist Hausfeld (1963) in Woodenbong. He found that the remnants of Aboriginal culture that had been made

---

1. The universality of this belief was illustrated to me in November 1971 when I saw two consecutive patients in Bourke who told me that their ailments must have been caused by such curses. One was an Aborigine, the other a Yugoslav.

secret and hidden from whites would have been purely secular material in the tribal situation. These secrets seemed to have some importance for the Aborigines as a possession which they had managed to keep from the white man. By 1973 however there had been such a resurgence of interest in all things Aboriginal and a pride in their Aboriginal ancestry, that Aborigines began to enjoy talking about what they knew. Those few Aborigines who spoke Wanggumara would come together and speak in their own tongue with obvious nostalgia and a gleeful twinkle in their eyes as they made comments about white men who could not understand what they were saying.

A few of the older men still knew their Aboriginal name, but even if they could be persuaded to say it, did so in an almost inaudible whisper. Aboriginal people now carried the names of former white squatters, councillors and merchants. A few had modified nicknames probably given in meaningful jest by some early settler (eg. Bugmy).

Aboriginal folk medicine

There was still a belief in the power of some Aboriginal medical practices and one full-blood Aborigine from Weilmoringle (Mr Jack O'Lantern) was widely regarded by other Aborigines as having healing powers. I knew of three Bourke Aborigines who consulted him when their persistent headaches had not been relieved by Western drugs. All were cured after Mr O'Lantern removed the 'sickness-causing foreign bodies' from their heads.

There was a variety of other treatments which were common knowledge among Aboriginal adults and still occasionally used for treating illness or injury. Burns and dermatitis were treated by applying fat from either the pelican, ant-eater or the lace monitor (*Varanus varius*) to the affected part. Warts were treated by applying sap from the cotton bush plant and boils or carbuncles were drawn with an antiphlogistic made from the marshmallow flower. Impetigo was treated by applying an extract made from dogbush leaves (*Eremophila bigoniiflora*). The leaves of the same plant were also burnt to rid a place of the spirit of a dead person (*see* chapter 5). Rheumatism was treated by rubbing in either fat from the goanna or an extract of lily-root and if that did not produce relief, hot sandalwood was applied to the painful joint. The tuber of the wild potato was reputed to cure kidney troubles and a drink made from the bark of the kurrajong tree was said to have a similar curative effect on diabetes. Another practice which I saw used only once was the application of a small clay cap to protect the soft part of a baby's skull.

The sentiments of the Bourke Aborigines

Sentiments are the beliefs and feelings which structure the way in which people view their world. Without an understanding of these sentiments it is impossible to understand what makes people 'tick'.

I intended to administer an attitude survey to a random sample of whites and Aborigines. This was never completed but the few results that were obtained are worth mentioning since I consider them to be a reflection of the general attitudes of whites and Aborigines in August 1971.

Aborigines believed that white people and especially government and police personnel would not give them a fair go. They tended to distrust white people even though they stated that most were friendly towards them. They were pessimistic about their future but were confused as to whether to try to influence it or to just hope for a lucky break. The attitudes to and beliefs about Aborigines held by white people were almost directly opposite to those held by the Aborigines themselves. Bourke Aborigines were angry, and until recently had not been able to express their anger. This ranged from the massacre of their forebears to their present humiliated condition. In trying to describe the life view of the Bourke Aborigines I can do no better than to quote verbatim some of their statements to me.

X. D.—town male, age 36

I guess we're living in the ashes because we ain't got no pride. Instead, we got shame. We don't know whether we're black or we're white. The kids know. The four year old she sees a white fella and she says 'There's a white fella'. We got too much shame, we worry too much about what the other person thinks of us instead of what we think about ourselves. We worry about what white people think about us, and they only put a great store on material things. Our way is better than theirs because the Aborigine values [human] relationships.

D. T.—town male, age 54

I've lost my language and the dances and the corroborees and the legends have all been warped by the white men and lost in the misunderstanding. I think we shouldn't waste time going back to this past because we don't know enough of what belonged to our people. We should be proud of being children of our ancestors and that's all. It means a lot to me to be what I am because I'm a Christian and I can say with Paul in the Bible that

I am what I am. I'm pleased whenever I see an Aborigine dressed up in the street but we're fortunate in Bourke because when someone [a white] sees you making the attempt he reaches out to help you up.

D. H.—town female, age 28

The whites just want to make you feel dirty. I bust my guts to make everything clean and the welfare come in and make me feel dirty. My friends come in and they say 'Shame, shame' and we laugh. It's a sort of a joke. You laugh because if you didn't you'd cry all the time.

P. E.—reserve male, age 50

People look at us like some sort of substandard way of life. The old Aboriginal way is gone and it can't be revived. We can dream, let's get the old fellows together and revive some of the Abo culture, but that's not real, it's just not real to fit into society today. We aren't going to fit into society today, so why shouldn't we build something of our own. We don't want to be Uncle Tombells or Jackie Jackiebells, we're scared of the white fella way. You know how black fellas are scared of the white fella forms. They don't understand them. They put them in a drawer, they hide them.

P. I.—reserve male, age 36

Sure we live down the reserve and we're happy. Someone comes down and asks us to work and we say no, not today, and we're happy and we take out a fag and we smoke it and we say not today, we're happy, but we're not happy we're bloody miserable and now we're getting some opportunity we've come here to learn how to use it.

O. G.—reserve male, age 27

I don't want my kids to grow up in this shit [the reserve]. It's OK for C. G. to say he'll never move, but what about his kids. Look at H., she's my age, she hasn't progressed much. What will her kids have, bingo, kids at 15, run off with some fellow and then more kids.

Not unexpectedly, there was a smouldering resentment about the massacres of their forebears. Calley (1957) has claimed that Aborigines on the north coast of New South Wales discuss this topic without displaying any sentiments of outraged justice. This however was not true in Bourke. I had the moving experience of seeing more than thirty Bourke Aborigines in tears when discussing how and where their ancestors were shot by white graziers and their white employees. One Bourke woman even suggested that all Aborigines should emulate the Brisbane Tribal Council and wear a red head band to remind them of the spilt blood of their ancestors.

White racism

When the Star-Belly Sneetches had frankfurter roasts
Or picnics or parties or marshmallow toasts,
They never invited the Plain-Belly Sneetches,
They left them out cold, in the dark of the beaches.
They kept them away. Never let them come near.
And that's how they treated them year after year.

Dr Seuss, 1965:7

Like the Plain-Belly Sneetches in Dr Seuss's book for children, Bourke Aborigines were excluded from white society and placed in an inferior relationship to it. Any attempt to understand their attitudes and their situation must take this into account.

With few exceptions, white people in Bourke held a variety of stereotypes about Aborigines. One of the most common was that all Aborigines were dirty. I was frequently asked if I had found much venereal disease in Bourke Aborigines and when I answered in the negative it was obvious that I was not believed. It appeared to me that Bourke had an inordinate number of white women whose obsession with cleanliness was compromised by the presence of the Aborigines.

Another stereotype was that Aborigines were unintelligent due to having small heads and brains. This was 'confirmed' by children's poor performance in IQ tests and their clustering in O.A. (Occupation Activities) Classes. Stories of their ineptitude in doing such things as spending $50 on a taxi ride to pick up $40 of back wages circulated through the town to provide the week's funny story. At the same time Aborigines were regarded as cunning due to their admixture of white blood.

They were alleged to be lazy, drunk, neglectful of their children and prone to go 'walkabout'. Worse still they were ungrateful. It seemed to me that almost every grazier around Bourke had paid 'his' Aboriginal workers well and had given them enough galvanised iron to build a reasonable humpy only to have the Aborigines leave him the following week.

Nearly all the white people of Bourke portrayed the Aborigines by their apparent faults. Only a handful of whites were aware of their not inconsiderable (but not so obvious) virtues. These stereotypes were

41

reinforced by the local press which without being overtly racist succeeded in conveying a picture of Aborigines as diseased incompetent trouble-makers who lived entirely on handouts.

It is well known that residents in small country towns whose economic status is depressed and in which there are large numbers of Aborigines, exhibit the most unfavourable attitudes to them (Gale 1964; Mitchell 1968). The 'undeserving' Aboriginal serves as the scapegoat for the insecurities and uncertainties of the 'deserving' whites. There is also little doubt that the depressed social condition of the Aborigines reflects upon the conscience and the humanity of the white community. By distorting or denying the Aboriginal experience the whites absolve themselves of their feelings of guilt. They reinforced this blamelessness by placing Aborigines in a double-bind situation. They were rejected by white society which at the same time expected them to accept the values of the rejecting society. An added insult was that their artefacts and the cave and rock art of their predecessors were used as tourist attractions by those same racist whites.

Whatever the underlying causes for the perpetuation of racial prejudice against Aborigines it manifested itself by a dehumanisation of Aborigines which allowed whites to exploit them in a manner which would be regarded as unChristian if applied to fellow whites. This exploitation was commercial and it was also through official channels. It approached a peak in the Court of Petty Sessions with a steady stream of Aborigines being fined and/or gaoled for such misdemeanours as 'unseemly words', bald tyres, and committing a nuisance.

In my eyes this exploitation reached its peak at a boxing tournament run by the Rotary Club of Bourke as part of a festival of sport over the Easter period, 1972. Fifteen Aboriginal boys were readily induced to participate in the preliminary contests. These boys were totally untrained, unequipped and without boxing experience. I, and they, understood that they would be sparring with each other. Instead they were served up as cannon fodder to the well trained, fully equipped and experienced white representatives of the Dubbo and Narromine Police Boys' Clubs. Only one Aboriginal boy scored a victory and most of the others were severely outclassed. Barracking during the fight was strictly along colour lines with the Aborigines urging their boys on with shouts of 'give it to Whitey'. This was regarded by the whites in the audience as a manifestation of black racism.

Aborigines in Bourke were commonly spoken of as 'boongs' and 'coons', not infrequently to their face. The more genteel called them 'blackfellas'. These terms were common vocabulary to most white children by the time they were five years old.

At best the relations between white and black were a combination of mutual distrust and mutual ignorance. The greatest white ignorance was the lack of awareness of how racial antipathy affected Aborigines. This was exemplified by one male primary school teacher who complained to me about the apparent lack of interest shown in his school by Aboriginal mothers.

Those women can talk to me at any time. I'm less frightening than you are. I can't stand the way they just stand there and hide their head. I feel like hitting them. But I've told them ten times to come to the Mother's Club but they don't seem to listen to me. I suppose I'll have to keep telling them until it gets through their thick scones that they are welcome to come along.

The American psychiatrist, E. B. Brody, has drawn attention to the effects of cultural exclusion in reducing a person's already low self esteem. He has described how his inferior status is accentuated by being excluded from the possibility of attaining membership in, and being accepted by, those who control the institutions which control his existence (Brody, 1966). The effect of white racism on Bourke Aborigines was to emphasise this loss of self esteem and was a major force in perpetuating their under-attainment. Bourke whites were always surprised when an Aborigine expressed any bitterness over his past or present situation. With few exceptions they failed to understand that the Aborigines were angry and humiliated and that the racist attitudes and actions of Bourke white society made angry Aborigines angrier. With even less insight Bourke whites had failed to recognise how much their racist attitudes and actions had contributed to the problems of the 'problem Aborigines'.

Conclusions about the Bourke Aboriginal situation, 1970–71

It was the misfortune of Australian Aborigines to be colonised by a people who at that time believed themselves to be chosen by God to civilise the heathen races of the world. It was the time of the Industrial Revolution and the potato famines of Ireland. Children of nine years of age were still being sentenced to death for stealing twopennyworth of bread. The Protestant ethic was at its height and the quality of humaneness was at a low ebb. In the west of New South Wales the land and woman hunger of the colonisers and their ruthless determination to prosper was compounded by their ethnocentric incomprehension of the Aboriginal way of life. At the same time the Aborigines' social system was so different from that of an industrial society that they lacked the means to use the new culture. The result of the contact of the two cultures was catastrophic for the Aborigines. They were dispossessed of their land by disease and by violence. The authority of their elders collapsed, together with the cultural practices that had sustained them for at least 30 000 years.

The new settlers made few places available in their economy for 'Bourke Aborigines'. In order to survive they had to become dependent upon paternalistic charity from welfare or mission organisations. In their paternalism these welfare agencies further insulated the Aborigines from learning and developing new skills.

The result was that in Bourke as in the rest of Australia, Aborigines had come to occupy the status of the lowest caste, excluded by behaviour as well as by colour from the mainstream of life in the town. They were generally despised, socially disparaged and their positive attributes were devalued. Their political and economic powerlessness gave few of them hope for the future. They exhibited the psychology of a persecuted and rootless people. In this age a black man who had to get a white man to read for him, write for him and dial a telephone for him, was hardly likely to feel competent or to exhibit much self esteem.

Their functional unit was the extended family but each family mistrusted the other and communication between them was poor. There was no real leadership, no common goals or leisure activities and the Aborigines of Bourke could not have been considered a community except in the sense of their common rejection by the white people of the town.

In brief, most Bourke Aborigines were not beneficiaries of the basic freedoms from want, disease, ignorance, squalor, idleness or of the right to determine their own destiny. They exhibited all the criteria of a socially disintegrated society (Murphy and Leighton, 1965). The effects of deculturation were the same as had occurred to those born losers of the movie screen—the North American Indian and the descendants of those still admired sailors, the Vikings (Berg, 1971).

Most Aborigines regarded their circumstances as beyond their control and reinforced this view by pointing out that those Aborigines who had conformed to middle class white norms were still not accepted by whites and in particular still lacked the self confidence to drink in the private, instead of the public, bars of the local hotels.

The most commonly found individual responses to these sentiments were rebellion, retreatism, conformity and a lack of innovation, a situation described in other poverty groups (Merton, 1957). Many younger men rebelled against white values by fighting, drinking and working only when any other course was impossible. Most older men and some of the younger ones escaped from the problems of their existence by a heavy consumption of alcohol. A few men and women (less than 30) achieved a measure of stability and acceptance by their adherence to and attendance at religious and church ceremonies. Almost ten per cent of adolescent and pre-adolescent youths achieved some measure of unity and esteem in each other's eyes by forming gangs and innovating goals (usually petty theft) which were disapproved of by the majority society.

Whichever way one looks at the situation of the Bourke Aborigines in 1970–71 they were fringe people. They lived on the fringe of the town, on the fringe of the economic system, on the fringe of the education system, and as will be shown, below the fringe of adequate health. They were participators in few of the benefits or the responsibilities that go with being a part of present day modern society. All the processes of white life with which they had to contend helped to make them feel nobodies. The decline of the Aborigines was summed up for me by Mr George McDermott, a full-blood Aboriginal of the Wanggumara tribe, shortly before he died at the age of 88. He said 'When the white man came, he sort of mucked things up'.

Chapter 2
Community development in Bourke

Initiating change—Small beginnings

I arrived in Bourke on 14 July 1970. In August 1970, I began making contact with the Aboriginal people by providing them with some of their medical services. By November I felt confident enough to arrange an evening meeting with fifteen Aborigines to discuss ways in which I could be of any assistance to them. Two of the people present wanted to know why I had chosen Bourke and I explained that the University of New South Wales had taken an interest in Bourke through the invitation of Dr Teddy Coolican a local general practitioner for 22 years. This brief explanation seemed to be accepted at its face value.

With the help of Pastor Bill Reid who had previous dealings with academics from the University of New South Wales, I had organised a further two meetings by the end of the year. An extra ten people attended on each occasion and it was apparent from their discussions that many of them had ideas, desires and ambitions which they wanted to put into action but did not know how. The most common topics raised were housing and the need to get enough education to run a smallgoods shop or to be able to fill in a log-book so they could get a job driving a truck or a bulldozer.

I had a premonition that my task as an agent of change was not going to be easy when I invited a senior teacher to one of these meetings to discuss vocational and adult education. He took almost two hours to read out the relevant (and irrelevant) sections of the Education Department handbook and finished up by telling the Aborigines present that he could offer some help with English and needlework!

One Aboriginal man who suggested that woolclassing, shearing and carpentry might be more appropriate, was told with absolute finality that since these were not specifically mentioned in the departmental regulations it was not possible.

The first act of self determination

By January 1971, a committee had been elected and its members called an urgent meeting to discuss what they regarded as a derogatory article about Bourke Aborigines which had appeared in a Sydney newspaper the *Daily Mirror*. Thirty-eight people attended. This article contained such inaccuracies as:

There are few virgins on the reserve older than 13. A doctor found no girl of 15 who was a virgin. Pregnancy occurs no later than 17 years . . . Of the girls, 80% are unemployable . . . Of the men, 95% have been in gaol at least once by the time they reach 19 . . . Once the symbol of Bourke's fringe-people was a wine bottle rolling in the dust . . . One Aboriginal child from the Bourke reserve was buried every fortnight. (Burgess, 1971)

Feelings at the meeting ran high. As Bill Reid summed up, 'We build ourselves up and this stranger comes and knocks us down and breaks our ego'. It was agreed amid loud applause, that Pastor Reid write a letter to express 'the angry feelings of the Bourke Aborigines'. This letter was duly written, but it was not published despite my telephoning the editor of the *Daily Mirror* to explain how important it would be to the Aboriginal community of Bourke. It was eventually published in the now disbanded Aboriginal newspaper *Origin*, February 1971, under the heading: 'Praise for nuns was "kick in guts" for Bourke Aborigines.' The letter from Pastor Reid was:

The Aboriginal community of Bourke is annoyed with an article that appeared on Thursday, January 14, in the *Daily Mirror*. The article, as we understand it, was in praise of the Indian Nuns and the work which they hope to accomplish among our people.

In praising the nuns, Mr Burgess accomplished a double purpose that could have far-reaching and lasting effects on the lives of our people, not only in this area, but in other places where the article has been read.

The Aboriginal people are suspicious of the white man, and we feel that Mr Burgess, whilst praising the little Nuns, has also belittled the Aborigine.

We resent the statement that our daughters have lost their virginity at the age of 15, and we wonder what purpose Mr Burgess hoped to accomplish other than to draw the unwelcome attentions of the undesirable element of this area to our girls.

We feel Mr Burgess is exaggerating to some extent in mentioning that a child has been buried fortnightly prior to the arrival of the Nuns.

We resent too, the statement that the symbol of the Aborigine is a wine bottle rolling in the dust; also that 80% of our girls are unemployable, and 95% of the men have been in gaol at the age of 19.

Mr Burgess is certainly wrong in saying that the town people have no further dealings with the Reserve Aborigine, for until recently we, too, were part and parcel of the shanty town with its dogs, flies and fights. Many of these people are relatives and live there only because there is no other place to live.

We are fully appreciative of the work done by the little Indian Nuns, and feel sure that they will eventually be able to work successfully among our people, especially the children and old people[1].

But we feel that Mr Burgess, in his praise of the Nuns, has overlooked just how sensitive the Aborigine is, and that his feelings can also be hurt.

The thing that Mr Burgess has overlooked is that a body of Aborigines had already began meeting to discuss problems in the Aboriginal community, together with ways and means to best overcome these problems.

The result of these meetings is that a committee has been formed. This committee will deal with the problems of our people, by bringing them to the notice of those in the best positions to deal with them.

It is on a motion of this committee that this letter has been written, in order that individuals like Mr Pat Burgess should realize that they fail to consider the feelings of others, and the effects of what they write may create.

Let us remind Mr Burgess that a pat on the back has a greater effect in accomplishing some goals than a kick in the guts.

This had been an important meeting in that it was the first time that the Aborigines had decided to express their angry feelings to an open audience, and the first time that the Aboriginal people of Bourke had ever undertaken any political action. They also decided to form the Aboriginal Advancement Association of Bourke (A.A.A.). The President was elected on the grounds that she could write and because she lacked the confidence to chair a meeting it was agreed that several other members should share this duty. By May 1971, 44 different people had attended at least one meeting. The majority of these were members of the United Aboriginal Mission Church which was led by Pastor Bill Reid.

Human Relations Workshop: a turning point

In May 1971, I received an invitation from Dr Ned Iceton, a medical doctor turned adult educator, to attend an Aboriginal Human Relations Workshop at the University of New England. This is an intense learning experience aimed at increasing a participant's insight and interpersonal skills. It is described more fully on page 77. I asked three Aboriginal men who were on the committee of the Aboriginal Advancement Association to attend with me. For two of the Aborigines Armidale was the furthest they had ever been away from Bourke.

1. Six Indian nuns belonging to Mother Teresa's Sisters of Charity were attracted from Calcutta to Bourke to work with the Aborigines. One of the underlying rationales was that people of like skin colour would form a rapport with each other.

The visit to Armidale turned out to be a milestone in the development of the Aboriginal community. The Human Relations Workshop showed them that other Aborigines had similar problems to their own and similar feelings of anger and inadequacy. It also showed them that some of the white 'resource people' also had their emotional 'hang-ups'. They were most surprised to see that some of these white people could be helped by Aborigines. Two of the Bourke Aborigines remained silent throughout the ten days at Armidale and the third participated in an intellectual, but not apparently in an emotional way.

On the way back from Armidale, we visited several towns and my Aboriginal companions displayed interest in the sort of things that were happening in those towns regarding Aborigines. This journey gave me my first real human contact with Aborigines. On returning to Bourke my companions expressed their confidence in me to other Aborigines who began to communicate with me in a more real and trusting manner.

A month after their return from Armidale, the three Aborigines who had participated in that experience decided to start a human relations group with some other Aborigines in Bourke. The two Aborigines who had been silent in Armidale, were now quite talkative and had developed some deep insights into the problems of those people who attended these groups. They displayed increasing skill at conducting sessions with their own people.

I suggested that the human relations groups now be extended to meetings between school teachers and Aboriginal people. Although these were not successful as human relations groups mainly due to the desire of the teachers to argue intellectually amongst themselves about Aborigines, they did serve the purpose of providing the Aborigines and teachers with their first experience of actual contact with each other.

These meetings reached a frequency of three times a week with up to 50 people attending so that they had to be divided up into four groups. More selected white people were invited to attend and they sat in with whichever Aboriginal group decided to invite them. A youth group with about 30 members spontaneously sprang up and chose as their resource people an American high school teacher with experience as a civil rights activist, and Pastor Bill Reid. These meetings were also reinforced by the visit of four Aborigines from Armidale who had been present at the Human Relations Workshop in May.

49

The beginnings of community

A year after I had come to live in Bourke, the A.A.A. was showing signs of some corporate life. Money was being collected through cake stalls, raffles, and at the suggestion of one Aboriginal, through the ubiquitous bingo schools. The A.A.A. had organised a picnic at an old tribal ground 80 km from Bourke which was attended by 250 people. There was considerable interest in A.A.A. affairs; it now had more than 60 regular participants (although few were financial members) and 130 different people had attended at least one meeting. More people from the Bourke Reserve were becoming involved and the meetings were no longer an extension of the United Aboriginal Mission Church.

Application for registration of the Aboriginal Advancement Association and a setback

Because the A.A.A. was not a registered association, the bingo games were theoretically illegal. It was feared that the police might break them up and it was decided to seek registration as a charity. The application to the Chief Secretary's Department was refused without explanation, but probably because more than half the members of the committee had recorded convictions for petty misdemeanours. This refusal was regarded as a major setback by the Aboriginal people, some of whom took the view that the A.A.A. as a whole was not legal and therefore had no power to do anything. This view was propagated by the then secretary who promptly resigned and refused to have any further part in the A.A.A.

The failure to be registered as a charity by the Chief Secretary's Office was only one cause of a sudden loss of momentum among the activists in the Aboriginal community. The treasurer also resigned, partly because of his own internal insecurity at handling money and his inability to manipulate figures, and also because his brother-in-law, who was now employed as a health aide, kept attacking him at meetings. His wife could also see no importance in the work he was doing and begrudged him the time that he spent doing it. A feeling of frustration was evident amongst those Aboriginal people who were attending meetings and human relations groups. This was expressed as almost total apathy to an Abschol[1] project for building a playing field on the Bourke Reserve and equipping it with swings and monkey bars. It

1. Abschol is a university students' organisation aimed at assisting Aborigines.

seemed that the community needed a concrete problem to solve in addition to working out their own interpersonal problems.

However, some things were still going such as the smallgoods and grocery shop opened by two Aboriginal women, the employment of two Aboriginal health aides, the employment of a young Aboriginal woman in one of the pharmacy shops, the setting up of a co-operative funeral fund, and the beginnings of an adult education class. Planning on a building project had started in conjunction with an architect and his four associates.

During 1971, spokesmen from the A.A.A. made several contacts with their Federal Member of Parliament, Mr J. FitzPatrick, the N.S.W. Minister for Child Welfare and Social Services, Mr J. Waddy, and the State Director of Aboriginal Affairs, Mr I. Mitchell. On one occasion many of their views were incorporated in a speech that Mr J. FitzPatrick M.P., made to Parliament (FitzPatrick, 1971). They also had a meeting with a mixed parliamentary committee visiting Bourke. At all of these meetings, housing was discussed and plans were put forward by the A.A.A. about ways to improve housing and also to build a community hall.

One of the most promising signs was the attempt by a shire official to persuade two of the Aboriginal activists to 'leave the black-fellers alone. Look after yourself. You won't do any good for them. They are hopeless. You are just wasting your time and energy. They will use you up. You will do all right for yourself if you come along with the shire'. One of the Aboriginal activists replied: 'Well, I think I can please myself. I am not married to the shire'. This small incident was of some significance in that it was seen and reported by the Aborigines concerned as a sign that the shire was worried about Aboriginal power and therefore, it must be that the A.A.A. in fact had some power.

'Freedom From Hunger' aids community development

As early as August 1971 there had been some discussion about trying to get an Aboriginal field officer working in Bourke. It had been agreed to approach the Foundation for Aboriginal Affairs in Sydney[1]. However, one member of the A.A.A. strenuously objected to this on the grounds that he considered the Foundation to be a 'white man's organisation' and the move was dropped.

1. The Foundation of Aboriginal Affairs was an Aboriginal welfare organisation set up by interested whites and blacks in Sydney in 1965.

51

The Abschol movement of the University of New South Wales had adopted the Bourke A.A.A. as its current interest[1]. They notified the A.A.A. that the Australian Freedom From Hunger Campaign was thinking of supplying money for Aboriginal development projects. At a meeting held to discuss this, Mr Wally Byers (one of the Aborigines who had come with me to the Human Relations Workshop at Armidale) pointed out that other organisations such as the golf club, bowling club and Rugby League Club, all had permanently employed officers to run their affairs. He added that the A.A.A. had more potential members than most of these clubs and should therefore have a permanent officer. He drew attention to the fact that Armidale had an Aboriginal field officer who was employed by the local university. It was agreed to make a submission for funds to the Freedom From Hunger Campaign for the employment of two field officers, one to represent the town and the other the Reserve.

The National Executive Officer of Freedom From Hunger, Mr Alan Smith, visited Bourke and established good rapport with A.A.A. members. In December 1971 eight representatives of the A.A.A. visited the Australian Freedom From Hunger Campaign Executive in Sydney to discuss their submission. This was successful and a grant of $27 000 was made to the A.A.A. to employ two full-time field officers for a period of three years.

After three months of debate it was affirmed in February 1972 that one field officer should be elected on the basis of his association with the town and the other based on his association with the reserve. The A.A.A. selected two of its own members to be the field officers. One A.A.A. committee member was particularly upset at being passed over. He pointed out that the way in which the proposed field officers had been selected did not come from the people and that without the people behind him a field officer would be 'pushing his own shit uphill by himself'. He accused me of being partial to both of these proposed field officers and of engineering their election.

This was a fairly true interpretation of my subconscious and not-so-subconscious manipulations. It was eventually agreed by the A.A.A. that a secret ballot should take place and that all Aborigines over the age of 16 years should be eligible to vote. The Vice-President of the

1. This was because in their search for a project to support, the secretary of Abschol had written to several people working with Aborigines, and I had been the only one to reply.

52

shire was sympathetic to the Aboriginal cause and he and the Deputy Shire Clerk were asked to conduct the election. Candidates had to be nominated and seconded in writing and the nominations given to the Electoral Officer before 14 February 1972. The Committee of the A.A.A. drew up their own electoral roll which contained the names of 225 people over the age of 16 years.

Four trusted white people and one Aboriginal who was not a candidate were asked to go in pairs from house to house with the ballot box and collect votes. The voters had the choice of filling in the voting cards themselves or telling the collectors how they wanted them to be filled in. (It must be remembered that a large majority of the population over the age of 16 years was illiterate.) This method was similar to the Mobile Presiding Officer Scheme in New Guinea.

All votes were taken between 18 and 21 February, and 182 of those eligible cast a vote. There were eight candidates and a preferential voting system was used. The patterns of voting which I had suspected would occur did not eventuate. Families did not vote for candidates from that family. The younger activists received few votes and one of the members previously nominated by the A.A.A., and who in truth was favoured by me, received only two votes.

This election had aroused a lot of interest among Aboriginal people both in town and on the Reserve. It was the first time that they had ever voted. The care with which votes were cast showed that when they understood the qualities which were thought desirable in a field officer, the Aborigines had exercised thoughtful and adequate choices.

Most votes were obtained by Mr Wally Byers who had not been nominated previously by the A.A.A. and he received his support from the Reserve. The second field officer was Pastor Bill Reid who received most of his support from the town.

A grant of $2600 was also received from the Australian Freedom From Hunger Campaign for the purchase of a mini-bus. This seemed to be taken by many white people in Bourke as a material manifestation of Aboriginal power. Some pointed out that this was going to put the taxi drivers out of work and was a clear sign of racism against whites.

Involvement of Reserve people

The interest aroused by the election and the thought that they had a representative began to bring more people from the Reserve into the A.A.A. As a result, it was agreed that some of the meetings should be held on the Reserve. The first such meeting was conducted in the open around a burning tractor tyre and this made any personal interaction impossible. Not all Aborigines from the Reserve held out much hope for the A.A.A. and a spokesman from the Reserve expressed the view that Aboriginal Advancement was rubbish and that 'we got nothin', and them in town in houses got nothin' either. They pay so much rent they don't eat proper and they have to borrow the money off pensioners to buy a gallon of petrol'.

Flexing their muscles

Despite this not uncommon viewpoint, a distinct change was noticeable in the behaviour of Aboriginal people in that they appeared to be more secure and more able to discuss their different points of view. In particular the A.A.A. and their field officers were becoming more confident. An Aboriginal woman complained at an A.A.A. meeting that a Child Welfare Officer had taken over the control of her pension and was rationing out the money to her little by little. The field officers promised to find out whether this was legal by writing to the Minister for Child Welfare and Social Services. The facts were that the woman had actually asked the Child Welfare Officer to administer her pension so that her husband would not get the money and spend it on alcohol. This was not known to the field officers. The Child Welfare Officer was enraged at having to answer questions from his Minister about his alleged misconduct. He accused me of firstly, putting the Aborigines up to writing the letter and secondly, of writing it myself. He refused to believe that the secretary of the A.A.A. could write such a letter, and called him into his office where he gave him a dictation test. The secretary reported that although he 'passed the dictation test with distinction' the Welfare Officer still refused to believe that he had written the letter.

The A.A.A. also began replying to letters in the opinion column of the Bourke and capital city newspapers which contained derogatory or racist remarks about them. These letters were read out at the meetings to the delight and approval of members. The letters appeared to epitomise a change from their previous powerlessness to a new position of greater influence.

A place of their own

By May 1972, many Aboriginal people were expressing interest in the affairs of the A.A.A. Meetings had first been held in the United

Aboriginal Mission Church. They had shifted to a large room in the Child Welfare Office and then to the University of New South Wales pre-school. None of these venues had been satisfactory. Behaviour which was permissible at a political meeting was often not acceptable in a church. The Child Welfare Office was owned by the police and many Aborigines were ill at ease in it, even at night when it was empty. Despite the efforts of several Aborigines, my wife and I, to clean up the pre-school after our meetings, we were never able to achieve the standards required by the teachers and the white mothers who had been rostered for duty on the following day.

After Mr Bernie Coates and Mr John Luckens arrived in Bourke to assist with the building programme, they were able to obtain permission to meet at the old and now derelict and deconsecrated Methodist Church. With the aid of several helpers from the A.A.A. they made the necessary repairs. This old church seemed to be regarded by most Bourke Aborigines as a place of their own and the first two meetings held in it attracted over 100 Aboriginal people on each occasion.

Enhanced self-esteem

The most notable feature was that the Aboriginal people were showing signs of being a community. They organised a newsletter, film evenings, and a small library. Some children were attending an after-school play group run with the aid of two white helpers from Sydney, Trees Wescott and Julie Janson. They had active football and girls' basketball teams.

They were organising 'busy bees' to keep the old Methodist church as a functioning hall and were running barbecues for themselves and for visiting people. They also had a funeral fund. When Mrs Frost and Father Glynn, President and Secretary respectively of the Australian Freedom From Hunger Campaign, visited Bourke to officially hand over the mini-bus to the A.A.A., a barbecue was held for them on the Bourke Reserve. The two guests were served by Aboriginal people and one of the Bourke whites remarked that this was a departure from the usual practice of the whites having to fight for their food like everybody else. Pastor Reid replied that 'In the past, we would have liked to have served you your food, but we would not have been sure that you would have accepted it'.

The further use of human relations workshops

In May 1972, 34 Bourke Aborigines journeyed to Armidale and 21 actively participated in another human relations workshop. This

Plate 8   Members of the Aboriginal Advancement Association at a meeting held in the Bourke pre-school, 1972.

joint venture added to community feeling and solidarity and was manifest in more rational discussion about the difficulties being encountered by the A.A.A. and ways to overcome them. School teachers were remarking that Aborigines were looking them in the eye and that their children seemed more confident in school. This confidence had extended to Aboriginal school children delivering lecturettes to their white classmates, on the Aboriginal way of life of some of the older Aboriginal identities in the town. A summary of the events which had occurred in Bourke since my intervention as a change agent (July 1970 to May 1972) is shown in Table 6.

Political activism

On 10 July 1972 there was much discussion amongst Aborigines about whether to support the moratorium in Sydney to mark National

Table 6 Summary of events in Bourke from July 1970 to May 1972

	Physical health	Psychological health	Political, social and civic
Established	Health Survey	Human relations	Aboriginal Advancement
	Eye Survey	groups	Association
	Nutrition	adults	2 elected full-time Field
	Survey, diet	youths	Officers
	and vitamin	Consultation	Political lobbying: Local,
	levels	with school	State, Federal levels
	Family Planning	teachers	Community owned transport
	Clinic	Psychiatric first	Parents-teachers Human
	General Practice	aid	Relations Group
	Clinic		Pre-school (directed by Dr B.
	Female Peer-		Nurcombe)
	Related		Three regional conferences
	Health Aides		with Armidale Aborigines
			Mr Coates and Mr Luckens
			to supervise, organise and
			train people for housing
			project
			Smallgoods shop
			Adult education—typing,
			literacy, art
			Newsletter
			Abschol support
			Sporting teams—rugby;
			water polo; cricket;
			basketball
			Dances, barbecues

Table 6 Summary of events in Bourke from July 1970 to May 1972— *(continued)*

	Physical health	Psychological health	Political, social and civic
In process	Integration of paramedical agencies: Far West, Community Health, District Hospital Weight Watchers Club	Behaviour disorders in children	Housing (low cost self help)
Being planned or discussed	Health Education Nutritional Education	Married couples human relations group Women's group Alcoholism programme	Beef fattening farm Management—Aboriginal consultation groups— meatworks Family resettlement programme (Prof. J. Cawte, Mr E. Cockburn) Handicraft workshop Co-operative to cover medical, ambulance, funeral, dental, travel expenses and housing
Failed or discontinued	Male Peer- Related Health Aide Hospital- Reserve nursing aid scheme		Legal Aid Service Police-Aboriginal forum

Aborigines' Day. The women were all against it since they said 'We have to eat'. At 7.15 am on Tuesday 11 July, Bill Reid went to the meat works and called on all the Aboriginal employees to stop work and come to a meeting in the Bourke Memorial Park. This extended to those Aborigines employed on the Shire and by the Main Roads Department. The headmaster of the primary school was also approached and agreed to give the Aboriginal children a school holiday. All the people congregated in the Bourke Memorial Park and listened to an oration

Plate 9 Pastor Bill Reid and committee members of the Aboriginal Advancement Association.

Plate 10 The late Ray Johnson serving a roast porcupine to Sister Bernadette of Moree, a participant in the Armidale Human Relations Workshop.

delivered by Bill Reid on land rights and the need to support their own people. White civic leaders had been invited to attend but they all declined. This walk-out caused great inconvenience to all the employing bodies, especially the meat works which had to close down for the day. The managers of all these enterprises were unaware that this was National Aborigines' Day and that this was the Aborigines' way of showing that the withdrawal of their labour could cause great inconvenience to the economy of the town. It was beyond the comprehension of white managers to think that Aborigines could do this of their own volition and they blamed me (who knew nothing until after the walk-out) for the event. During that and the following day, there was an increase in the arrests of people drinking on the Reserve, and most Aborigines who owned cars reported being stopped as many as three times in the two-day period to have their cars examined for roadworthiness. The police also demanded to know why children were not at school and the mothers told them to ask Bill Reid. One policeman replied, 'His name stinks around here'.

Progress continued with the A.A.A. having its ups and downs depending upon the amount of interest shown by Aborigines in Bourke. The first prototype house was under way, but it did not produce the interest nor the involvement of the Aboriginal people for which I had hoped.

Dr H. C. Coombs, one of Australia's most respected civil servants and ministerial advisers, visited Bourke in October, and this created an upsurge of activity in the Association. It was apparent that Aboriginal people needed the approval of white authority figures. When they got this, it in some way legitimised their endeavours in their own eyes.

The A.A.A. was being increasingly seen as a legitimate and even powerful body in Bourke. Part of the illusion of power was that white people regarded it as having almost unlimited access to funds from the Department of Aboriginal Affairs.

The Apex Club had formed a joint committee with A.A.A. and other interested members of the town to talk about setting up a Youth or Police Boys' Club. This was the first time that any white group had ever consulted with an Aboriginal group in Bourke. Committee members of the A.A.A. were also being invited to school speech and prize-giving days as official guests.

The field officers began to agitate over things they thought were injustices. They complained about such things as discrimination

Plate 11   Members of the Aboriginal water polo club.

against Aborigines in the use of unemployment relief monies and about the gaoling of children from as young as eight years of age (W. Reid, *Sydney Morning Herald*, 21 March 1973). They also protested to officers of the Department of Aboriginal Affairs about the zealous enforcement of the *Aborigines Act* 1969 which prevented even social drinking on the Reserve and they began to prepare a case to test its legality.

Regression

Nevertheless, the cohesion which had begun to develop in 1972 had not shown evidence of growth in 1973. Various factions arose in the community, centring around those who were employed on the building team and those allying themselves with the liaison officers. In part this was associated with the relative failure of the building programme which seemed that it would not produce any real change in the housing status of Bourke Aborigines. Many white people were being too influential in Bourke Aboriginal affairs, and not allowing the Aborigines to make their own decisions in their own time. Bill Reid had been appointed an adviser to the Minister for Aboriginal Affairs and was devoting the majority of his efforts to this end and was often away from Bourke. Some of the leading activists in the A.A.A. had decided to go to Newcastle as part of a re-settlement scheme and their know-how and more stable influence were missed from the affairs of the Association. A.A.A. meetings had become formal in the extreme and usually bogged down with the reading and passing of minutes of the previous meeting. This stifled discussion and fading interest was reflected in falling attendances.

However, the social side of the process of community development continued to advance, and this prevented the factionalism from progressing beyond a mild degree. More joint functions such as barbecues and dances were being held and the basketball and football sporting teams continued to function, both in Bourke and making trips to other country centres. A cricket team 'The Koalas', had been formed and entered in open competition and Wally Byers began a water-polo club with the help of a recently arrived Child Welfare Officer. This latter club was particularly successful in that it attracted Aborigines of all ages. Also the easiest way for white people to play water-polo was to join the Aboriginal club. Those who did included a shire official, a policeman and one of the most racist white youths in the town. Their views on Aborigines were much modified by this human contact.

Increased liaison was occurring between the Aboriginal field officers, the Aboriginal health aides, the hospital and the community health and Royal Far West Health Sisters. This enabled A.A.A. officers to organise such things as immunisation campaigns in which the Aborigines themselves could play an active part. It was significant that these immunisation clinics took place in the A.A.A. community centre.

Farewell

In order to reduce the degree of dependency of some members of the A.A.A. upon me I had taken a decreasing part in its affairs for at least a year before my departure in June 1973. This was at the end of a three-year term. I had expected that my departure would be regarded by some Aborigines as a form of betrayal, since despite my efforts and those of the University of New South Wales, I had no successor and their future medical care was not catered for to the degree that I had been able to provide. However, apart from a handful of people who expressed concern that I was going to write about their (Aboriginal) secrets, I did not detect any feeling that I had let them down. The A.A.A. hired a hall for a farewell party for my wife and myself. This was a generous affair attended by over 250 people and included a 'champagne' supper, speeches, a band and dancing. Beside two collective presents, we received a variety of individual gifts particularly meaningful to us because of the thought which had gone into choosing them and the financial sacrifice which people had obviously made to purchase them. I was sorry that more white people from the town did not see this event. It showed so clearly that, given the chance and the confidence, Aboriginal people were as capable as whites of organising a large function and of showing their appreciation of what really amounted to a normal, warm human interaction between them and two now departing friends.

Community development after the departure of the change agent

The A.A.A. continued to meet and conduct its affairs with fluctuating vigour over the next four months. They felt that they should have more control over the building programme and not be influenced by the two whites, Mr John Luckens and Mr Bernie Coates, who were still helping them. The fortuitous appearance of an Aboriginal carpenter was the answer to their desire for black control. He was greeted with unanimous acceptance from both the blacks and the few whites still involved in Aboriginal development.

Eighteen months previously, at the suggestion of the Department of Aboriginal Affairs, the A.A.A. had initiated the establishment of a housing co-operative as a legally incorporated body. On 1 November 1973 the Widjeri[1] Co-operative became a reality with a board of control elected by secret ballot. This election was poorly organised and was seen by some Aborigines and whites to result in a large 'donkey' vote. Mr Wally Byers, the first choice of the Reserve Aborigines in the election of field officers for the A.A.A., had his name at the bottom of the list and was not elected. Although the Widjeri Co-operative was regarded by some white helpers as a development of the A.A.A., it was seen by many Aborigines as being competitive with the A.A.A. The housing money, business and decision-making were taken over by the Co-operative board which became a self contained and

1. A Gamilaroi word for good.

64

elitist body. Its decisions were not relayed to the A.A.A. so that the older body lacked information and the power of decision. The whole basis of the A.A.A. (ie. a forum for discussion and the involvement of the people) was negated. Consequently it ceased to meet as there was no longer anything to discuss.

A power struggle developed between members of the Widjeri Co-operative board. Those who had been activists previously on the A.A.A. became frustrated by being unable to make their newly-involved fellow board members, led by the Aboriginal carpenter, hear their point of view. Considerable personal animosity resulted ending in the resignation of Pastor Bill Reid and the two white members of the board, Mr Luckens and Mr Coates.

This factionalism was aided by the visit of an officer of the Department of Aboriginal Affairs. Whatever his intentions, he left the impression that the Aboriginal carpenter had to leave, which he did (the same day); that the building programme had to be frozen because the books did not balance; and that the A.A.A. had to be reconstituted. It was a measure of the lack of sophistication and confusion of the Aborigines that they meekly accepted these directives. Admittedly, the departmental officer was supported by Pastor Reid who believed that the Department of Aboriginal Affairs official had powers to enforce his suggestions. Mr Wally Byers was probably the only Bourke Aborigine who could have successfully opposed the Canberra official. Ironically he had postponed his annual holiday twice to fit in with the changing plans of the departmental officer and in the end he did go on holiday and so was absent from Bourke.

The result was that the old activists had triumphed over the new, the building programme stopped despite still having $29 000 in the bank, the people began to see the hope of a house as a pipe-dream and all the Aboriginal activists suffered a severe loss of confidence, expressed by the view that 'we can't do anything without Gubs'.

Despite this there were still signs of corporate Aboriginal activity expressed through the resumption of Aboriginal adult education, the formation of a play-school group on one morning a week, sporting team activities and the planning of a vegetable garden on the Bourke Reserve. The retention of the ability to express collective displeasure was obvious from the considerable community excitement and letter writing that was engendered by the alleged poor health care received by one Aboriginal in mid-1974.

65

Wally Byers who at first had been the less dominant of the two field officers had developed into a leader with a firm grasp of the democratic process and of the needs of his people. He was responsible for gathering together the pieces of the A.A.A. and the Widjeri Co-operative. A new board of the Co-operative was reconstituted, all the members having, at some time previously, held office in the A.A.A. The standard of discussion, participation, problem solving and planning at the two meetings which I attended during my two visits to Bourke in 1974 would have been surprising in even the most educated company. Mr Luckens was hired as secretary to the Co-operative for a period of three months. It was stressed to him that he was an employee and that they (the Aborigines) would be the ones to make the decisions.

In August 1974 it seemed that the process of referring decisions of the reconstituted Widjeri board back to the people for discussion was beginning. The board was also aware that its job was to involve the people in the process of development. They were especially concerned to help those still on the Reserve who were asking what Aboriginal advancement had ever done for them. A new round of meetings with a variety of black and white politicians had occurred and this had focused further attention on the necessity to complete the unfinished projects.

In November 1974, the two field officers decided that they had to keep faith with those who had elected them. They used all the available money they could find, including their salaries for the next six months, and put deposits on four houses. They then went to Canberra, declared their actions as a *fait accompli*, obtained financial help to complete their transactions, and returned to Bourke. Then they announced that things were moving again, that the houses which had remained unfinished since the beginning of 1974 would be completed and that at least four other houses would be available.

It was ironic that Wally Byers who, more than any other person in Bourke—black or white—had understood, stressed and practised the necessity for consultation and participation, had had to revert to the white man's method of management and pressure to obtain the objectives necessary to restore Aboriginal activity in Bourke.

A few of the events contained in this chapter as seen through the eyes of some of the Aboriginal leaders are recorded in chapter 14, in particular Wally Byers' summary of change in Bourke is valuable for the insights it can give white people working with Aborigines.

Since that time further materialistic progress has been made. By the end of 1976 a total of 27 families were housed as a result of efforts by the Widjeri Co-operative, seventeen in the town and ten on the Bourke Reserve. The building programme was continuing with the Widjeri Co-operative employing a white carpenter who was also in charge of the training of three Aboriginal apprentices. The Co-operative also employed two full-time Aboriginal field officers previously funded by the grant from the Freedom From Hunger Campaign and an Aboriginal girl as a secretary-typist.

Aborigines were employed as health aides and as teaching assistants in all of the schools in Bourke. One Aboriginal woman provided lunches for mothers and children as part of a nutritional programme aimed at maintaining health.

Bourke Aborigines had become prominent in the sporting scene and their cricket team, 'The Koalas', was winning a few matches. Aborigines were competing in white football teams and the children of some of the more integrated Aboriginal families were having some success in the previously non-Aboriginal sport of tennis.

A summary and brief analysis of the projects undertaken by Bourke Aborigines are shown in Table 7. Despite this materialistic progress the cohesion of the community was less than it had been in 1972. This was partly the result of despondency that has arisen from massive unemployment due to world-wide inflation but also partly due to the channelling of power away from the people into the hands of the employed field officers.

Table 7   Summary of projects undertaken by Bourke Aborigines 1971–76

Project	Result 1974	Reasons for result	Conclusion and statement of principles involved
Aboriginal Advancement Association	Slow beginning, crescendo effect involving a third of adults (>15 years) in the community in 1972.	Original apathy replaced by the feeling that this body could right grievances. A.A.A. was active and successful in expressing an Aboriginal viewpoint. Replaced white welfare organisations as a place to ask for help in righting grievances. Had an active social programme, eg. sports, socials.	People felt a genuine need to better their lot. A.A.A. supplied a forum for the interchange of views and was a political organisation whose aim was to fight for the rights of the Bourke Aborigines.

67

Table 7 Summary of projects undertaken by Bourke Aborigines 1971–76— (continued)

Project	Result 1974	Reasons for result	Conclusion and statement of principles involved
	Declined and merged into Widjeri Co-operative in November 1973.	Many participants alienated and bored by the ritualisation and formality of the meetings which denied them the opportunity of expressing their views. Failure of the executive to carry out resolutions of previous meetings. Meeting topics became irrelevant to their needs, eg. one meeting was bogged down by the secretary trying to convince people of the importance of signing a petition to keep the Torres Strait Islands in Australian territory.	Leaders need to be sensitive to encouraging those with opinions or grievances to air them. White oriented 'motioning and seconding' meetings were foreign to the consensus method of the Aborigines and had the effect of gagging them. Widjeri Co-operative, a white man's idea, set up at suggestion of Department of Aboriginal Affairs and executed by one white helper. Organisationally too complex to be run by Aborigines without white help.
	Still viable 1976. Represents an increase in Aboriginal influence.	Core group from original A.A.A. still active and concerned. Increased capability in making decisions and understanding white society organisations. Recognised as influential by white organisations including the Department of Aboriginal Affairs. Lack of wider community involvement leaves organisation shaky.	With a recognised and intact leadership there is an organisational nucleus around which a resurgence of community interest could eventuate. White organisations still see this nucleus as capable of political action.
Full-time Aboriginal Field Officers	One failure.	Chosen by change agent not by people! Became authoritarian and was rejected by other Aborigines.	Aboriginal leaders should be elected by their peers.
	One partially successful.	Figurehead, scribe and spokesman.	

Table 7 Summary of projects undertaken by Bourke Aborigines 1971–76—
       (continued)

Project	Result 1974	Reasons for result	Conclusion and statement of principles involved
		Strong and willing to stand up for Aboriginal rights. Had skills to communicate with whites and with white organisations. Tended to forget to involve other Aborigines in his work.	
	One successful.	Democrat. Involved other Aborigines. Worked for benefit of other Aborigines without any attempt to gain from his position. Could negotiate with whites in an atmosphere of humour. Began to show effects of work pressure in 1976.	Aborigines need workers who can devote their full time to organising Aboriginal affairs and who can act as a focus for Aboriginal dealings with white organisations. These workers need friends to support them against the anxiety of being criticised by their constituents.
Human Relations Workshops and Groups	Success in 1971–1972.	Filled a felt need for people to have a say in what was happening. Provided a structure in which it was 'safe' to have this say. Proved a more natural medium for reaching decisions than the white 'committee' method. This led to the confidence to express ideas and grievances and to be increasingly articulate in both Aboriginal and white company. Provided a learning medium and insight into the motives and difficulties of other Aborigines and whites.	Change agent needs to encourage the formation of structures which help Aborigines to express themselves and reach consensus and to discourage structures which produce uncertainty and inhibit discussion, eg. the white 'motioning and seconding' committee meeting. Human Relations Group is a method of obtaining and maintaining the interpersonal cohesion needed for effective action.

69

Table 7 Summary of projects undertaken by Bourke Aborigines 1971–76—
(continued)

Project	Result 1974	Reasons for result	Conclusion and statement of principles involved
	Not functioning in 1974.	Too successful in 1972. Utilised too much of the time of the Aboriginal leaders and the change agent. Departure of change agent whose presence was still needed to make these groups 'safe'. Failure in 1973 and 1974 to reinforce the human relations process by a residential workshop as had previously occurred in 1971 and 1972.	Human Relations Groups are a potent method of initiating inter-racial understanding.
	Discussion in 1976 to invite Dr Iceton and Max Kamien to run a further workshop in Bourke.		Running Human Relations Groups requires learned skills and without a facilitator to steer a conflict situation they can be a threatening experience. The insights and experience gained at Human Relations Groups needs to be reinforced at least yearly.
A.A.A. minibus	Success. Provides a means of easy transport for sporting and social functions and hospital or doctor.	Enables Bourke Aborigines to travel to other towns.	Aborigines need material possessions to increase collective community esteem especially in the eyes of other Aboriginal communities.
	Regular bus run not working in 1974.	Not able to charge a fare under terms of licensing. Taxis still more convenient even if more expensive.	Ease of transport increases participation in meetings, sport, etc.

Project	Result 1974	Reasons for result	Conclusion and statement of principles involved
	Traded in for station-wagon 1976.		Sporting clubs have learned to use station-wagon and cars responsibly and to reimburse Co-operative for long distance trips
Housing	1974 Three houses built; two houses partially built; two houses purchased, but large interest in housing. 70% Aborigines on Reserve 1971 in houses in 1974. Failure in itself but resulting in partial success with regards to housing the Aboriginal population.	Not what people really wanted, more akin to what architects wanted. Process of building too slow. Too much central interference from Canberra. Prospect of obtaining a house built by the Widjeri Co-operative less than 5% per annum.	Providing resources to only a few Aboriginal families tends to be divisive and accentuates family factions. Large projects such as housing should aim to provide for the whole community even if this means that houses are smaller and cheaper to begin with.
	1976 17 houses bought or built in town. 10 small houses erected on Reserve. Still demands for community hall.	Better functioning of Housing Co-operative. White carpenter gave Co-operative stability and buildings quality.	Widespread approval for small houses on Reserve since this is what Aboriginal people have asked for but which whites did not want. Housing Co-operative is now a cohesive force in the community even if arbitrary allocation of new houses results sometimes in division.

71

Table 7 Summary of projects undertaken by Bourke Aborigines 1971–76— *(continued)*

Project	Result 1974	Reasons for result	Conclusion and statement of principles involved
Adult education	Failure 1972.	Teachers ambivalent to the programme. Teachers lacked knowledge about this type of education. Aboriginal wives objected to husbands attending mixed classes.	Need to understand cultural norms of the community.
	Limited success 1974.	One teacher, Mr T. Buckman, motivated to teach small groups of Aborigines. He discovered an American method for teaching literacy skills to illiterate adults.	Another case of the 'singer, not the song?' Teachers who lack experience in adult education especially in teaching literary skills need a programme to guide them.
	Ceased 1975.	Mr Buckman transferred.	
Smallgoods shop	Success. Run at an equal standard to other shops in Bourke. Did not go bankrupt as most whites predicted. Transferred business to another Aborigine in 1974.	Two hard working Aboriginal women who were able to refuse credit to other Aborigines when this was necessary. Both women accepted by whites in the town. Back-up support from change agent and capital grants officers from the Department of Aboriginal Affairs.	Given the support and goodwill of their sponsors such enterprises can succeed. Owners need be able to withstand the pressure of relatives and friends to run their business on extended credit.
	1976 Still success. First owner now runs successful and independent meals on wheels as part of a nutrition programme.	Obtained the idea from attending a conference of Aborigines about nutrition.	Aborigines, like whites, need the opportunity of exposure to new ideas.

Table 7 Summary of projects undertaken by Bourke Aborigines 1971–76—
(continued)

Project	Result 1974	Reasons for result	Conclusion and statement of principles involved
Handicraft workshop for making artefacts and children's toys	Failure. Three years after money was made available for it, workshop was unused except by one member of the community.	People did not ask for it. No consultation with members of the community on whether it was needed. Parents were not involved in the type of education of their children in which toys would be useful. No fixed centre to house the workshop.	Project must be a felt need and preferably the request for aid initiating it should come from a number of people in the community.
	1976—Some minor activity.	Due to interest in copper work by Community Health Sister and woollen toys by Indian Nuns.	
Recreational facilities on Bourke Reserve			
Football ground	Ground cleared, grass planted. Watered for one week— failure.	Abschol project. Boy Scout approach. What can I do for you without really finding out by discussion and consultation? Students seen by Aborigines as a manipulable resource if placated by apparently agreeing with their project. No adequate watering facilities made available for use by volunteer Aboriginal caretakers. No immediate result. Would take a year before a playing field was ready.	Abschol students in Bourke only two weeks. Lack of real consultation. No committee elected by Reserve people to have responsibility for looking after the grounds, ie. no social pressure on the two volunteer caretakers. Small projects with long gestation times are more liable to fail than those which yield quick results.

Table 7 Summary of projects undertaken by Bourke Aborigines 1971–76— *(continued)*

Project	Result 1974	Reasons for result	Conclusion and statement of principles involved
Children's playground	Success. Frequently used and apparatus repaired by Aborigines. 1976 upgraded due to special works programme asked for and organised by Aborigines.	Abschol project. Adequate consultation. Project suggested by Aborigines. Swings purchased by Abschol but transported and erected by Aborigines after a 'thinking period' of two months after purchase. Repaired by Aborigines to prevent accidents to their children.	Aborigines' decision after original idea by Abschol. Immediate benefit to children. Immediate benefit of keeping it in good repair.
Sport			
Football, cricket, water polo, basketball	Successful. Began as social competition between Aborigines in other towns. Now teams entered in general competition with whites.	Felt need of Aborigines, especially children. Aborigines already had the skills to participate. Social support of fellow Aborigines. Increased community participation and self esteem beginning to decrease stereotyping by whites through increased human contact.	Utilisation of available skills resulting in immediate success. Social support by other Aborigines enabled participation in the wider world to occur without having to reject norms. Resulted in an ability of those Aborigines involved to organise themselves with funds, equipment, Bingo money used purposefully for the first time.

Nevertheless, change for the better was still taking place. The Bourke Aborigines had developed some self-confidence and an increased ability to organise themselves. In November 1976, Wally Byers who was still a field officer put it this way, 'So you see, Bourke is only a little place, but the Murries are there and the white people are learning to live with it and learning that we are people. We still have a long way to go before white people learn that Murries of Bourke are becoming more than just second-class citizens.'

The process of change

The social development of the Aboriginal community of Bourke has resulted in some measure of success. There were five main factors responsible for this. These were the intervention of a change agent, the emergence of Aboriginal leaders, the formation of a power base in the A.A.A., the increase in insight, social functioning and co-operation through the use of human relation groups, and the broadening of skills and horizons through increased contact with whites and other Aboriginal communities. The role of the change agent is described in chapter 12 and the emergence of Aboriginal leaders in chapter 14. The last three factors are discussed in the remainder of this chapter.

The Aboriginal Advancement Association

It has been often said power corrupts. But it is perhaps equally important to realise that weakness, too, corrupts. Power corrupts a few, while weakness corrupts the many. Hatred, malice, rudeness, intolerance and suspicion are the fruits of weakness. The resentment of the weak does not spring from any injustice done to them but from the sense of their inadequacy and impotence. We cannot win the weak by sharing our wealth with them. They feel our generosity as oppression. (Hoffer, 1964:12)

At the end of 1970 the Aborigines of Bourke lacked any cohesive organisation through which they could negotiate with white governmental bodies. They were, in a word, powerless. They were at the mercy of the official actions or the unofficial whims of the police, the welfare officers, the shire council, the New South Wales Housing Commission and any other person or organisation who wished to exploit or to wield authority over them (*see* chapter 1). At the end of 1974 this degree of powerlessness had diminished. A major reason for this was the formation of the Bourke Aboriginal Advancement Association which, as has been mentioned, later became a legally incorporated body known as the Widjeri Co-operative.

The frequent meetings of the A.A.A., which at its peak attracted over a third of the Aboriginal adults in Bourke, had several important internal effects on the functioning of the community. The meetings provided a forum for the dissemination and discussion of information from which Aborigines could make collective decisions regarding their future plans of action. The discussions also provided a medium through which Aborigines upset over some particular issue or action taken against them by white people, could publicly express their anger. This in itself led to the learning of new ways of dealing with problems in place of the previous head-on collisions with white administrative bodies or the dissipation of frustration and anger through getting drunk.

The process of collective decision making meant that Aborigines gained some collective courage. This was nurtured through small successes such as having their letters to the editors of local and Sydney newspapers published, acquiring a mini-bus and organising some enjoyable social and sporting events. The Aboriginal leaders also began to observe that some white authority figures had begun to take notice of them and that some were unsure of their ground when confronted about their actions. The A.A.A. slowly developed into a political pressure group capable of voicing the feelings of a large proportion of Bourke Aborigines. The A.A.A. became the power base of the Bourke Aborigines from which they could get access to federal, state, and through them to local government bodies.

This organisation was never an influential or a powerful body as are some white organisations in Bourke such as Rotary, Apex and the Returned Services League. Through sheer lack of numbers and economic power few Aboriginal groups in Australia could ever hope to wield much power. Even so, most white authorities and organisations were not sure just how much sway the A.A.A. did have. The fact that they no longer regarded Bourke Aborigines as powerless made for a greater readiness to accommodate and compromise with Aborigines.

To be taken notice of instead of being ignored or ridiculed, to succeed occasionally instead of always to fail, allowed for the development of an increased personal status in the Aboriginal which in turn led in some to a new found dignity. In addition, the fact of having to run their own affairs led some members to learn the skills of negotiation, compromise and pressure needed to succeed in a white man's world.

Bourke Aborigines like nearly all Aborigines in Australia, have been appealing to the altruism of whites for over 100 years, without success. The A.A.A. represented a new strategy in the fight by Aborigines to help themselves. One of the American social activist Saul Alinsky's chief lieutenants in organising oppressed American communities for social action, has pointed out that 'The important thing to remember is that the powerful and the powerless cannot negotiate. If both should come to the same bargaining table, the latter is simply a beggar'. (Peabody, 1971:527)

The A.A.A. provided enough support and cohesion for its representatives to approach the bargaining table with at least a semblance of bargaining power. The A.A.A. did not raise Bourke Aborigines into a powerful group; it did, however, lift their status and their perceived degree of influence above the level of the mendicant and so achieved gains that one-sided white altruism had never been prepared to grant.

Human relations groups

A human relations workshop is a specially created environment to enable a person to have an intense learning experience through discussing interpersonal and material problems and learning new ways of relating to himself, his family and his predicament at the level of his deepest and frankest emotional feelings about a variety of issues. It is a mechanism through which people can bare their emotions, really listen to, understand, and hear what other people are saying and learn more self awareness by seeing themselves through the eyes of others. It is a process by which in the space of about a week people can get to know and understand each other better than most people do after many years of ordinary social contact. Whereas the A.A.A. was predominantly concerned with task oriented material problems, the human relations groups were concerned with the way in which faulty or unresolved interpersonal conflicts affected group efforts at solving the collective problems which affected them.

For most Aborigines the human relations workshop experience was a major one in which they externalised their feelings of inferiority. Through sharing these feelings, and seeing that other people had similar worries to themselves, people began to gain greater personal security and greater trust in each other. They began to see how capable they could be in understanding another person's viewpoint and contributing to the general learning experience of a group. Some wives even expressed surprise at the 'brains' shown by their husbands.

These workshops and their continuation on returning to Bourke were significant in the development of Bourke Aborigines. They provided the beginning of self insight and personal growth and understanding of others (and of reality) and enlightenment into the thinking and motivation of other people, especially whites. The changes in attitude to others resulted in decision making and in many

77

cases to behavioural change and to action. The greatest change was in the ability to express emotions, to be articulate in public and to express personal dissatisfaction.

The extension of these groups to include whites was also important. It allowed Aborigines to see that despite the difference in schooling and literacy they were as intelligent as whites, and that they could stand up to whites and question their authority. It also enabled Aborigines to see that many of the stereotypes held about whites lacked reality. For example in 1970 a Welfare Officer was, to an Aboriginal, the ultimate authority. They assumed, for instance, that eviction, conviction, the confiscation or control of a pension, the placing of a child in care, were all done from the malevolence of the officer's hard heart.

After human relations meetings, with myself, the change agent, as emotional support, Aborigines began to feel they could assert their feelings in safety. The Welfare Officer was seen on the defensive for the first time and disconcerted by trying to justify himself and some of his actions. But most important Aborigines learnt that the Welfare Officer was a cog in a wheel, that he had a boss who in turn had a boss. They also learnt that the Welfare Officer did not always like what he had to do. In short, the Aborigines developed insight into three things. The first was that the Welfare Officer was human as they were human. The second was that he was much more fearful of authority than they were, and thirdly they learnt a little of the complicated workings of the white man's bureaucracies and his ponderous and often inflexible methods of invoking policy. They also realised that they too had to understand these ways in order to cope better with them.

This led to much less hostility to welfare and to housing authorities. The Welfare Officer almost became a 'regular guy'. In times of disagreement with me (the change agent) the virtues of the Welfare Officer would be extolled in comparison with my iniquities. The human relations groups proved to be a nourishing medium for Aborigines to develop insight into themselves and about others and through this to increase their self confidence.

White helpers

Prior to 1971, no Aboriginal in Bourke had ever experienced a relationship of mutual equality with a white. The psychological effects of this cultural exclusion were discussed in chapter 1. The social effects were that Aborigines were denied the opportunity of learning about the white man's world and how the white man coped with it.

One positive side effect resulting from my efforts at social intervention in Bourke was that I was responsible for attracting outside white people to help in the building and other projects and I was also a nucleus around which a few interested Bourke whites could become involved with Aborigines. The relationship which these people developed with Aborigines was one of greater respect, interest, acceptance and eventually of equality, than Aborigines would have believed to be possible from whites. By making themselves available to Aborigines these voluntary white helpers assisted Aborigines in their individual personal growth. The confidence acquired in social relationships with some whites spread to their dealings with other not so sympathetic whites.

By mixing, discussing and travelling with some of these white helpers the horizons of the Aborigines enlarged (as did those of the white helpers). Some of the skills necessary for social functioning in white society were passed on, at first passively but later at some Aborigines' request more actively by these white friends.

Those Aborigines who had close personal contact with me through the A.A.A., and those who had even greater individual exposure to the building team helpers, John Luckens and Bernie Coates, underwent a process of considerable personal development as well as growth in social, organisational and, in the building team, manual skills. They nearly all developed and maintained a high degree of competence in human relationship skills and also an increase in self esteem.

The white backlash

Up until now I have dealt with the events which occurred in the Bourke Aboriginal community as if it were a closed system. It will be obvious from what I described in chapter 1 that the small and largely excluded Aboriginal community was part of and dependent in varying degrees upon the larger white community. How did this larger system react to the early and uncertain forward steps of Bourke Aborigines? In general they obeyed Newton's third law of motion: 'For every action there is an equal and opposite reaction'. In terms of social action this law of physics can be restated: 'When an oppressed group begins to act, their oppressors begin to react'.

This white backlash took the form of rumours about the rise of 'Black Power' and the probability of racial violence. The chief evidence for this was that Aborigines had become 'cheeky'. That is, they had begun to exhibit more self confidence and had stopped lowering their eyes and hiding behind their left hand when approached by a white. There was a rural recession in Bourke between 1971 and 1973 and this accentuated the general dissatisfaction of many whites. They maintained, in spite of factual evidence, that all Aborigines were living on Social Service payments three times greater than that paid to a white in similar circumstances. Although, in 1972, only 12 Aboriginal children were in receipt of a secondary schools grant of $200 per annum, this was regarded as the height of discrimination against whites. The fact that the school hostel (for 30 whites and 3 Aborigines) was subsidised by the state government to the tune of many thousands of dollars was ignored. This feeling of anti-white discrimination was one of the reasons (and perhaps the chief) for the inception in Bourke of the Isolated Children's Parents' Association which succeeded in the space of one year in obtaining a federal government subsidy of $400 a year for children who were disadvantaged by living distant from secondary schools. To enumerate all of the stories and rumours about Aborigines (and those whites who assisted them) would be to labour my point. It is enough to say that they were totally unrealistic in comparing the 'affluence of the government supported Aborigines' with the 'undeserved poverty of the whites'.

The Bourke Aborigines were regarded by most whites as a thing and a commodity. At best they could be granted patronage but not equality and expected to realise they lived in Bourke under the sufferance of whites. As one influential citizen stated to the Rotary Club of Bourke 'I am prepared to put up with those [Aborigines] who live here but not with those who come from elsewhere'. To many whites it was intolerable that an Aborigine should now become a person and expect equality and civility from whites as a right and not as a bonus. When the A.A.A. obtained a bus, whites expressed anger against the Aborigines for trying to put the six taxi drivers out of business. They were incredulous when two Aboriginal women purchased a smallgoods shop. As one antagonistic primary school teacher said, 'You mean Abos are going to be competing with whites'.

The white backlash was also expressed by one woman collecting a petition to keep Aborigines out of houses in the town and by letters to the local and Sydney newspapers, of which the following are examples.

To the Editor, the *Western Herald*

Travelling conditions for children

April 4th, 1972

Dear Sir,—I would like to draw to the attention of our Darling Shire Council, plus all ratepayers in such, to the deplorable state in which approximately 90 school children returned this day to their various Schools.

These children were jammed into two box carriages on the Bourke-Brewarrina train, which also had 7 sheep vans attached, giving the sheep much more room than these children.

Our Shire won the Bluett Award[1] last year and I am led to believe stand every chance of a repetition this year.

After considering the assistance given by the Aboriginal Welfare Board to the Aborigines in the form of Government Grants whilst working on Darling Shire, Baby Benefit Bonuses, School Subsidy Allowances, plus Modern Housing surely our Darling Shire could induce the Department of Railways to make some attempt to provide better and more comfortable travelling arrangements to return these children of ours to their respective Schools.

Respectively yours. Jack Bye, Kenmere Bore, Bourke.

To the Editor, *Daily Telegraph*

February 25, 1972

End racism

I think it is high time racial discrimination in Australia was stamped out. By this I mean discrimination against the white people.

Here in Bourke I see it every day. Periodically we are invaded by idealistic students who tell the Aborigines that 'black is beautiful', buy them grog and then leave the townspeople to suffer the consequences.

Aboriginal kiddies always have enough money to buy hot chips and lollies but you can count on one hand the white kiddies who have this kind of money.

Every now and then teams of specialists come here and give their services free of charge to the Aborigines but the whites who suffer under the same conditions pay through the nose.

The men are given more than $50 a week for doing nothing so why should they work? I say—take away this handout, let them work for their money and let them have some pride in themselves as a nation.

True that some live in deplorable conditions on the Reserve, but they don't want to move. New Housing Commission homes are being built for them which they proceed to destroy.

I am not anti-Aborigines; they are as intelligent and as capable of good things as most whites, but not while everything is handed to them on a plate.

I am definitely 'anti' this sort of racial discrimination.

Reader, Bourke, N.S.W. [Name and address withheld at writer's request.]

---

1. An annual award for the most progressive shire in New South Wales.

Children repeated the views of their parents and one Abschol student visiting Bourke in mid-1972 reported that a group of eight year olds he met when playing a trumpet on the river bank opposite to my house, told him to 'watch out for the bad guy who lives over there'. When asked to explain in what way I was bad they said 'He likes blackfellas'. One then repeated the current racist joke of the town which had been thought up by a school teacher. 'There are only four things wrong with Bourke and they all start with C. Camien, Coons, Cockburn, and Cunts like Phil Ayre[1].'

For over 100 years white people in Bourke have been exhorting Aborigines to be more like them. At the same time the Aborigines have fulfilled the role of the scapegoat in that rural society. No matter how far down the social scale a white may be, he could always point to Aborigines as being lower. No matter how much his dignity was impugned by being out of work there were always those with apparently less dignity. This was another instance of whites placing Aborigines into a classical 'double-bind' situation. They have exhorted them to be more like whites and then when some Aborigines begin to make the attempt they have cried 'racial discrimination against whites'.

For many whites the beginnings of the social development of Bourke Aborigines was not a state of temporary anxiety or a challenge to adapt to change; it was a warning of further anxiety to come, with a possible loss of power, prestige and the reduction in the gains from their vested interests in maintaining the *status quo* of Aborigines.

The American psychologist Morton Deutsch has drawn attention to the fact that social scientists have,

too often assumed that the social pathology has been in the ghetto rather than in those who have built the walls that surround it, that the 'disadvantaged' are the ones that need to be changed rather than the people and the institutions who have kept the disadvantaged in a submerged position. (Deutsch, 1971:569)

I have already pointed out how the A.A.A. shifted the power equation in Bourke a little way from the established white hierarchy and how I hoped that this shift would become stabilised and accepted before further changes took place. The entry of Aboriginal sporting

---

1. Camien—A mis-spelling of Kamien; Coons—A commonly used term of derogation for Aborigines; Cockburn—A Child Welfare Officer who often sided with Aborigines; Phil Ayre—The Employment Officer for Aborigines in the Western Shires area who was active in Aboriginal affairs.

teams into open competition with white teams also aided this process by increasing social interaction between blacks and whites and caused some whites at least to examine the existing negative stereotypes they held about Aborigines.

My endeavours at changing the views and actions of 'those who built the walls' will be described in chapters 10 and 12. I also made an attempt through my role as a psychiatrist to help the other 'helping agents' such as teachers and policemen to understand and so to manage better what they often regarded as the aberrant behaviour of the Bourke Aborigines (*see* chapter 13).

Chapter 3
The patterns of illness

In order to define the health needs of Bourke Aborigines it was necessary to acquire a comprehensive picture of their patterns of illness. I did most of this work in the latter half of 1971 by which time I had been resident in the town for more than a year and was providing most of the general medical care to the Aboriginal community.

My data were collected by interviews, physical examination of subjects and from the records of the Bourke District Hospital. The methods I used and the results are described in more detail in various medical publications (Kamien, 1975a and b; 1976a and b).

Mortality

In the five years from 1967 to 1971 there were 18 infant deaths out of 204 live births—an infant mortality rate of 88 per 1000. This was very close to the estimates calculated by Moodie (1973) for part-Aborigines in the whole of New South Wales. Twelve of these children died after the first month of life (their mean age of death was 5 months) and in theory their deaths would have been preventable had medical care been sought earlier. Seven of these children died from pneumonia, three from gastroenteritis, one from whooping cough and one from internal haemorrhage. During the same period only five white children died out of 532 births—an infant mortality rate of 9.4 per 1000. Only one of these children died after the first month of life.

In the same five-year period, 26 Bourke Aboriginal adults died out of an estimated mid-period adult population of 280. Ten men and four women died from heart attacks and nearly half of them were under the age of 50 years. This was probably related to the high frequency of diabetes, high blood pressure and increased blood fats found in this particular community. All but three of the remaining deaths were due to kidney failure, motor vehicle accidents, homicide and suicide. The death rate for all of these last mentioned conditions was far in excess of what would be expected in the Australian community as a whole. Nevertheless, the death rate for Bourke Aboriginal adults was similar to that for part-Aborigines in New South Wales between 1955 and 1964 (Moodie, 1973). Few Bourke Aborigines reached old age and the proportion of those older than 65 years was only 1.5%. In comparison Bourke white people older than 65 years made up 6.4% of the white population of the shire.

In his book, *Aboriginal Health*, Dr P. M. Moodie argues that one of the most sensitive indices of a community's state of health is the proportion of its members who, at death, are aged over 50 years. For instance, from 1958 to 1960, 84% of white Australians were over the age of 50 years at death, but for Northern Territory Aborigines the figure was only 35%. The proportion of Bourke Aborigines who died after the age of 50 years was similar to that of the Northern Territory. Between 1962 and 1966 the proportion was 29% and from 1967 until 1971 it had improved to 39%. Even so such a figure compares unfavourably with many of the poorer developing countries of the 'Third World'.

Physical illness

I questioned 343 mothers about their children's health. They reported that 17% of the children were generally unwell and that 20% of the children had contracted an illness in the previous month from which they had not yet fully recovered. The most common diseases found in Aboriginal children were intestinal parasites, trachoma, dental caries, running ears and perforated eardrums, bronchitis, school sores (impetigo), ringworms and anaemia (*see* Table 8).

Of the 282 adults that I interviewed, 31% complained of persistent ill health and 34% said that they had an episode of illness in the previous month from which they had yet to recover. In adults the most common diseases found were dental caries and gum infections, a variety of eye disorders, fungal infections of the skin, chronic bronchitis, urinary tract infections, intestinal parasites, high blood pressure and anaemia (*see* Table 9).

Intestinal parasites

Intestinal parasites were found in the stools of 63% of those children tested, even though the majority had been treated for 'worms' at least once in the previous two years. The most commonly found parasite was the protozoa *Giardia lamblia*. This parasite lines the upper part of the gut and can prevent the absorption of food, leading in turn to the

85

Table 8 Proportion of Bourke Aboriginal children aged 1 to 14 years with a recent history of illness and/or with abnormal findings in October 1971[1]

System	History of illness		Physical or laboratory examination	
	Number questioned	% with recent illness	Number tested	% in need of medical attention
Intestinal parasites	357	44%	158	63%
Iron deficiency blood film			260	51%
Anaemia			260	13%
Eye disorder	350	18%	350	50%
Dental disease	253[2]	27%	261	38%
Height < 10th percentile[3]			344	28%
Weight < 10th percentile			344	25%
Ear disorder	351	21%	370	23%
Recent illness without full recovery	343	20%		
Respiratory disorders	315	27%	369	17%
Generally unwell	343	17%		
Gastrointestinal disorder	250[2]	12%	369	16%
Skin (infective) disorder	346	27%	369	16%
Hair (pediculosis)	346		369	3%
Urinary tract infection	357	1%	111	5%
Total in need of medical attention			370	72%

1. Percentages rounded to the nearest whole number.
2. Children 5–14 years only.
3. A percentile chart is a way of comparing an individual child with a standard for other children in the population. In the white Australian population only 10% of children will fall below the tenth percentile.

Table 9 Proportion of Bourke Aborigines older than 15 years, sexes combined, with a recent history of illness and/or with abnormal findings in October 1971[1]

System	History of illness		Physical or laboratory examination	
	Number questioned	% with recent illness	Number tested	% in need of medical attention
Tooth disorders	285	68%	244	70%
Recent illness without full recovery	282	34%		
Generally unwell	282	31%		
Eye disorders	288	31%	268	31%
Gastrointestinal disorders			263	31%
Skin disorders	288	10%	263	30%
Aching muscles, bones or joints	288	29%		
Respiratory disorders	266	22%	264	21%
Urinary tract infection	284	16%	158	19%
Intestinal parasites			56	18%
Anaemia			199	15%
Hypertension			262	15%
Recurrent headache	287	14%		
Gynaecological disorders	123	14%		
Obesity			233	13%
Ear disorders	288	13%	264	12%
Diabetes mellitus			268	5%
Total in need of medical attention			292	79%

1. Percentages rounded to the nearest whole number.

production of voluminous loose and foul-smelling stools and a failure of the child to thrive. These children were also more prone to develop anaemia. During the three years that I was in Bourke only one white child was found to be infested with *Giardia lamblia* and he was a white infant from Sydney who became ill while on a caravan holiday in Bourke. This parasite is easily spread and is ubiquitous in many populations throughout the world and the fact that it was so common in Bourke Aboriginal children and so uncommon among Bourke white children was another indirect measure of the social distance between them. *Giardia lamblia* were also found in 7% of the stools of asymptomatic adults. Whipworm, threadworm, roundworm and the dwarf tapeworm were also found in children and adults but of themselves did not appear to cause any major symptoms.

Dental disease

Of the children aged 5 to 14 years, 38% had fairly gross dental disease. All of them had active caries and approximately one third of the children had easily visible inflammation of their gums. Although 27% had complained of a toothache in the previous year only 11% of the children had ever attended a dentist.

A survey carried out on the white children at one school in Bourke showed that their dental state was not much better than the Aboriginal children despite having received more dental care in the form of fillings and extractions. However, the white children had much less gum infection and this was presumably a reflection of their greater opportunities to practise dental hygiene.

Toothache was a major source of discomfort to Bourke Aboriginal adults and three-quarters of the men and almost two-thirds of the women reported having had at least one toothache in the previous year. Despite this, only 45% of the men and 56% of the women had ever received dental treatment at any stage of their lives. Easily visible dental caries were found in 66% of the men and 74% of the women. About half of them also had severe infection of the gums and teeth so destroyed that they were unable to be used for mastication (*see* Plate 12). Professor Tasman Brown of the Department of Oral Biology at the University of Adelaide has placed the blame for the increasing rate of caries in Aborigines on poor food habits, poorly fluoridated water and an absence of dental treatment (Brown, 1972). In Bourke, the Aboriginal people drank rainwater, which is deficient in fluoride, or

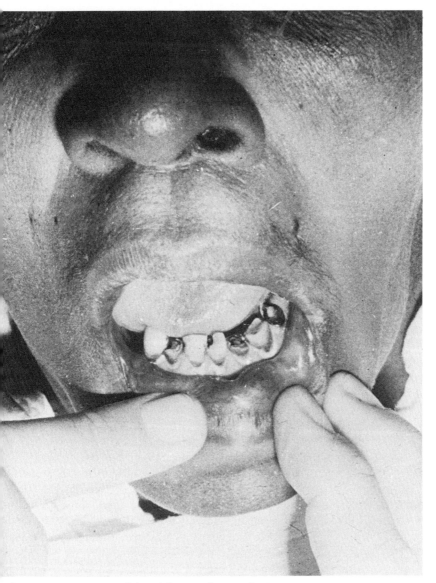

Plate 12 A severe case of dental decay and gum infection.

water from the Darling River, which has a fluoride content of 0.25 to 0.75 parts per million, depending on the amount of recent rain in the area[1]. Their diet was very high in carbohydrate and dental treatment was not easily accessible. No attempt had ever been made to encourage or educate them to seek proper dental care. I was able to discover only one toothbrush on the Bourke Reserve, and that was used for cleaning a gun. Besides using Bex or Vincent powders the Aborigines tried to relieve their toothaches by keeping their mouths full of water. I discovered three women who used methylated spirits instead, in the belief that this would rot out their hollow teeth.

Eye disease

Trachoma is an eye disease caused by chlamydia, an infective agent with properties half way between that of a virus and a bacteria. Trachoma is associated with overcrowding, uncontrolled breeding of flies and poor facilities for adequate hygiene. Since these conditions are common to many Aborigines throughout Australia it is not surprising that surveys in Western Australia and South Australia have shown a frequency of trachoma that has ranged from 49% to 96% of the children studied. In Bourke 50% of the children had trachoma and the greatest frequency was found in those children under 5 years of age (see Plate 13).

Although acute trachoma was endemic in the children, chronic trachoma was found in only nine adults and only three of them had enough distortion of their eyelids to require surgical correction. Chronic trachoma results in scarring of the cornea and is the world's major cause of blindness currently affecting over 20 million people. It was surprising that its effects were so mild in Bourke Aborigines. This is not true of other Aboriginal communities in Australia and it is probable that in Bourke treatment of severe superimposed bacterial infections with antibiotics over the last 30 years, has tended to limit the development of scarring of the cornea and eyelids.

White people in Bourke like white people throughout Australia had a low frequency of trachoma. In the absence of an effective vaccine it is probable that trachoma will remain endemic in Bourke Aborigines until their general health and living conditions approach that of the

1. To prevent tooth decay the recommended concentration of fluoride in water is one part per million.

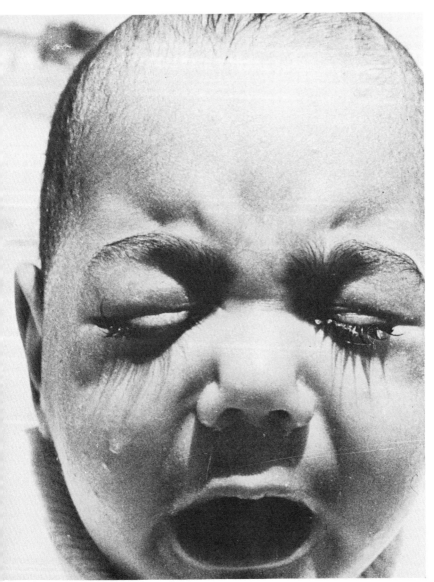

Plate 13　An Aboriginal child suffering from trachoma.

majority of white people in the same town.

It is also possible that simultaneous antibiotic therapy of the entire Australian Aboriginal population could eradicate trachoma. Professor Fred Hollows from the Prince of Wales Hospital in Sydney is at present attempting such an approach.

Besides those with chronic trachoma, a further 25% of all Bourke Aboriginal adults were in need of ophthalmological attention. The most common eye disorders found were cataracts, large fleshy growths across the cornea due to chronic exposure to dust (pterygia), refractive errors of the eyes requiring glasses and disorders of the retina at the back of the eyes due to hypertension and/or diabetes.

Ear disease

Acute middle ear disease is a common disorder of children. An English survey involving 47 500 children showed that in a third of them it resulted in at least one visit to a doctor in the first ten years of their life and that 30% of all attacks of middle ear disease were associated with a discharging ear. However, follow-up six months later showed that nearly all the perforated ear-drums had healed (Medical Research Council Working Party for Research in General Practice, 1957). The main difference between middle ear disease of middle class children and that of poorer class children is that the disease in the latter is more indolent. A high frequency of chronic ear disease has been found in children of socio-economically deprived backgrounds irrespective of their ethnic origin. It has been described in slum children in Glasgow, Eskimos in Alaska, Maoris in New Zealand, disadvantaged children in New York and in Navajo Indians on the Colorado Plateau. This relationship with poverty is also seen in the historical context.

Hippocrates (460–375 BC) wrote that 'watery discharges from the ears' were often found in 'little and new-born children'. In England at the turn of this century ear nose and throat specialists expressed concern at the continuing accumulation of middle ear disease which they attributed to 'a public neglect of discharging ears as long as they were painless'. At the same time Dr R. Arthur, a surgeon at Sydney Hospital stated that 'from the false perspective of an outpatient clinic, one is tempted to affirm in his haste, that every second child among the poorer classes possesses such an [running] ear' (Arthur, 1902:314).

Since Bourke Aboriginal children are socially and economically deprived it might be expected that they too would suffer from chronic ear disease. Eleven per cent of the children had a suppurative discharge from one ear and another 5% from both ears. A further 5% of children had a dry, unhealed perforation of one ear-drum and another 3% of children had a dry, unhealed perforation of both ear-drums. These unhealed perforations could be expected to become re-infected and begin to discharge after children had acquired a 'cold' or some other upper respiratory tract infection.

Many fanciful hypotheses have been voiced by doctors and nurses about the cause of chronically discharging ears in Aboriginal children. Some have blamed the shape of the Aboriginal (and part-Aboriginal) skull for supposedly causing the tube connecting the middle ear with the back of the throat (the Eustachian tube) to be more horizontal and thus less efficient at draining the middle ear. Another commonly held theory is that because Aboriginal children often bottle feed lying down, infected milk runs from the back of their throat into their middle ear. Other causes that have been postulated are allergy to milk, deficiencies of vitamins, iron and immunological resistance. Failure to blow the nose or a lack of skill in doing so has also been blamed. Evidence in favour of any of these hypotheses is generally lacking. Chronic ear disease begins many years before Aboriginal children are allowed near a pool or a river so that it is unlikely that swimming was a causative factor in itself although it may perpetuate existing ear disease.

This chronic ear disease resulted in partial deafness and had an effect on language development in young children and later on their ability to benefit from schooling. Hearing tests were performed on 236 children aged 5 years and older and 11% were found to have appreciable hearing loss (that is greater than 20 decibels loss) in their better ear. Four of these children were obviously deaf and had a hearing loss of more than 40 decibels in their better ear. Seven children aged 5 to 7 years were found to have a combination of severely discharging ears, deafness and speech defects. A further 9% of the children had a hearing loss of greater than 20 decibels in only one ear. Hearing tests are an arbitrary tool especially in middle ear disease which has seasonal fluctuations. Had these hearing tests been performed in the winter when upper respiratory tract infections were more common, it is probable that many more children would have been found with chronically discharging ears and further hearing loss.

In general the teachers of these children did not realise they were deaf. They regarded them as inattentive and often placed them at the back of the classroom where they would cause the least disruption to the rest of the class.

Educational deprivation was not the only serious social effect of running ears in Aboriginal children. The easily visible discharging ears played their part in accentuating racial prejudice. White mothers feared that their children would catch this infection and the proposed school purchase of audio-visual equipment with attached earphones caused alarm in some generally fair-minded white women.

Chronic ear disease was one of the main causes for evacuating children to Sydney hospitals for treatment. Although this was done with the best of motives it seemed to me to be contra-indicated, both from the point of view of unnecessary separation of children from their parents and because unless the children had been carefully selected it proved to be a useless exercise. I was able to follow up eleven children who had spent an average time of 138 days in Sydney hospitals before their eighth birthday because of chronically suppurating ears. All of them still had perforated ear-drums and seven had profusely running ears. A further seven Aboriginal children had surgery performed to repair their ear-drums in the previous five years. Four of them had a re-perforation of their ear-drums due to reinfection and the failure to seek medical attention at that time. Voluntary agencies which bypassed the local medical practitioner in what really amounted to a form of kidnapping service, were contributing little to improving ear disease in the Aboriginal children of Bourke.

Although the frequency of chronically suppurating ears became less as children grew older about one quarter of the children affected could expect to be troubled by active ear disease in later adult life. Of the 264 adults that I examined, 8% had a perforation of one ear-drum and 4% a perforation of both their ear-drums. Half of these subjects had at least one running ear. Hearing tests showed that 6% of the adults had a hearing loss of greater than 20 decibels in their better ear and all of them had obvious and socially inadequate hearing.

Respiratory disease

A history of recurrent coughs, sore throats or bronchitis was obtained in 27% of the children. This was more common in the younger children and was found in 56% of those children aged one to four years. Despite the fact that children were examined in October when the total population was generally free of 'colds', 28% of Aboriginal children were found to have a running nose. Abnormal respiratory sounds were heard in the chests of 17% of the children examined. This was particularly common in children under the age of 5 years of whom 40% were so affected.

The respiratory diseases of chronic bronchitis, emphysema (over-distension and rupture of the air spaces in the lungs), and pneumonia were major causes of disability in Bourke Aboriginal adults. Between 1967 and 1971, 24% of the adult Aboriginal population of Bourke were admitted to hospital on at least one occasion with one of these diseases and 5% of the total population had three or more hospital admissions for respiratory disease in the same period. In 1968, Dr Coolican recorded that pneumonia and bronchitis accounted for 15% of all disease episodes in Aborigines and only 5.5% of disease episodes in Europeans who attended his practice in Bourke. A loose productive cough was found in 21% of adults and abnormal lung sounds were heard through a stethoscope in 17% of adults. This is between two and three times the frequency of respiratory disease that might be expected in a community of white Australian smokers (Gandevia, 1967).

The cause of this troublesome repiratory disease is a matter of speculation, but such factors as poor nutrition, over-crowding and

Table 10 Smoking habits in white inhabitants of Prahran, Canberra and Busselton compared with Bourke Aborigines and expressed as a proportion of their adult population

	Percentage of non-smokers		Percentage smoking 1–14 cigarettes per day		Percentage smoking > 15 cigarettes per day	
	M	F	M	F	M	F
Prahran[1]						
(Melbourne)	44.5%	65.1%	20.7%	14.0%	34.8%	20.9%
Canberra[2]	48.1%	65.0%	12.7%	16.6%	39.2%	18.4%
Busselton[3]						
(W.A.)	56.0%	76.0%	38.0%	12.0%	22.0%	12.0%
Bourke	13.3%	29.4%	26.6%	34.7%	60.1%	35.9%

1. Rankin and Wilkinson, 1971.

2. Hennessy et al., 1973.

3. Cullen and Woodings, 1975.

living conditions which offered only minimal protection against the cold, wind, dust and smoke were almost certainly contributors. In addition, Bourke Aborigines were very heavy smokers. Only 22% of the adults were non-smokers and a third of them had formerly been heavy smokers. The men began to smoke at an average age of 13 years and the women at 16 years. By the time they were 12 years old, 49% of the men and 11% of the women were regular smokers and by the age of 16 years, 95% of the men and 53% of the women smoked regularly. This adult pattern of smoking was established ten years earlier than that recorded in the most recent surveys of white populations in Australia (*see* Table 10).

Tuberculosis was one of the serious diseases that Aborigines acquired through white contact and until recently it was a frequent problem for Bourke Aboriginal adults. I found only six subjects with tuberculosis and only one of these was a newly discovered case. The living conditions of most Aborigines in Bourke were ideal for the spread of tuberculosis, therefore my finding of only one new case was a tribute to the effectiveness of the previous state and Commonwealth tuberculosis eradication programme.

Diseases of the skin and hair

Recurrent skin sores were a fact of life in people with poor facilities for personal hygiene and whose living conditions exposed them to mosquito and sandfly bites (*see* Plate 14). Sixteen per cent of the children examined were found to have skin infections. Half of these had ringworms and the other half impetigo (staphylococcal skin sores) (*see* Plate 15). Both these infective skin troubles tended to flare up into small epidemics and if not treated early often required hospitalisation. Ringworm was almost certainly caught from infected dogs which roved around nearly all Aboriginal dwellings in Bourke (*see* Plate 16).

Although only five boys and fifteen girls were found to have head lice (*Pediculus humans* var. *capitus*) this condition warrants further discussion because it arouses such emotive reactions in white Australians who regard lice as synonymous with a lack of hygiene. These attitudes towards lice have been handed down for several generations and probably originated in Australians from the time of World War I when epidemic typhus, spread by the body louse (*Pediculus humans* var. *corporus*), was responsible for the death of many

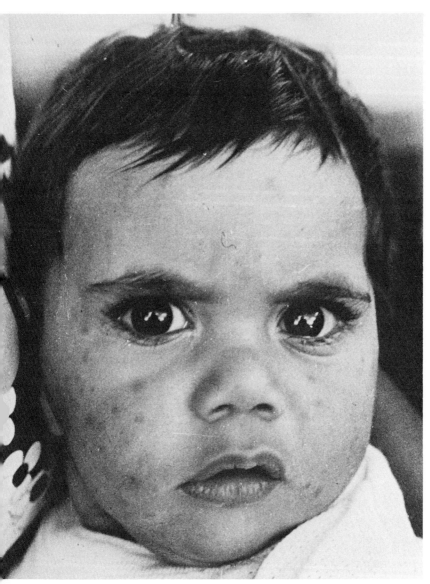

Plate 14 An Aboriginal baby with severe mosquito bites.

Plate 15   A child suffering from ringworm.

Plate 16   Dogs were a common source for ringworm infection.

soldiers who fought in the trenches of Europe. Although the head lice found in Aboriginal children were asymptomatic and were not associated with any secondary infection, the social consequences for those school children were out of all proportion to the severity of the infestation. The almost hysterical reaction to lice by some of the school teachers must have cemented in the minds of the children the feeling of being a 'dirty Aborigine'.

The most common skin disease found in adults was a form of tinea (tinea versicolor) which occurred in 33% of men and 20% of women. Although this caused minor itching in most of the people who had it, they had had it for so long that the only time any notice was taken of the condition was when it caused widespread pale patches on the skin and they became worried that they would turn into white men (see Plate 17). This disorder is spread by body contact and as it is resistant to most antifungal medication, it is almost impossible to eradicate.

I did not find any cases of scabies in 1971. However, early in 1973 a family with scabies arrived from Sydney and the mites spread rapidly through the Aboriginal, and to a lesser extent through the white, community.

Cardiovascular disorders

Studies in white populations in Australia have shown that about 15% of adults have hypertension. The prevalence of hypertension in Bourke Aborigines was similar with 14% of the men and 16% of the women being affected. The main difference was that hypertension was found at an earlier stage in Aborigines than in whites and this was especially so for women of child-bearing age. The other main difference was that only four Aborigines were being treated for their hypertension and they reported that they took their tablets only when they felt they needed them. This, most often, was when they had a headache.

The two main causes of heart disease were hypertension and rheumatic fever. Seven subjects had episodes of angina—nearly all the result of underlying hypertensive heart disease. The most common cause of valvular heart disease found in Australia used to be rheumatic fever. Since World War II it has become much less common in white Australians mainly as a result of their improved social conditions and the rapidity with which they receive treatment with antibiotics for

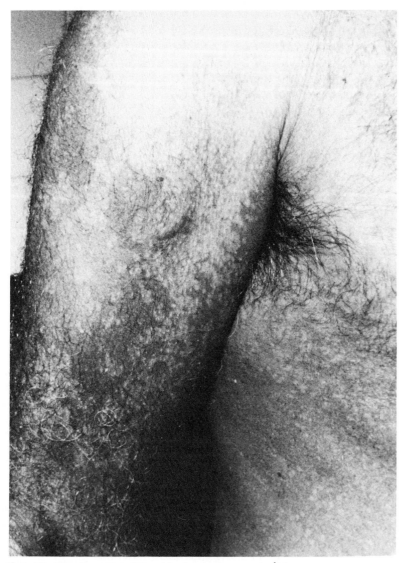

Plate 17   Discolouration of the skin due to tinea versicolor.

streptococcal sore throats[1]. A high prevalence of rheumatic heart disease is now found only in people living under conditions of poverty. Three men and eight women had heart murmurs probably resulting from previous episodes of rheumatic fever and one of them was so severely incapacitated that she was referred for immediate replacement of her damaged mitral valve.

Five children were found with heart disorders. Two had known congenital heart disease for which they were receiving surgical treatment and the other three probably had small holes between their right and left ventricles.

Urinary tract disorder

Another health hazard for people who live in sub-standard conditions is a high frequency of urinary tract infections (*Lancet*, editorial, 1970). Bourke Aborigines were no exception to this common finding. In the twelve months before my survey, 7% of the men and 25% of the women remembered having at least one episode of burning when passing urine. An examination of the urine of 158 adults showed that 10% of the men and 25% of the women had a urinary infection. This was 16 times that found in white people in the rural town of Busselton in Western Australia in which 0.6% of men and 1.9% of women had such an infection (Cullen, 1972). A high prevalence of urinary tract infection was also found in Bourke Aboriginal children of whom 4.5% were affected.

Gynaecological disorders

Of 123 women whom I interviewed, 14% complained of menstrual disorders of which the most common were painful or excessive menstruation. Although no women complained of vaginal discharge or irritation, the protozoal infection Trichomonas vaginalis was found in 6% of the women during microscopy of their urine.

Cancer of the cervix was found in two women (1.6% of the potentially fertile female population). As with urinary tract infection the incidence of both *Trichomonas vaginalis* infection and cancer of the cervix is higher in those of lower socio-economic status. In the

1. Some types of streptococcal infections result in the body forming antibodies which not only destroy streptocci but also react against heart valve tissues.

middle-class living conditions of Busselton, Western Australia, trichomonal infection was found in only 0.3% of women and a positive cervical smear test in 0.2% (Bird *et al.*, 1970).

Diabetes

It has been postulated that possession of the diabetic gene would have been an advantage to a hunting people whose dietary pattern was that of feast and famine (Neel *et al.*, 1965). This would have assisted the deposition of fat when food was plentiful and this would protect an individual against starvation when food was scarce. The process of acculturation with its change in eating habits and reduction in physical activity could produce symptomatic diabetes in those people possessing this genetic makeup. There is epidemiological evidence to support this hypothesis in Pima Indians in Arizona, who had a prevalence of diabetes of 42% in those over 25 years of age. A high prevalence of diabetes has also been shown in other American Indian tribes, in native Hawaiians and in New Zealand Maoris (Bennett *et al.*, 1971). One survey of an urbanised Aboriginal community in South Australia showed that 19% of the subjects over the age of 20 years were diabetic (Wise *et al.*, 1970). In Bourke, seven men and seven women were found to be diabetic. Half were known to be diabetic before my survey, four were discovered as a result of the survey and I found a further three in the course of clinical practice. All had late-onset diabetes and except for one, who needed insulin by injection, were controlled by the use of oral drugs. Eleven of these subjects had a family history of diabetes and most of them were markedly obese. The prevalence of diabetes in the total Aboriginal population over 30 years of age was 8.3% and for those over 40 years of age it was 12.6%. These diabetic subjects were discovered by urine testing alone and had I given them a drink with sugar and then measured their blood sugar levels it is probable that the prevalence of discovered diabetics would have been much higher.

Anaemia

Iron deficiency anaemia was very common in Bourke Aboriginal children. Of the 260 who were tested, 13% had a haemoglobin level below 10g/100ml which is commonly accepted as the lower limit of normal. A further 38% of the children had diminished iron stores as judged by their blood film and serum iron levels even though they were not anaemic. A comparison between Aboriginal and white children under the age of 5 years who were admitted to the Bourke District Hospital, showed that 36% of the Aboriginal children and only 7% of the white children had a haemoglobin of less than 10g/100ml. This high frequency of iron deficiency anaemia in Bourke Aboriginal children appeared to be due to a diet low in iron and to repeated intercurrent infections and intestinal infestations which are known to damage the intestinal mucosa. In these circumstances ingested iron is probably poorly absorbed and this is one reason why so many sick Aboriginal children did not respond to medication with oral iron preparations. This lack of response to oral iron has also been noted among some Maori children (Tonkin, 1970). There is mounting evidence linking iron deficiency with morbidity in children (Tonkin, 1970; Lammi and Lovric, 1973). This suggests that replenishing the iron stores of these Aboriginal children would be a good preventive health measure and Jose and Welch in Queensland have shown that correcting iron deficiency anaemia by medication and the treatment of intestinal infestations produced a growth spurt in malnourished Aboriginal children (Jose and Welch, 1970).

In adults the criteria I used for anaemia was a haemoglobin of less than 11.5g/100ml, together with a blood film indicative of iron deficiency. Three men and 26 women were found to be anaemic. The Aboriginal women in Bourke therefore ran the risk of developing an iron deficiency anaemia during pregnancy. However, this rarely occurred and was almost certainly due to their compliance in taking the iron tablets that were prescribed for them.

Both the children and the adults had mean white cell counts above 10 000 per ml^3. These figures are higher than those found in surveys of white populations. It is possible that this could represent 'normality' for Bourke part-Aborigines, but it more likely reflects the persistent chronic infection from the chest, ears, skin and teeth which were so prevalent in this community.

Other abnormal findings

A variety of tests was performed on the blood of volunteering Bourke Aborigines. Most of the results found are of little interest to the general reader but those who are specifically interested are referred to the medical literature (Kamien, 1976b).

There were however two findings of specific interest. The first was that although venereal disease is reported by the lay press as being rife in various Aboriginal and some white communities I discovered only one new case of syphilis during the three years that I was in Bourke.

The other interesting finding was that 19% of the men and 20% of the women had a high level of cholesterol in their blood, and 51% of the men and 49% of the women had a high level of plasma fat which in many cases showed up as milky plasma when their blood had been collected. This high level of blood fats was probably a reflection of their tendency towards diabetes together with their high carbohydrate and high alcohol intake. An elevated blood fat level is recognised as a significant risk factor for developing a heart attack and as has been mentioned earlier in this chapter, this was the commonest cause of death especially in those Aborigines under 50 years of age.

The incidence of disease

When planning a health service, it is necessary to know the number of new cases of a disease which may be expected in a given period of time. This information is difficult to collect unless a researcher has a large team of helpers and an exceptionally compliant target population who can and will keep records of any new symptoms which afflict them. Both of these situations did not exist in Bourke, so I was forced to make a rough approximation of the incidence of disease and disability by recording the number of consultations that members of the Aboriginal population made with me in the first six months of 1971. During this period, 142 Aboriginal children consulted me on 358 occasions and 70 adults consulted on 179 occasions.

Throat and chest infections, ear ache and diarrhoea accounted for over one half of all the consultations made by children. There was a high incidence of infective disease in Bourke Aboriginal children and this is shown in Table 11 where a comparison is made between the consultations that they made with me and the consultations made by white patients who attended a selection of 377 doctors in Australia over the same period of time (Australian Morbidity Index, 1971). For children, most of the accidents were burns from the open fires used for cooking and for warmth on the Bourke Reserve. In adults, accidents accounted for 20% of all medical consultations and nearly all these injuries were the result of fighting when drunk. The other common causes for adults seeking medical attention were acute bronchitis (13%

of all consultations), infections of the kidneys and urinary tract (11 % of all consultations) and toothache (7 % of all consultations). Compared with white Australians, few consultations were made for heart disease, arthritis, back pain, the symptoms of mental stress or for antenatal care (Australian Morbidity Index, 1971).

Hospitalisation

Frequent and lengthy hospitalisation of their children was an unpalatable fact of life for Bourke Aboriginal mothers. This was due to the tendencies of doctors to play safe and admit children who were marginally sick and for the necessity to admit those children who presented for treatment only when they were very ill. Of the 380 children aged 1 to 14 years in the total population, 70 % had been admitted to hospital at least once in the preceding five years, 26 % more than three times and 14 % more than five times. I performed an ongoing analysis of all children under the age of 5 years who were admitted to the Bourke District Hospital between 1 September 1971 and 31 August 1972. Seventy-two per cent of all Aboriginal children and 15 % of all white children in the Bourke Shire were admitted during that time. The most striking findings were that every Aboriginal child under the age

Table 11 The most common diseases in Bourke Aboriginal children compared with the Australian Morbidity Index, January to June 1971 both expressed as a percentage of total consultations made with children aged 0 to 14 years

Disease entities	Percentage of total consultations[1]	
	Bourke	Australian Morbidity Index
Upper respiratory tract infection[2]	20%	13%
Otitis media (suppurating ears)	21%	6%
Accidents	9%	5%
Gastroenteritis	10%	4%
Skin infections	13%	3%
Conjunctivitis and acute trachoma	7%	2%
Chickenpox, measles and mumps	6%	1%
Failure to thrive[3]	5%	1%
Total percentage of all consultations	91%	35%

1. Percentages rounded to the nearest whole number.
2. Royal Australian College of General Practitioners Australian Morbidity Survey Nos 145, 146.
3. Royal Australian College of General Practitioners Australian Morbidity Survey Nos 48, 49, 176.

of 2 years and 92% of all Aboriginal pre-school children from the Bourke Reserve, were admitted to hospital at least once during that 12 month period. On a population basis Aboriginal children had proportionally ten times the number of hospital admissions as did white children. In addition, the average length of an admission for an Aboriginal child was six times longer than that for a white child (Kamien and Cameron, 1974).

Conclusions

These surveys of the health of Bourke Aborigines showed that in 1971 approximately 30% of all the Aboriginal children had a history of recent discomfort from illness and that 72% were in need of medical attention. Although 39% of all children had only mild disease conditions, the correction of these was important for the general comfort of the children and the effect that multiple minor infections and infestations had on their health. The more visible minor conditions such as skin infections, running noses and head lice warranted special attention since their presence was a factor in perpetuating prejudice against Aboriginal children by white Australians.

The state of health of the Bourke Aboriginal adults differed little from that of their children. Almost 70% of the adults complained of recent discomfort from medical or dental disorder and 79% were found to be in need of medical attention. Minor conditions which caused subjective discomfort were found in 40% of men and 48% of women. More severe illness which caused chronic ill health was present in 30% of the men and 39% of women. The need for medical attention increased with age from 70% in those aged 15 to 29 years to 96% in those aged more than 50 years.

All these data indicated that despite a high level of dedication by health personnel, the traditional white health services were relatively ineffective in combating the mortality and the morbidity of both children and adults and that the reasons for this needed to be examined further in order to plan for more effective health care.

Chapter 4
Nutrition and the 'Secret Bread Tests'

In the previous chapter, I showed that the general health of Bourke Aborigines was similar to that currently found in most of the developing countries of the Third World. The Medical Statistician, H. O. Lancaster, has shown that this state of health was also found in white Australians in Sydney between 1900 and 1910 (Lancaster, 1956a and b; 1957a and b). One of the chief factors underlying the ill health of all these populations is poor nutrition. Many Bourke Aboriginal children were small and thin, their diet and that of their parents was deficient in several essential nutrients and their blood vitamin levels were the lowest yet recorded in any at risk group in the Australian population.

Indices of poor nutrition

Using the standards issued by the Australian Institute of Anatomy (1957), 28% of the Bourke Aboriginal children were in the lowest tenth percentile for height and 25% were in the lowest tenth percentile for weight. The corresponding figures for Bourke white children were 8% and 5% respectively. In more concrete terms, Bourke Aboriginal boys aged 5 to 13 years were on average 4 cm shorter and 3.7 kg lighter and Bourke Aboriginal girls aged 5 to 15 years were 3 cm shorter and 2.8 kg lighter than New South Wales white children of the same age (Jones et al., 1973). It is of course possible that part-Aboriginal children are genetically smaller than white children. However, further confirmation that malnutrition was a contributing factor was obtained by measuring the skin-fold thickness of Aboriginal children and by the finding that between birth and the time of their first admission to hospital (usually before their first birthday), their mean weight had dropped by 10%, while for white children under the same circumstances it had remained the same (Kamien and Cameron, 1974).

In the absence of adequate Australian data, the desirable weight for adults was calculated from tables used by the Metropolitan Life Insurance Company of America (Diem, 1962). No Bourke Aborigines

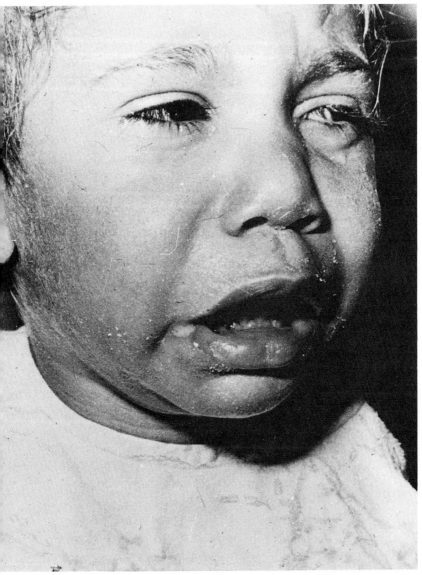

Plate 18 A child showing the effects of multi vitamin deficiency. This is particularly noticeable by the sores at the corner of the mouth and bleeding gums.

were found who were less than 70% of this desirable weight, ie. none was exceptionally thin. On the other hand, 5% of the men and 19% of the women were obviously obese being more than 140% of their desirable weight. The women had a tendency to become fatter with age and multiple pregnancies and of those aged 20 to 29 years, 15% were markedly obese and this increased to 50% for all women over 50 years of age.

In addition to these basic anthropometric measurements, physical examination of the Bourke Aborigines produced further evidence of nutritional deficiency. Fissures at both angles of the mouth were found in 14% of the children and in 31% of the adults (*see* Plate 18). A red, raw tongue was found in 3% of children and in 6% of adults and dry, scaly skin was found in nearly half of the total Aboriginal population. All these signs are associated with deficiencies of the B group of vitamins. Further indications of the extent of vitamin deficiency in this community were the detection of three children with the skin lesions of pellagra[1]; four young children with bruising due to vitamin K deficiency; and a further four infants who, because of vitamin C deficiency, developed pin-head sized bleeding spots in their skin when the veins in their arms were occluded by a tourniquet prior to collecting a specimen of blood.

One of these children was a seven month old girl. She was small and had been breast-fed since birth. The only supplementary food that she had been given was canned spaghetti which contains no vitamin C. Her mother's breast milk contained only half the minimal desirable level of vitamin C and an analysis of the mother's diet showed it to be low in calories, calcium, iron, vitamin A, vitamin B_1, vitamin B_2, and very low in vitamin C.

This widespread vitamin deficiency in Bourke Aborigines was confirmed by measuring the blood vitamin levels of a randomly selected sample of various age groups in their population. Multiple, subclinical vitamin deficiencies were common throughout all age groups and the most inadequate blood vitamin levels were found in toddlers and women of child-bearing age (*see* Table 12).

The measurement of blood vitamin levels is useful because it can detect deficiencies before they have resulted in medically detectable

---

1. Pellagra is due to a deficiency of the vitamin nicotinic acid and is manifest by pigmented dermatitis on those parts of the body exposed to sunlight.

Table 12 Distribution of vitamin deficiencies in the Bourke Aboriginal population by age group

	Number of subjects by age group (years)						
Age group	0–2	3–9	10–14	15–29	30–54	55+	
No. of vitamin deficiencies							Total
0	0	0	1	0	0	0	1
1	1	1	0	2	0	0	4
2	3	2	1	1	2	3	12
3	5	6	5	7	5	2	30
4	6	1	5	9	5	3	29
5	0	1	0	3	0	1	5
6	3	0	0	1	0	0	4
7	0	0	0	0	0	0	0
Total	18	11	12	23	12	9	85

signs. The results can also be used as a base-line against which to assess the results of various measures aimed at improving nutrition. Figs 3 and 4 summarise the results of the blood vitamin analyses in the Bourke Aboriginal population. The blood levels of the vitamins B-carotene (a precursor of vitamin A found in green and yellow vegetables), folic acid (a B group vitamin found in green leafed vegetables) and vitamin B12 found in liver and kidneys (a lack of which causes pernicious anaemia) were also assayed. Low levels were found for B-carotene in 63% of subjects, for folic acid in 42% of subjects and for vitamin B12 in 5% of subjects.

Diet

The staple diet of Bourke Aborigines was predominantly white bread, damper made from white flour, without yeast, and baked in ashes, and johnny cakes' made from the same dough and fried in dripping (Plate 19). These were usually eaten with golden syrup, jam or honey and washed down with large quantities of sweetened tea whitened with full cream powdered milk. An analysis of the available white bread showed that for a person to approximate his daily needs of vitamin B_1 he would need to eat about one kilogram of the bread per day.

Meat from the local butchers was expensive and so Aboriginal people preferred to buy a live sheep and kill it themselves. The mutton was kept fresh for four or five days in a wet hessian bag which was

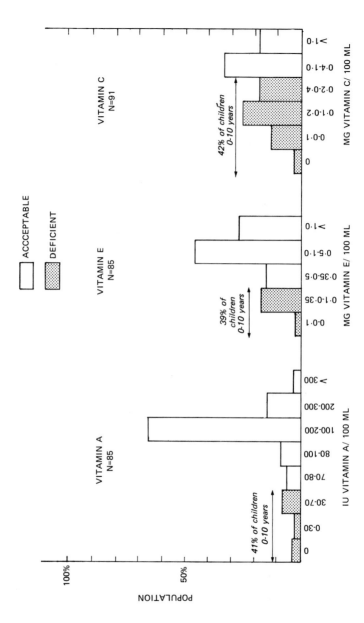

Figure 3 Percentage distribution of Bourke Aboriginal subjects according to plasma levels of vitamins A, E and C.

hung on a tree during the day and placed on the roof every night to keep it cool and protect it from dogs. All the meat was either fried or made into a stew and cooked for a very long time. Cooking facilities were generally primitive and nearly all relied on a wood fire. Once the fire had been lit it was kept burning and the stews were often left cooking for many hours. Other sources of protein were fish and eggs. The fish were usually caught by line or by trap in the Darling River. About 20% of families had one member who could be relied upon to catch fish at least once a week. Eggs were all bought at the local shops and, when money was available, fried or scrambled eggs were eaten each day with each person averaging between half and one egg per day.

Fruit and vegetables were obtained once a week, usually on a Wednesday, from a visiting green-grocer and were all eaten on the day of purchase or at most the day after and none was left for the rest of the week. Although Bourke has about 100 ha of citrus orchards, the Aboriginal people did not feel comfortable going there and so did not purchase the ample and cheap citrus fruits that were available. The local wild fruits were prized by the Aborigines and were a good source of vitamin C. These included bush bananas, gruie apples, bush lemons, bush oranges and quandongs. These however were real luxuries and were available for only a short time during their growing season.

Except for the 280 ml of fresh milk made available through the School Milk Scheme, Aboriginal children had only full cream powdered milk which they had in their tea. Although there was little difference in price between this milk and vitamin-fortified milk powder, the mothers bought the former because it was packed in 1 lb [c. 450 g] tins and so appeared cheaper than the fortified variety which came in $2\frac{1}{2}$ lb [c. 1135 g] tins. The adults also preferred the taste of the unfortified milk powder in their tea.

Ice blocks, ice creams, sweets, potato chips and aerated drinks were consumed by children in large quantities. When money was available children were given between 20 and 40 cents each to buy their lunch at school and, like children everywhere, they preferred to buy these particular food items.

A detailed dietary survey

In order to get more accurate data about the food consumed by Bourke Aborigines, I organised a detailed dietary survey of two families whom I considered to have the best dietary habits of the Aborigines in Bourke.

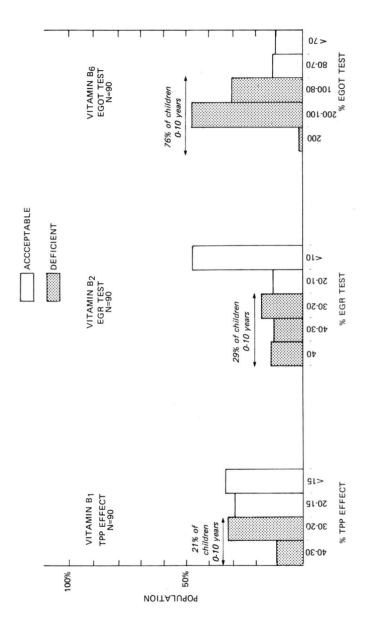

Figure 4 Percentage distribution of Bourke Aboriginal subjects according to enzyme reactivation tests for vitamins B_1, B_2 and B_6.

Plate 19 'Johnny cakes' a popular Aboriginal food made from flour and water.

One family was from the Bourke Reserve and the other was from the town. Ms Pamela Rosevear, Mrs Joan Winston and Mrs Lillian Puchta of the Vitamin Laboratories of Roche Products Pty Ltd, obtained each family's permission to sample, weigh and later analyse the food consumed by each of the seventeen members of the families over a period of six days. The percentage contribution made by the various food groups to the intakes of calories and protein for these two families is shown in Table 13. Combining this survey with the dietary information previously obtained, it was apparent that the dietary intake of Bourke Aborigines was low in calcium, calories, iron and vitamins. Similar surveys have been done in white stress groups in Sydney and none has shown overall daily food intakes as deficient as was that of Bourke Aborigines (Nobile and Woodhill, 1973).

> *The effect of fortifying flour on the nutritional state of*
>
> *Bourke Aborigines*

There were two ways of trying to enrich the nutrition of Aborigines in Bourke. The first way was to provide them with information which

115

Table 13 Percentage contribution of various food groups to the intakes of calories and protein of the two families during the six day dietary survey in April 1972

Food		Family 1		Family 2	
		Calories %	Protein %	Calories %	Protein %
Bread (from white flour)	Mean	33	30	30	25
	Range	19–44	12–43	22–35	14–32
Milk	Mean	14	20	5	7
	Range	3–22	6–27	0.3–10	0.4–14
Meat (mainly stews)	Mean	19	36	29	53
	Range	9–44	20–68	20–49	44–71
Eggs	Mean	2	3	5	8
	Range	1– 4	1– 7	1– 8	2–13
Vegetables (mainly potatoes)	Mean	4	4	4	2
	Range	2–16	2–11	2– 8	2– 4
Fruit	Mean	4	2	2	0.8
	Range	1– 8	0.1– 3	0.6– 5	0.1– 2
Fats: dripping, butter, margarine	Mean	12	0.4	11	0.5
	Range	6–15	0.2–0.5	10–14	0.3–0.6
Sweets: cakes. chocolate, jams, honey	Mean	10	2	11	2
	Range	3–16	0.01– 7	4–20	0.01– 6

might in the long run lead to a change in their dietary habits. The second way was to fortify their staple foods with those nutrients lacking in their diet. A good diet is obviously better than adding artificial supplements to food. However, programmes of nutrition education are difficult to mount and even if successful, are notoriously slow at remedying an acute public health problem. Bread was the staple diet of Bourke Aborigines in that it contributed nearly 30% of their intake of both calories and protein. I reasoned that the only quick and practical way of ensuring that they obtained sufficient of their needed nutrients was to add these to the flour used in making their bread There is legal provision made for such measures under the New South

Wales Pure Food Act which specifies the upper limits of the allowable additive.

After taking independent advice on this matter from the Australian Bread Research Institute in Sydney, the local baker, Mr Alan Morrall agreed, as a public health measure, to add iron and the vitamins B_1, B_2 and niacin to the white flour used in Bourke. This fortified bread was available from August 1973 until March 1974.

I re-examined a sample of Bourke Aborigines in April 1974, eight weeks after the fortification of flour had ceased. There had been a significant improvement in the blood levels of those vitamins added to the flour. Half of those who had deficient blood levels of B group vitamins in 1971, now had acceptable blood levels in 1974. In addition those physical signs of an inflamed tongue, fissures at the angles of the mouth and dryness of the skin attributed to B group vitamin deficiency, had virtually disappeared.

At the same time, the blood levels of vitamins not added to the flour remained unchanged or worsened. In particular, the blood levels of vitamin A in children had deteriorated markedly, probably as a result of the loss of their main source of vitamin A following the cessation of the School Milk Scheme at the end of 1973 (Kamien *et al.,* 1975).

A lesson for the unwary

My plan to fortify the bread in Bourke was one measure which I, as a doctor, took to help improve the health of those so obviously in need. It did not occur to me that this could be blown up into a controversial issue in which I would be labelled by some as 'a secret experimenter on human beings'.

Since the prime aim of this book is to present my experiences and insights to others involved in the process of change, I have thought it worthwhile to include here the original newspaper report and some subsequent correspondence which tell their own story. They are not included to induce a state of paranoia in would-be change agents, but to show the necessity for these agents to try to anticipate, and so avoid, even the most unapparent complications. Had I been more wary, I would have written a letter of explanation to the local newspaper before the bread was fortified. This would have prevented any controversy and the Aborigines of Bourke would not have lost the benefit of eating fortified bread.

117

From the *National Times*, 25 February–2 March 1974

The guinea pigs of Bourke: the secret bread tests

By Michael Ross

The question of compulsory enrichment of bread, subject of medical controversy in the United States, is surfacing in Australia, one of the few developed countries in the world which has so far resisted the trend.

The nutrition committee of the National Health and Medical Research Council in Australia has recommended a major survey to find out if Australians suffer nutritional deficiencies from a lack of thiamine, niacin and riboflavin in our national diet.

The survey yet to be endorsed by the Council's food standards committee, is likely to lead to a recommendation that Australian bread be fortified with vitamins.

But in the meantime an experiment in enriched bread has already been conducted in Bourke, a far-west New South Wales country town, without the knowledge of it inhabitants and without the permission of public health authorities.

The experiment is also contrary to a 1959 ruling by the National Health and Medical Research Council. The ruling was made following a survey of Canberra housewives and their nutritional standards which led to the belief that enrichment was not necessary to give Australians the necessary nutrients.

However, this ruling has since been criticized because the survey was not carried out among poorer groups who were more likely to show signs of vitamin deficiency.

The experiment in enriched bread has been going on in Bourke for the past year. Iron and three of the vitamin B group—thiamine, niacin and riboflavin—have been added to the entire bread supply of the town's only bakery. Iron additives are a major subject of medical controversy today in the U.S. where it has been claimed some people have suffered from an excess intake of iron.

The experiment was part of a research survey to find out what impact enriched bread would have on the low nutrition standards of Aborigines in the town and neighbouring areas. The Aborigines have in the past suffered serious vitamin deficiencies.

The experiment was started by Dr Max Kamien, who is now senior lecturer in medicine at the University of Western Australia. He spent one year in Bourke as part of a research fellowship from the Institute of Psychiatry to study human ecology in the arid zone.

He was joined in the experiment by Roche Products Pty Ltd a vitamin chemical company which is working on a new technique of analysing blood samples from selected Aboriginal volunteers to show up not only vitamin deficiencies, but how vitamins work within the human body. Roche's nutrition scientist, Dr Sylvia Nobil worked with Dr Kamien on the Bourke experiment.

The *Morrall Bakery* at Bourke agreed to join in the experiment after contacting the Bread Research Institute, which is now examining results of the experiment.

But because there is only one bakery in Bourke, all residents of Bourke and the neighbouring district have been eating enriched bread without their knowledge.

While New South Wales does not prohibit limited amounts of vitamins and iron to be included in bread, normally the producer labels the enriched bread with the specific items included.

But because the *Morrall Bakery* does not use the additive as a selling point, it is under no legal obligation to declare through packaging information what vitamins or iron are in the bread.

Dr Kamien admits that a statement should have been made in Bourke about the experiment. 'This is a pilot trial scheme in which I, as a doctor, am trying to work a social change, because the Aboriginal people suffer a considerable level of vitamin deficiency', he said.

Dr Kamien says that the addition of riboflavin was stopped after complaints—the first from the local hospital—that the bread colouring was yellowy.

Dr Kamien said he accepted that there was a moral question which might be raised as to how far a medical research project can be carried out without proper participation with the government health authorities.

He said he himself fully appreciates the researchers' rights conflict with those of individuals. He agreed also that his nutritional studies at Bourke could be misinterpreted by laymen.

However, if Dr Kamien and Dr Nobile are forced to abandon their project, much needed data on nutritional deficiency will be lost.

This includes one finding that may lead to a conclusion that oral dosages of iron have little effect on Aboriginal children because of a gut worm, while injections achieve a 'spurt' in growth even at advanced child ages.

Since the War, the United States has by compulsion used bread as a national carrier of vitamins and iron into the diets of the American people.

A decision by the U.S. Food and Drug Administration ordering bread manufacturers to double the iron content in bread up to 40 milligrams per pound next April has brought criticism that it was not based on medical knowledge, is arbitrary and even critical.

It has been estimated that 200 000 sufferers from the fatal genetic disease of Cooley's anaemia, who suffer from an excess of iron, will be endangered.

Excess iron, according to one American expert could cause cirrhosis of the liver, pancreatic damage, diabetes and heart failures.

In Australia attitudes to the vitamin enrichment of bread vary.

Dr F. W. Clements, principal medical officer at the School of Public Health and Tropical Medicine at Sydney University, is neither opposed nor in favour of bread enrichment at this stage. He said there was a great deal of work required to be clarified before many questions could be answered. 'We can't use overseas studies because no studies were done before their enrichment policy. The Americans can only say they reduced the number of people on Skid Row,' he said. 'If you are going in for a national policy, you need some relative data to show that what you have done is effective.'

Professor Laurie Powell, senior reader in medicine with the Department of Medicine at Queensland University, said it was a fact that where there was an iron deficiency it was more common to women than men. He surmised that if iron was added to bread, some people may get too much.

Iron excess causes haemochromatosis (an uncommon disease, but more common in Australia than overseas) and Cooley's disease. Professor Powell agreed it was reasonable that some American opinions in regard to its sufferers of Cooley's disease could have some significance in Australia because of similar migratory schemes from Italy and Greece.

119

Plate 20 Cartoonist Peter A. Garvey's interpretation of 'The Guinea Pigs of Bourke, Secret Bread Tests' (by courtesy of the Editor, *Sunday Times*, Perth, 3 March 1974).

Dr Joan Woodhill, chairman of the division of nutrition and dietetics at Prince Henry Hospital in Sydney, like Dr Clements, has no definite opinion for or against general food enrichment in bread. But she is convinced that if the population would accept wholemeal bread this would give them sufficient iron and nutrient levels. Dr Woodhill did support a recommendation by the head of the Arid Region Study, Professor John Cawte, which has been made to Professor Henderson's poverty committee, that enriched bread should be made available to Aborigines. A member of the 1959 committee which decided against enriching bread, Dr Woodhill agrees that their finding is now open to question.

Spokesmen for Australian bread-making organisations say there is no move to press for vitamin and iron enrichment policies. Director of the Bread Research Institute, Mr F. Bond, said anything that has to be done of an enrichment nature has to fulfil the needs of the public, based on proper nutritional evidence and not give way to exploration for promoting foodstuffs.

The institute which is interested in the Roche project at Bourke, has been involved before in helping with another additive. When C.S.R. developed Anticay as a protection in sugar against tooth decay the institute was involved in preparing bread samples with Anticay for C.S.R.'s test-feeding programs. Anticay is being used in bread manufacturing in Tasmania, Victoria and South Australia, despite its effectiveness being questioned by the Australian Dental Association.

This article produced a number of responses, the most succinct being that shown in Plate 20.

At the risk of boring the reader I am including some of the correspondence which followed the above article because I feel that it does have a lesson for would-be change agents.

Secret bread tests: the facts

To the editor, *National Times*

Sir—May 1, in fairness, claim the space to correct the nine errors of fact and five half-truths and innuendos in the article 'Secret bread tests' by Michael Ross (*National Times,* 25 February–2 March).

During the three years that I was in Bourke it appeared that many members of the lower socio-economic groups (including Aborigines) had a poor nutritional status. In order to test this I organized a study and asked the Roche Vitamin Laboratories (the only laboratory in Australia with the expertise) if they would perform the vitamin assays. Fortifying the bread was done in good faith as a preventive health measure. If Mr Ross considers that this makes people in Bourke into guinea-pigs then he must agree that the entire populations of Britain, U.S.A., all the Scandinavian countries and most of Europe are in the same category. In Canada, bakers can fortify bread on a voluntary basis and 86% of them do so. It was not intended as an experiment and the paper describing this survey (which is in publication) merely says that the data found could be used as the basis for longitudinal study into the effects of fortified bread on the nutritional state of a community.

This study was not initiated by Roche. I have not received a single cent in payment or in kind from them and they had nothing to do with the decision to fortify the bread.

Should the survey be completed it is quite possible that the results would show that iron and vitamin supplementation of bread is not indicated and so the insinuation that a multinational pharmaceutical company would benefit through duping an unsuspecting Australian doctor is unproven and uncharitable.

It can hardly be claimed that these tests are secret since it is widely known and approved by all the health agencies in Bourke and by the Bread Research Institute.

Very senior doctors in both the State and Commonwealth Health Departments are aware of it, and I delivered a paper about it to the nutritional section at the last ANZAAS Conference as well as giving a copy of that paper to newsmen covering that conference. An article on the study is also in preparation for the *Australian Journal of Food Technology*. The subjects who were selected at random for the survey were fully aware of its objects and four separate discussions totalling 12 hours were held with representatives of the Aboriginal people so that they fully realised what was entailed before they gave their permission to be surveyed. The section of the survey concerning Aboriginal people was then organized by the Bourke Aboriginal Advancement Association. Full details of the results have been given to them at their request and all disease found has been treated.

The National Health and Medical Research Council was appointed in 1958 to review the nutritive significance of Australian bread. It did not fulfil its terms of reference in that by never once considering the Australian Aboriginal it did not take into consideration the health of all socio-economic classes. It also had no power to make a ruling, it was simply an advisory body. It did not conduct a survey, it reviewed the available literature and stated that there was no study available to enable them to offer an opinion of the incidence of thiamine deficiency in the community. The law regarding the fortification of bread is clearly stated on pages 8 and 9 of the New South Wales Pure Food Act and Regulations Number 31, 1908, which Mr Ross can obtain from the Government Printer in Sydney. Public Health Authority permission is not needed nor is it sought by all those companies which fortify cake mix and breakfast cereals.

The amount of iron added to the bread in Bourke brings the total iron content to one-sixth of the allowed amount. This is assessed independently by Roche Vitamin Laboratories and by the Bread Research Institute. This is less than that now found in normal wholemeal loaves and a person eating 8 oz. bread would obtain just over one half of his recommended minimum daily intake. The evidence coming from the United States of America on the dangers of iron is highly speculative and unproven. The fatal variant of Cooley's anaemia does not exist in Bourke and the disease is inherited and is fatal, irrespective of diet.

Haemochromatosis is a very rare disease which also does not exist in Bourke. A paper by Professor Powell found the prevalence of it in Australia to be 30/100 000 which is less than that found in Europe and the U.S. Since Mr Ross quotes him as saying that the prevalence of this disease was more common in Australia than in other countries, it appears that he has got that telephone conversation as garbled as the names he mis-spells and the quotes which he attributes to me.

What I did say to Mr Ross was that if he was trying to make the point that communities among whom medical research was being carried out should be fully aware of what was being done, then I agreed with him. The only oversight on my part and the only part-truth in his article was that the fortification of bread was not officially advertised in the local press or on the wrapping on the bread. This had been intended and was not done simply because the baker, Mr Morrall, felt that if he was doing a community service he did not want to be seen to profit out of it, in exactly the same way as he does not seek credit for the other considerable services he performs on behalf of his community. I did agree with Mr Ross that these nutritional studies could be misinterpreted by a layman only if presented to him in an unfair, out of context manner by an irresponsible newspaper reporter after a 'sensational revelation' who deliberately misinterpreted facts.

It would add perspective to the argument to say that severe iron deficiency anaemia affects the growth and well-being of children and in Sydney has been found in a prevalence of 3000/100 000 and in Bourke of 79 700/100 000.

If, as Mr Ross says, much-needed data on nutritional deficiency will be lost if this project is abandoned, why does he try to ensure this by misrepresenting the facts and using such untrue and emotive headlines. Perhaps it no longer matters since as he has already predicted the results of a proposed nutritional survey recommended by the National Health and Medical Research Council in Australia, I could use his clairvoyant powers to tell me if fortifying bread in Bourke made any difference to the health status of that 30% of the population who may need it. (M. Kamien, Department of Medicine, University of Western Australia, W.A.)

The editor replied:

(The point made by our story was that the experiment was secret as far as the general population of Bourke was concerned and as far as the Department of Health in New South Wales was concerned. Both points were correct. Given the secrecy of the experiment, the people of Bourke were clearly guinea pigs. While the *National Times* did not claim that the experiment would cause harm to the people of Bourke we did make the point that such experiments should be cleared with the public health authorities given the dangers of unsupervised experiments. We stand by this point. *Editor*).

Correspondence, the *Western Herald*, Friday, 8 March 1974, page 12

Misleading article—bread tests

Dear Sir,—Due to the manner in which an article was presented recently in the *National Times*, I would respectfully request that the following comments be printed to correct any wrong impressions that may have been formed.

I quote the following from Mr Eric E. Bond, A.R.M.T.C., F.P.A.G.I., Director, Bread Research Institute of Australia, North Ryde, N.S.W.

The headlines of an article in the *National Times* of 25.2.74 concerning bread tests in Bourke are misleading, far from factual and carry wrong implications as far as *Morrall's Bakery* is concerned. Some of the statements in the article could also cause unnecessary concern and apprehension to some people in that town.

What Mr Morrall has done is to improve the nutritive value of his bread well within the limits and requirements of the N.S.W. Pure Food Regulations. These permit the addition of essential nutrients, such as vitamins of the B group eg. thiamine and niacin, and the mineral iron, to a number of foods including bread.

123

To protect the public against unfair advertising, the Regulations provide that where any claims concerning added nutrients are made they must be stated in a specified manner. Where claims are not made or the enrichment is not advertised, no statements are required. There is no obligation of the manufacturer to label his products or to make any public statement in this regard.

The nutrients that Mr Morrall has added to his bread are naturally present in wheat and, to a lesser extent, in flour. What he has done in effect has been to raise the nutritive value of his white bread in respect to these nutrients which are present in the whole grain.

When people eat a wide variety of foods in sufficient quantity there is little likelihood of nutritional deficiencies occurring and all types of bread provide an adequate supply of nutrients. Those people, however, who consume a very limited range of foods, particularly if these include large quantities of sugar and alcohol, may not obtain the amounts of vitamins of the B group and iron recommended as necessary for maintaining good health and may develop malnutrition. Normally, well nourished people do not suffer in any way from consuming additional quantities of these nutrients which are present in a number of other foods, but enrichment of a basic and cheap food such as bread, can be beneficial to those suffering from malnutrition.

As far as we know the whole basis of the involvement of *Morrall's Bakery* is a willingness to co-operate in the study of improving the food value and diet of some people in the Bourke district. Because of this we feel that Mr Morrall is worthy of commendation rather than condemnation of any kind.

Morrall's Bakery, per Alan H. Morrall.

The final result of this small saga is that at the beginning of 1977 bread is not fortified in Bourke and the debate as to whether bread should be fortified with vitamins and iron throughout Australia continues. The people of Bourke, black and white do not care whether their bread is fortified or not. On my last visit to that town I could discover only two exceptions to this general feeling. Both of them were white men who stopped me in the street and said, 'Gee we've been feeling crook since they took the vitamins out of the bread'.

Chapter 5
Psychiatric and behaviour disorder

At the beginning of this book, I showed that Aborigines occupied the lowest rung in the social and economic ladder of the total Bourke community. In addition, they were excluded from the life of the dominant white society, their community was socially and culturally disintegrated and they were politically powerless. Similar factors have been shown to have a negative relationship to mental health. It was important to assess the frequency of psychiatric disorders in the Bourke Aboriginal community for two reasons. The first was to identify individual Aborigines who might benefit from psychiatric help. The second was to test a hypothesis put forward by the American psychiatrist, Alexander Leighton, that a high rate of psychiatric disorder in a community would inhibit planned change (Leighton, 1965).

My method of case finding and the way in which I defined psychiatric disorder are fully discussed in two separate papers (Kamien, 1976c and d). I hope that it is sufficient to say that my criteria of abnormality were conservative and would be accepted by most practising psychiatrists. In the case of children, their mothers and close relatives recognised that the child's behaviour was abnormal for his or her age and in the case of adults nearly all had been reported by their fellow Aborigines as 'sick in the head', 'nervy', 'he's a funny man . . . a bit peculiar' or 'he is off his head when he has had a few'. Furthermore I only classified an adult as suffering from a psychiatric disorder when I had estimated that his degree of mental impairment had reduced by at least 25% his ability to function with his work, his family or his community.

Behaviour disorders in children

In 1972, 28% of boys and 35% of girls had at least one category of frequent and persistent behaviour which was regarded by me and their families as abnormal for their age. The numbers of children in each descriptive category of behaviour are shown in Table 14. I arbitrarily

Table 14 Number of children aged 5–14 years in each category of behaviour disorder

	Boys $n=129$	Girls $n=121$
Emotional behaviour		
Temper tantrums	20	19
Physical disorders		
Abdominal pain	11	19
Headaches	15	19
Disorders of sleep		
Enuresis[1]	27	38
Nightmares or night terrors	2	
School centred problems		
School refusal	5	
Slow learner	3	1
Antisocial behaviour		
Destructiveness	2	1
Aggression to other children	1	1
Stealing	13	2
Running away	4	6
Other disorders		
Asthma		4
Epilepsy	1	1
Self poisoning		1
Hysterical fits		1
Anxiety	1	4
Depression		1
Compulsive eating		1
Total individuals	36 (27.9%)[2]	43 (35.5%)[2]

1. Number of subjects 6 years and older $=219$.
2. Some children exhibited several of these symptom complexes.

defined as severely disturbed those children who had three or more symptoms of longer than two years' duration in the broad descriptive categories shown in Table 14. There were eleven boys (8%) and ten girls (8%) in this category. The mean age of the boys was 9 years and that of the girls 10 years.

Temper tantrums

Nearly all children with temper tantrums were reported as having severe, uncontrollable outbursts of rage which occurred almost every day. Except for three teenage girls no temper tantrums were reported in children above the age of 12 years. The frequency of temper tantrums in Bourke Aboriginal children was twice that found in a survey in Buckinghamshire in England, where 6.5% of children aged 5 to 15 years were recorded as having temper tantrums at least once a week (Shepherd *et al.*, 1971). Child psychiatrists have noted that temper tantrums are more common in the children of those families who are 'emotionally explosive' and who, like most Bourke Aboriginal families, do not restrain their immediate feelings over a frustrating experience. Temper tantrums can be seen as partly manipulative and partly a reaction to an unpredictable disciplinary measure when the child usually expected a permissive response. Since Aboriginal mothers did not take these tantrums seriously or try to control them, they tended to persist. It is likely that children with temper tantrums will grow into quick-tempered adults unless they learn to control this behaviour.

Abdominal pain and headache

Recurrent abdominal pains and headaches were commonly found as a symptom complex in the same children. Younger children tended to present more often with abdominal pain and older children with headaches. Vomiting was not associated with either complaint. The occurrence of abdominal pain in Bourke Aboriginal children was almost three times that found in children of the same age in the Buckinghamshire survey.

Abdominal pain was a symptom which always caused concern in Aboriginal mothers, because they associated it with potentially severe gastrointestinal illness. Headache was twice as common in Bourke Aboriginal children as in the English survey. Headaches were also a frequent complaint in adults and it is probable that children learned to express their distress in this way.

Bed-wetting

Bed-wetting (enuresis) was common in all age groups. Eleven boys and twenty girls over the age of 10 years were bed-wetters; eight boys and six girls had wet their beds two or more times a week, and eleven boys and twenty-four girls were enuretic every night. Two boys and two girls under the age of 10 years were enuretic during the day and this always occurred shortly after their arrival at school. A figure of 30% with enuresis is one of the highest recorded in any such survey. Bed-wetting is regarded by some authors as a manifestation of anxiety, and in addition to a possible genetic component this would appear to be the major factor in Bourke Aboriginal children. In most families enuresis was regarded with benign acceptance, especially when the mother herself had been a bed-wetter until her early teens. Four families had resorted to forbidding the children to have drinks before going to bed and to a variety of punitive measures, including immediate cold showers, on the discovery of a wet bed. I was not sure whether the parents had a high tolerance threshold, were not concerned, were ashamed, or did not regard the cure of the symptom as being in the province of the doctor. Whatever the reason, Dr Coolican did not record any Aboriginal child as having consulted him because of bed-wetting in Bourke during 1968 (Coolican, 1973).

I used the anti-depressive drug Imipramine given at night in a dose of 50 to 75 mg depending on the child's size, to treat the condition. Alternative treatments such as a buzzer[1] were not feasible since there were often up to four children sharing the same bed. Superficial psychotherapy was also logistically difficult because of the number of children affected. Four children were not given their tablets. Of those who did take medication, 56 (92%) ceased bed-wetting within a week and had remained dry after ceasing to take the drug over follow-up periods ranging from three to eighteen months. Of those who were not cured, two children had a recurrence on ceasing to take the drug, and three, who had previously been wet every night, were now enuretic only on the nights when their father's drinking precipitated a major family upheaval. These results are surprising since controlled studies using Imipramine have shown it to be much less effective than in these Bourke Aboriginal children. A frequent objection to giving tablets to children is the risk of accidental poisoning. Despite the inadequacy of storage space in Aboriginal dwellings no cases of accidental poisoning occurred.

Antisocial behaviour

In the five years preceding this survey (from 1967 to 1971), 25 boys and 21 girls were reported as having been in some trouble with the law. Seven boys and 3 girls had been warned by the police, 8 boys and 3 girls had been taken to court, and 10 boys and 15 girls had experienced detention in either the town gaol or a reformatory in

1. A method of conditioning a child to wake up when he feels the urge to empty his bladder.

Sydney. The most common causes were petty theft and running away from home. Both stealing and running away from home occurred as gang activities, although the latter was nearly always precipitated by a severe family upheaval associated with physical violence from a drunken father. All children who exhibited repeated antisocial behaviour came from large families where the father was often absent or frequently drunk and indiscriminately punitive. Many of these children perceived their fathers as inadequate and exhibited obvious fear and often active dislike of them. The average number of children in the families of the antisocial children was 9.3 (range 4 to 15) compared with a mean of 5.4 for the total Aboriginal population of Bourke.

Of the antisocial boys 33% were small for their age and were chronic bed-wetters. All the antisocial boys and antisocial girls were alienated from their own families, the education system and the dominant white culture. They found both status and a role by belonging to a gang which actively rejected the value system of the majority society.

Although over 90% of the theft was petty and involved goods such as confectionery which were worth only a few dollars, the reaction of white society was unusually severe. Children as young as 8 years old were kept in a gaol cell while awaiting an appearance before a magistrate. While this caused much guilt and anxiety in the child's parents it also accentuated the child's status in his gang, especially when he accepted blame for misdemeanours committed by his gang colleagues.

Another source of conflict between Aboriginal children and the law was the early sexual experimentation of Aboriginal girls which began at about the age of 14 to 15 years. This was a social norm and some of these girls formed deep, emotional relationships with their boyfriends. The major concern displayed by the police and Welfare Departments over these liaisons were seen by the girls in particular as unwarranted interference in their affairs. It is probable that the punitive attitudes of Child Welfare Department officers, police and magistrates helped to further alienate Aboriginal children and adults from white society and perpetuated the antisocial behaviour which these very agencies were trying to eradicate.

Reports of cases of children with severe behaviour disorders

Antisocial and psychoneurotic behaviour disorder

Case 1   This 8 year old boy was the eighth of eleven children. His mother had also lost two infants from infective disease. The father worked on a property some 300 km from Bourke and visited home about once a month. Money was chronically scarce and the mother supplemented her income by working in the abattoirs or picking fruit. She had episodes of severe depression which resulted in bouts of drinking. During these periods the boy was cared for either by a maternal aunt or by his elder sisters. He was small, being on the third percentile for weight and height. He had an infected and running right ear and a small perforation of the drum in the left ear. His hearing in the better ear was normal. He exhibited frequent and severe temper tantrums at home, suffered from recurrent abdominal pains and headaches, wet his bed every night, disliked his teachers and often refused to go to school. He was the leader of the gang of older boys which had been responsible for episodes of petty pilfering from a variety of smallgoods shops.

He had appeared before the Children's Court on three occasions, had spent two nights in the town gaol and had been referred to a remand home for psychiatric assessment. He appeared an anxious and timid child in all situations except that of leader of his gang.

Case 2   This 10 year old boy was the fourth of ten children. His father was permanently employed and was affectionate when sober, but highly punitive when drunk. His mother was an attractive, permissive woman who had lost two children in infancy and whose energies were completely taken up in looking after her family and coping with her husband's heavy drinking. The boy was a healthy looking child whose only physical handicap was active and severe bilateral middle ear disease. His deafness was known to his parents and sisters but was not realised by his schoolteachers who regarded him as inattentive. He was a poor learner and often played truant. He was also a chronic bed-wetter. He belonged to the same gang as the 8 year old boy in Case 1 and since he was usually the executor of the stealing episodes, he was caught by the police more often than his companions. He had appeared before the Children's Court on at least five occasions and had spent two periods totalling five days in a cell in the local lock-up. He was sent to a reformatory for a spell of one year and on his return to Bourke immediately resumed his previous gang-oriented behaviour.

Case 3   This 12 year old boy was the sixth of seven children. His father was a plausible, verbal alcoholic whose behaviour was unpredictable and sometimes violent. His children were obviously frightened of him. His mother was an intelligent, long-suffering woman who more often than not exhibited physical signs of her husband's violence. She had three still-births and three of her infants had died before the age of one year. Although this boy was smaller than other children of his age group he was able at sport when he could be coaxed into competing. He had previously suffered from ear disease but this had healed. He exhibited frequent temper tantrums, chronic bed-wetting, and a marked dislike of school despite his position in the top stream. He had numerous encounters with the police, Child Welfare Department and the Children's Court, but apart from spending several evenings in the local police station he had never been sent to either a remand home or a reformatory. On occasion his antisocial behaviour took the form of gross vandalism. He was regarded by his teachers as an intelligent youth who was certain to become a habitual criminal 'unless someone did something'.

Antisocial aggressive behaviour

Case 4   This 14 year old youth was the youngest of four children. His father was in permanent employment and his mother was concerned and protective. Both parents were chronically ill, the father with heart failure and obesity, and the mother with diabetes. An elder brother had a mild spastic weakness of one side of his body and after drinking alcohol exhibited violent aggressive behaviour, which had caused him considerable trouble with the law. This youth had been a large baby and the delivery had been difficult. He too, was mildly spastic and was prone to sudden, unpredictable rages which led to difficulties with his peers at school. He had been assessed as falling into the watershed between those who were educationally subnormal and those who were eligible for an occupational activities class.

At home, he exhibited frequent temper tantrums and had episodes of marked anxiety. On clinical grounds, it was thought possible that he was suffering from temporal lobe epilepsy. He responded well to medical treatment and was able to go back to school, with few further episodes of violently aggressive behaviour.

131

Case 5 This 10 year old girl was the eighth in a family of fifteen children. The father was permanently employed and, apart from excessive consumption of alcohol, appeared on the surface to cope well with white society. The mother was chronically depressed and made little attempt to control and support her family. Five of the girl's older siblings were in reformatories and several of her younger siblings had already been in trouble with the police. She appeared a warm, friendly girl who made easy interpersonal relationships. However, she was known to have frequent and severe temper tantrums, to suffer from recurrent headaches and repeated bed-wetting, and to have difficulties with her school work which her teacher put down to inattention. She indulged in petty pilfering and vandalism. Her mother reported that she was also destructive of property at home. She appeared to have no internal controls over her behaviour and no insight into the effect that her destroying of people's property had on their reaction to her. She was mainly responsible for $2000 worth of damage to the goods and house of a white family where she had been a welcome visitor. She seemed perplexed and bewildered when she received a cool reception from them when she came to play on the day following her act of vandalism.

Traditional disorder

Case 6 This 12 year old boy was the youngest of twelve children. His father was a chronic alcoholic who was frequently absent from home for long periods of time. His mother, who exhibited much affection for him, was a large, able woman adept at managing the affairs of her family. Although not a full-blooded Aborigine, the mother spoke a number of Aboriginal dialects fluently and had a great knowledge of and belief in Aboriginal tribal customs. The boy was an obese and slightly timid child, who did not like school and would avoid going as often as possible. After the death of his two year old niece, of whom he was very fond, he exhibited recurrent episodes of severe headache and abdominal pain, marked episodes of anxiety and frequent night terrors. These symptoms were only partially relieved by tranquillising medicines, and his mother resorted to traditional Aboriginal methods of ridding him of the spirit of his dead niece. This was done by holding him over smouldering dog-bush leaves (*Eremophila bignoniiflora*) for about 20 minutes in company with his elder sister, who had also been affected by the spirit of her dead daughter. After this, his night terrors and abdominal pains disappeared, although he was still prone to mild episodes of anxiety.

Separation anxiety

Case 7   This was a 7 year old boy whose father was an intelligent man who suffered from migraine and marked hypochondriasis. His mother was aged 23 years and had borne five children, two of whom had died. She had herself been declared a neglected child and had been brought up in an institution. The boy had experienced numerous separations from both his parents and spent a considerable time being looked after by his paternal grandmother. He had had nine admissions to the local hospital with inpatient periods totalling 52 days, and four admissions to hospitals in Sydney with inpatient periods totalling 226 days. The latter admissions were for running ears. After discharge from a Sydney hospital he had severe behaviour problems at home and at school. He had frequent and severe temper tantrums and clung to his mother when brought anywhere near the vicinity of the hospital. This clinging behaviour also resulted in episodes of refusing to go to school. Although he was usually dry at night he had a recurrence of bed wetting after each episode of separation. This boy had severe behaviour disorders that were not helped by frequent prolonged and unnecessary admissions to a hospital geographically far removed from his family.

Psychoneurotic and psychosomatic disorders

Case 8   This was a 12 year old girl who was the second of three children. Her mother had been murdered in a drunken brawl and she had been adopted by another Aboriginal family. From the age of seven she had been separated from that family for 122 days owing to admissions to a Sydney hospital for ear trouble. She was a large, well groomed girl who exhibited marked shyness in all situations. She had recurrent headaches and abdominal pains, persistent bed-wetting and frequent crying attacks. She retained an infantile dependence on her adoptive mother. She was, however, regarded by her teachers as well behaved, co-operative and an example to the other children.

Case 9   This 8 year old girl was the third of a family of five children. She had never had contact with her real father and her mother had recently married a man much younger than herself. Since then the family relationships had been most unstable with the police being

133

called to intervene in arguments on numerous occasions. Her mother was very histrionic and suffered from episodes of hysterical paralysis. She used the law to control her husband, so that he spent a large part of each month serving prison sentences. This did not help the family finances and they were in a state of chronic poverty. The mother made frequent attempts to settle in a house in the town but these were always thwarted by the family upsets. The girl was warm, friendly and intelligent. She had spent 56 days in hospital for treatment of a slightly wasted arm resulting from poliomyelitis. She remarked that 'hospital was much better than the Bourke Reserve. No-one had fights.' She suffered from frequent abdominal pains and headaches and was a chronic bed-wetter. During the times of family upheaval she exhibited acute anxiety reactions with marked physical distress, culminating on one occasion with a hysterical paralysis of both legs.

Reactive depression

Case 10 This 14 year old girl was the eldest of six children. Her father was particularly strict, but not violent. Because her mother was permanently disabled, the main chores of the household fell to her. She was an attractive girl, who was in good physical health. She appeared to be extremely moody and depressed. She spent a large part of her day sitting by herself and crying, especially when her father was drunk and became verbally abusive towards her. These episodes of depressive behaviour were interspersed with emotional outbursts both at home and at school. She suffered from frequent abdominal pains and headaches and was already becoming addicted to analgesic powders. Her father attempted to undertake leadership roles in the Aboriginal community which produced so much anxiety in him that he found it necessary to relieve these symptoms with alcohol. Her moods were particularly dependent upon the achievements and hence the disposition of her father. After a move from the Reserve to a Housing Commission house and the publication of some of her poems in national magazine, her depressive condition improved.

Epidemiological studies of psychiatric disorders in different communities have shown that the traditional medical practitioner sees only the tip of the psychiatric iceberg. Where the community consist of depressed and reticent non-demanders of medical attention, this observation is even more relevant and this was shown in Dr Coolican's survey of his medical practice in Bourke where only one Aboriginal child was recorded as having consulted him with a behaviour disorder in 1968 (Coolican, 1973). Even after I had expressed an interest in the psychological and behavioural disorders of the children in the area by virtue of doing this survey only 37 children were referred to me, 26 by their mothers and 11 by either their teachers or the Department of Child Welfare.

Petrol sniffing by Aboriginal children has been reported in communities stretching from the Eastern Goldfields in Western Australia to Mornington Island in the Gulf of Carpentaria. No such cases were found amongst Bourke Aboriginal children. Neither were drug taking, glue sniffing and the regular consumption of alcohol before the age of 15 years found in this community.

Nearly all Bourke Aboriginal children exhibited fear of being alone in the dark, fear of dogs and anxiety when meeting white people. These fears were so universal and understandable that I did not regard them as abnormal in this particular sub-culture. Aboriginal people in this area still have a fear of ghosts and spirits and dogs evoke bad memories through being associated with guarding white people's properties and orchards. Aboriginal children suffered from a general feeling of insecurity and debasement which revealed itself in the mixture of anxiety and suspicion they exhibited in making contact with what they regarded as unpredictable white people. When viewed from the perspective of a white person, these children appeared anxious and inhibited. However, in the company of their own sub-group, this clinging, dependent behaviour disappeared.

Few of these Aboriginal children possessed the building blocks commonly regarded as desirable for the development of good mental health. They came from families in which quarrelling, alcoholism and physical violence were common, and in which the moods and actions of their parents, especially their fathers, were unpredictable and often inconsistent. When parental control of their behaviour was exercised, it was punitive and lacking in verbal reasoning and this probably contributed to a lack of internalised controls. Poverty was chronic and often deprived them of the bare necessities of life. Separation from their parents was common owing to the repeated hospitalisation of chronically ill children and also to the demands of seasonal work on their father's time Children also experienced racial discrimination at a very early age and this added to their low self-esteem. These child rearing experiences are described more fully in chapter 7.

It is probably owing to the struggles of and stability provided by the Aboriginal matriarch for her children and often her grandchildren that only 8% of the children in this community were assessed as being severely disturbed. This is a similar figure to that found by Dr Norelle Lickiss in her survey of behaviour disturbance in part-Aboriginal children in Sydney (Lickiss, 1970).

Dr Lickiss was critical of schools for alienating Aboriginal children by trying to force them to adopt the middle-class ideology of their teachers. She described how 'deviant' Aboriginal boys in Sydney had failed to negotiate the school as a social system (Lickiss, 1971b). With notable exceptions, the same situation existed in Bourke and was accentuated by the rapidity with which many teachers adopted the racist attitudes of most white people in the town to Aborigines.

It is a sad commentary on the conforming nature of white Australian society that it demands, through its schools and its laws, that Aborigines learn to become good, middle-class whites. It may be that is all that is left for part-Aborigines these days, but at the very least, such a decision should come from them and not be imposed by white policy makers. Until Aboriginal children feel there are genuine possibilities for them to achieve their needs of personal comfort and self-esteem, they will search for other methods of obtaining acceptance and prestige. If these other methods include belonging to delinquent or alcohol drinking groups, the spiral of emotional and material deprivation and low self-esteem will continue. Aboriginal children like other members of the community, need to have an occasional win in their lives. What is more, they need to see their parents also have an occasional victory. The doctor, teacher, welfare officer, or Aboriginal liaison officer who helps them to attain this occasional success, are almost certainly more effective forces towards their positive mental health than is a psychiatrist who treats them when they have become disturbed.

Psychiatric disorders in adults

Although I had anticipated some difficulty in formulating diagnoses in a cross-cultural situation, in practice this did not occur. The Aboriginal concept of being mentally sick differed little from that of the majority of white people in Bourke. This was possibly due to their partial internalisation of white values and the loss of most tribal Aboriginal beliefs. All the disorders I found, fitted readily into a Western system of classifying psychiatric disorder and their distribution in the Bourke Aboriginal adults is shown in Table 15.

The most common psychiatric condition found was a form of personality disorder. I made this diagnosis in people who did not have a major recognisable underlying psychiatric disorder but whose social conduct persistently interfered with their family and community life. This condition was found almost exclusively in men and was manifest by drinking alcohol with subsequent behaviour which was unacceptable to the families of these men (*see* chapter 6). Sixteen of these men and the three women in this diagnostic category were chronic alcoholics. The remaining men were periodic weekend drinkers who indulged in more frequent drinking when they were particularly angry, anxious or depressed. Included in this category of personality disorder were three men who usually reacted to minimal provocation with excessive hostility and aggression and two men whose interpersonal relationships were characterised by overt suspiciousness and unreasoned jealousy of their wives.

The second most common group of psychiatric disorders were either a depressive reaction or an anxiety state. These were almost totally confined to women. Those who suffered a depressive reaction complained of a persistently low mood and their self-esteem was so low that they regarded themselves as worthless beings. The people with an anxiety state were excessively apprehensive about many ordinary aspects of their life and exhibited a degree of fear in common situations which while understandable in terms of their past experiences, were still out of proportion to their current reality.

A further six people were diagnosed as suffering a psychoneurotic disorder. Two manifested the symptoms of hysterical paralysis of their legs, three had psychosomatic diseases such as migraine or duodenal ulcer and one woman exhibited severe hypochondriasis having made no less than 62 medical consultations in 1972 for a variety of bodily complaints.

The proportion of Bourke Aborigines who were severely mentally disturbed and had both lost touch with reality and who exhibited a major disintegration of their personality (ie. who were psychotic) was high by comparison with other population studies. However half of these people were psychotic due to another underlying disease such as brain damage or liver failure.

137

Table 15 Distribution of psychiatric disorders in Bourke Aboriginal adults by age and sex in 1972

Diagnosis	15-19 M	15-19 F	20-29 M	20-29 F	30-39 M	30-39 F	40-49 M	40-49 F	50+ yrs M	50+ yrs F	Total	Proportion of total population
Personality disorder	1		16		14	3	9	1	8		52	16%
Depressive reaction				5		3	1	5		4	18	6%
Anxiety state		1		5	2	4		1		3	16	5%
Other psychoneuroses	2	1	1			1					6	2%
Psychoses		1		1	1	1	1	4	1	1	10	3%
Total persons with a psychiatric disorder	3	2	17	12	17	12	11	11	9	8	102	32%
Percentage of each age group with a psychiatric disorder[1]	9%	6%	37%	23%	46%	37%	58%	48%	37%	38%		

1. Percentages rounded to the nearest whole number.

138

The case history of one of these women with psychosis is of special interest since she is to my knowledge the first Aborigine to have undergone psycho-surgery. This woman had been almost permanently disabled from a severe manic depressive illness. During periods of depression she would become markedly agitated and had attempted suicide on several occasions. The manic phase of her illness was less frequent but had occurred on three occasions in fourteen years. All Western and some traditional Aboriginal methods of relieving her distress had failed. After careful and prolonged consideration involving her family, the operation of prefrontal leucotomy was performed. This restored her to a fully functioning capacity. The last communication I received from her was a Christmas card in 1976, in which she mentioned that she had just had a poem published in a widely circulated newspaper.

The pattern of psychiatric disorder exhibited a marked sex difference. Women reacted to stress with anxiety and depression and the men defended against similar feelings by denial and sociopathic, addictive drinking behaviour. For Bourke Aborigines, the period of greatest risk for developing psychiatric disorder began in their middle twenties and continued into later life. The first five years after leaving school were a time of great freedom for Bourke Aborigines. The men were part of a group from which they drew support and status. They enjoyed travelling to other centres, working a while and moving on. Alcohol had begun to play a large part in the social life of the group and the flagon had gradually become a focal point of their common interest.

At this time, white society began to show active disapproval of them through its various institutions, and the vicious circle of drunkenness—aggression—prosecution—loss of dignity—impotent anger—drunkenness would begin to wear down whatever spirit the young Aboriginal men had previously possessed.

For girls, the period of freedom was much shorter. By the age of 19 years over 50% had had their first child, which was a desired event. By 25 years of age over 50% again would have had their fourth child. The women became weighed down by their ever increasing number of children who were often ill, and the burden of having to shoulder the family responsibilities with little support from their menfolk.

Psychiatric disorder was significantly more common in both men and women who were separated, women who were regular church attenders and women who lived in a town house (see Tables 16, 17 and 18).

139

Thirty-one women with an anxiety state or a mixture of anxiety and reactive depression came from houses with two white neighbours. Seventeen of these women lived in Housing Commission houses and nine of them claimed that their psychiatric symptoms had begun since they had moved to this better, but more isolated accommodation. Aboriginal people were not welcomed by their white neighbours. Their reception was often so hostile that they lived in a state of virtual siege. Their anxieties were increased by the complexities of electrical appliances which no-one had shown them how to use. The self-image and confidence of an Aboriginal woman was further eroded by the censorious attitude of her neighbours to her lack of basic material goods such as furniture and curtains. Not only had she lost the support that she had formerly obtained from her peers on the Reserve, but she was sometimes ostracised by them for trying to be 'flash'. The man on the other hand was forced to work regularly so he could pay the rent and he still had contact with other Aborigines at work. The social pressure of his peers on the Reserve to join in drinking parties was reduced by his geographical distance from them, and this resulted in a decrease in his consumption of alcohol. However, the negative effect of geographical

Table 16 Conjugal status of Bourke Aboriginal adults with a psychiatric disorder

| | Population | | Psychiatric disorder | |
	Male	Female	Male	Female
Married	59	59	24	21
De facto stable	33	33	7	5
De facto unstable	13	13	4	4
Separated	13	10	10	8
Widowed	3	6	3	3
Single	35	43	9	4
Total	156	164	57	45

Test of difference between married males with psychiatric disorder and 'normal' married males	$\chi^2 = 0.732$ N.S.
Test of difference between married females with psychiatric disorder and 'normal' married females	$\chi^2 = 3.463$ N.S.
Test of difference between separated males with psychiatric disorder and 'normal' separated males	$\chi^2 = 6.238\ \rho < 0.05$
Test of difference between separated females with psychiatric disorder and 'normal' separated females	$\chi^2 = 7.230\ \rho < 0.01$

Table 17 Active religious affiliation in Bourke Aboriginal adults with psychiatric disorder

	Population		Psychiatric cases	
	Male (%)	Female (%)	Male (%)	Female (%)
No	113 (72.4)	86 (52.4)	43 (75.4)	7 (15.6)
Yes	43 (27.6)	78 (47.6)	14 (24.6)	38 (84.4)
Total	156	164	57	45

Test of difference between active religious women with
   psychiatric disorder and active religious women who were
   'normal' $\chi^2 = 32.551$ $p < 0.001$

Table 18 Place of residence of Bourke Aboriginal adults with psychiatric disorder

	Population		Psychiatric disorder	
	Male (%)	Female (%)	Male (%)	Female (%)
Town	99 (63.5)	106 (64.6)	22 (38.6)	37 (82.2)
Reserve	57 (36.5)	58 (35.4)	35 (61.4)	8 (17.8)
Total	156	164	57	45

Excess psychiatric condition of males living on Reserve $\chi^2 = 21.261$ $p < 0.001$
Excess psychiatric condition of females living in town $\chi^2 = 8.911$ $p < 0.01$

and social isolation on the women outweighed the positive effect on the men. Similarly, adverse effects on mental health have been reported in English people who have lost their old family and friendship supports by moving to new development areas (Martin *et al.*, 1957) and in marginal groups which are culturally excluded from participating in the life of the majority society (Brody, 1966).

If it is the policy of the New South Wales State Housing Commission to spread selected Aboriginal families throughout the town as a method of integrating them into the white community, I would suggest that this is sociologically and psychologically short-sighted and will probably result in producing the opposite effects to those which they intend.

The 'personal discomfort' questionnaire

Professor John Cawte and his colleagues have modified the Cornell Medical Index (a commonly used questionnaire for detecting symptoms of ill health) for use in psychiatric field surveys. This

Table 19 Personal discomfort questionnaire percentage of 'yes' responses according to age and sex

Proportion of subjects answering 'yes'

Item	15 to 29 years M (n=48)	F (n=60)	30 to 49 years M (n=55)	F (n=53)	50+ years M (n=17)	F (n=17)	Total males (n=120)	Total females (n=130)
Somatic:								
Chest pain	40%	20%	38%	32%	35%	41%	38%	28%
Belching	19%	13%	33%	36%	29%	53%	27%	28%
Constipation		3%	2%	17%		12%	1%	10%
Stiffness	4%	7%	15%	17%	35%	47%	13%	16%
Skin sensitivity	2%		5%	6%	6%	6%	3%	4%
Headaches	33%	48%	24%	43%	6%	59%	25%	48%
Dizziness	13%	23%	9%	17%	18%	18%	12%	20%
Exhaustion:								
Morning fatigue	19%	27%	11%	47%	12%	29%	17%	41%
Other:								
Hypochondria	10%	12%	11%	23%		18%	9%	22%
Insomnia		12%	7%	23%	6%	24%	4%	18%
Anxiety:								
Xenophobia	10%	75%	9%	45%		35%	8%	58%
Inadequacy	8%	60%	4%	23%		12%	5%	39%
Continual worry	2%	13%	4%	32%		47%	3%	25%
Shyness	19%	40%	7%	23%	6%	12%	12%	29%
Shakiness	13%	23%	15%	26%	24%	35%	15%	26%
Cold sweating	8%	17%	5%	21%	6%	24%	7%	19%
Depression:								
Depression	6%	30%	20%	47%	12%	47%	13%	39%
Wish for death	4%	20%	9%	36%	18%	47%	8%	30%
Paranoid-irritability:								
Resentment of orders	65%	60%	73%	47%	18%	53%	61%	54%

questionnaire reveals clusters of psychiatric symptoms in a community as distinct from detecting psychiatric cases. It asks questions such as 'Do you have any pains in the heart or chest?'.

I administered this personal discomfort questionnaire to 250 subjects (78% of the total adult population). The results are shown in Table 19. Chest pain, headaches and resentment of orders were the dominant symptoms in both sexes. Chest pains were a common cause of absenteeism from work. In men the headaches were generally 'all over the head' and were related to tension and in women the headaches were unilateral and were accompanied by other symptoms associated with migraine. Diffuse pain was poorly tolerated by Aboriginal people in this area, whereas severe pain from injury was borne with stoicism.

When answering the question, 'Does it make you angry to have anyone tell you what to do?' many of the interviewees responded with a distinctly aggressive change in their tone of voice. This was an understandable response from people who had often been ordered about by members of the dominant white society.

Women scored higher on all items except chest pain and resentment of orders. The differences were especially marked in those symptoms which are components of the syndromes of anxiety and depression. It is probable that the low scores for the latter conditions found in men were due to a need to deny such unmanly feelings, both to themselves and to me. The emotions of self-pity and sometimes remorse not infrequently revealed themselves under the influence of alcohol.

Community development and psychiatric disorder

At the beginning of this chapter I mentioned that one of the reasons for measuring the prevalence of psychiatric disorder in the Bourke Aboriginal community was to test the hypothesis that a high rate of psychiatric disorder in a community would inhibit planned change. Few doctors would dispute that there was a high frequency of psychiatric disorder in this community. Similarly there was little doubt that those members of the community whose functioning was impaired by psychiatric disorder did have an inhibiting effect on the initiation and encouragement of social change. The alcoholic members disrupted, the depressed did not participate, and the anxious participated but could not execute their planning. However, it is a moot point at what level of non-participation of its members an organisation will cease to function. Even the late Saul Alinsky, who achieved world-wide recognition for his ability to organise the poor for radical social action, pointed out that in his most successful campaign in the Back-of-the-Yards slum area in Chicago, he was able to involve only 3% of the population (Thursz, 1966). Although 32% of the Bourke Aboriginal adults suffered from a psychiatric disorder, this did not inhibit the beginning of change in the community which began after my introduction as a doctor and an agent of social change.

Chapter 6
Alcohol and aspirin

The members of a disintegrated community are subject to high levels of stress. The universal, albeit maladaptive, responses of such people are to try to relieve their feelings of 'dis-ease', by getting drunk and by taking tablets which will either give them an emotional lift or tranquillise them.

Alcoholism is probably the major acute problem of Australian Aborigines. It disrupts their family life and interferes with the care of their children; it is a principal factor precipitating delinquency and crime and it is a leading cause of early death through physical disease, accidents and acts of violence. In many areas of Australia, alcohol is the main and the most immediate threat to the survival of Aborigines.

Although there has never been any proof that Aborigines are genetically vulnerable to alcohol, this belief is widely held by white Australians, partly because drunken Aborigines group together and are more conspicuous than drunken whites. The implication of this genetic view is that if Aborigines cannot hold their liquor they are an inferior species to the white man who can. These stereotypes contribute to the racial discrimination against Aborigines which is a feature of most country towns and many urban centres.

Any project aimed at helping Aboriginal communities has to contend with the disruptive effects of those members who are frequently drunk. The problem of alcohol abuse in Aborigines has not yielded to simplistic solutions such as prohibition, prosecution, education and forced separation from alcohol.

While it is apparent that men relieve their inner tensions through drinking alcohol, it is not widely known that many women attempt to achieve the same effect by taking analgesic powders. Both habits are detrimental to good health.

In order to seek solutions to these problems it is necessary to try to understand the underlying social and psychological causes and also how the Aboriginal drinker or analgesic swallower views and explains his or her addictive habits. My purpose in this chapter is to examine the

145

patterns of alcohol drinking and analgesic consumption by Bourke
Aborigines, the effect on their physical and social well-being and to
attempt to discover factors which may be of help in their management

Alcohol

A person who was dependent upon alcohol to the extent that it
frequently interfered with his family, community and/or economic life
was regarded as a problem drinker. A person who indulged in 'binge'
drinking every weekend but whose behaviour did not seriously impair
his relationships with his family or the community and who was able to
function in all spheres of activity during the week, was not classed as a
problem drinker.

I collected data on drinking habits as the number of glasses or bottles
of beer drunk, or the amount of fortified wine consumed in fractions of
a flagon. This was averaged out to a daily amount and converted into
grams of alcohol by taking each 7 oz (c. 200 ml) glass of beer and each
2 oz (c. 57 ml) of fortified wine as being equivalent to 10 g of alcohol[1].
Drinking was classified as light (1-10 g of alcohol per day) moderate (11
to 40g), moderately heavy (41 to 80 g) and heavy (81 g or more).

Alcohol intake in adults   Of the men surveyed only 12 (9.7%) were
teetotal while 66 (53.2%) were heavy drinkers consuming more than
80 grams of alcohol per day. Women were much lighter drinkers than
men and only four (3.1%) were found in the heavy drinking category
(*see* Table 20).

Table 20 Average daily consumption of alcohol by Bourke Aboriginal men
and women (20 years and over)

Daily alcohol intake (g)	Men		Women	
	Number	Proportion of total population	Number	Proportion of total population
Nil	12	9.7%	91	71.0%
< 10	14	11.3%	12	9.4%
11–40	12	9.7%	13	10.1%
41–80	17	13.7%	5	3.9%
81–120	22	17.7%	1	0.8%
121–180	31	25.0%	3	2.3%
180+	13	10.5%		
Not known	3	2.4%	3	2.3%
Total	124	100.0%	128	100.0%

1. I have since learned that 200 ml of Australian beer contains only 7.9 g of alcohol.

Table 21 Average daily consumption of alcohol in Bourke Aboriginal men by age group in decades

Daily alcohol intake (g)	Proportion of males				
	10 to 19 years (n=80)	20 to 29 years (n=41)	30 to 39 years (n=37)	40 to 49 years (n=19)	50 and over (n=24)
Nil	80.0%		5.4%	21.0%	25.0%
1– 10	12.5%	12.2%	21.6%		4.2%
11– 40	5.0%	14.6%	5.4%	5.3%	12.5%
41– 80	2.5%	19.5%	13.5%	5.3%	12.5%
81–120		19.5%	21.6%	21.0%	8.3%
121–180		46.3%	24.3%	31.6%	16.7%
180+		4.9%	8.1%	15.8%	20.8%

Table 22 Average daily consumption of alcohol in Bourke Aboriginal women by age group in decades

Daily alcohol intake (g)	Proportion of females				
	10 to 19 years (n=80)	20 to 29 years (n=49)	30 to 39 years (n=32)	40 to 49 years (n=23)	50 and over (n=21)
Nil	100.0%	73.5%	81.3%	60.9%	71.4%
1– 10		6.1%	9.4%	13.0%	14.3%
11– 40		14.3%		21.7%	4.8%
41–80		6.1%	6.2%		
81–120				4.4%	
21–180			3.1%		9.5%

The men began drinking between the ages of 14 years and 19 years with 36% of that age group being regular drinkers. By the age of 20 all the men were regular consumers of alcohol and this pattern of drinking remained constant except for those few who had decided to abstain. No women began to drink before the age of 20 years and except for seven of them, all other women were light or moderate drinkers (*see* Tables 21 and 22).

Most men consumed some alcohol each day. They drank beer in the public bar of hotels and fortified wines on the Reserve or by the river bank. With the exception of five women whose lives were overtly disrupted by alcohol, the other women rarely drank any other form of alcohol except beer. The percentage of alcohol taken as beer and as fortified wine is shown in Table 23.

147

Table 23 Proportion of alcohol taken as beer and fortified wine for each age group and sex[1]

| Age (years) | Proportion of total alcohol intake | | | |
| | Beer | | Wine | |
	Males	Females	Males	Females
10–19	72%		28%	
20–29	29%	70%	71%	30%
30–39	44%	44%	66%	66%
40–49	23%	62%	77%	38%
50+	38%	57%	62%	43%

1. Percentages rounded to nearest whole number.

Table 24 Proportion of male problem drinkers by age

Age (years)	Total population	Number of problem drinkers	Proportion of problem drinkers
15–19	32	1	3.1%
20–29	44	17	38.6%
30–39	37	12	32.4%
40–49	19	10	52.6%
50+	24	9	37.5%
Total	156	49	31.4%

Table 24 shows the age of the male problem drinkers. They comprised 31% of the total adult male population aged 15 years and over and all consumed an average of more than 80 g of alcohol per day. Five women (3.9% of the female population over 15 years) were problem drinkers. Three were aged 34–45 years and two were over 50 years. Only one had an alcohol intake of less than 80 g per day.

Sixteen men and one woman were dependent on alcohol to the extent that they drank every day. The remaining problem drinkers could and often did abstain from alcohol for varying periods of time. They indulged in episodes of 'binge' drinking in which up to 400 g of alcohol would be consumed in a day, usually in the form of fortified wines. Of the 57 males 15 years and older, resident on the Aboriginal Reserve, 35 (61%) were problem drinkers. The corresponding figure for the 86 men living in the town was 14 (16%). Two of the women problem drinkers lived on the Reserve and three in the town.

Psychiatric disorder Three male problem drinkers suffered from organic brain disease, two as a result of prolonged heavy drinking and one owing to a motor accident. One woman also had brain disorder due to liver disease. Only one male adult with an explosive psychopathic personality was found to have an obvious underlying psychiatric illness which might have resulted in symptomatic drinking. One woman who was a problem drinker had her drinking bouts precipitated by a recurrent depressive state. Five other women who averaged only a moderate daily intake of alcohol were noted to get drunk only when they experienced an underlying depressive or anxiety state.

The effects of alcohol

The degree of aggression released by the disinhibiting effects of alcohol resulted in a high incidence of physical injury. In 1971 and 1972, 22 men and 12 women were admitted to hospital with injuries sustained from fighting or, in the case of women, from being beaten by their drunken husbands. A young man who was a mild drinker died from a brain haemorrhage as a result of a knock-out blow delivered at a Christmas party. I recorded the greatest number of injuries resulting from drunkenness in September 1971, when 31 Aboriginal men sustained fractured bones or lacerations. All but seven of the 49 problem drinkers had an associated physical disease and 41 were admitted to hospital with an acute physical condition on at least one occasion in 1971 or 1972. Between them they had 209 hospital admissions which comprised 39.5% of all admissions for Aboriginal adults, and each of them spent an average time of 18 days per year in hospital.

Two men made serious attempts to hang themselves; one was unconscious for several hours and his face was covered in small skin haemorrhages for some days afterwards. Another cut his wrists and a fourth swallowed 40 tablets of aspirin. A minority of drunk men often exhibited self-pity rather than externalised aggression, but only these four gave expression to this by attempting suicide.

Occasional disruption of family life (less than one major family upset each month) in 1971–1972 was caused by 40 (32%) adult men and seven (5.5%) adult women and persistent disruption by 38 (31%) men and three (2%) women. Alcohol was regarded as the major family problem by the female head of 19% of all Aboriginal households and as a moderate problem in a further 28% of households.

149

Alcohol and the law

In the two years 1971 and 1972, 50% of the men aged 15 years and over and 8.5% of the women were arrested at least once by the police. Most arrests were for disorderly behaviour and the others were for misdemeanours committed while they were drinking. The only one which was not, was committed by a man who was caught driving a car during the period that his licence was suspended for a previous 'drunk-driving' conviction. When drunk, Aborigines were rarely amenable to a warning by a police officer, who was then forced to make an arrest in order to maintain the authority of his position. On the other hand the Aborigines Act of New South Wales (1969) encourages the police to abuse their powers by making even social drinking in a dwelling on an Aboriginal Reserve an offence. The simplistic view held by many rural whites and police that the zealous prosecution of drunken Aborigines will drive them to temperance was not only lacking in historical perspective but was almost certainly counter-productive, in that it ensured that Aborigines would register their protest by further drunkenness. A less interfering and more lenient policy together with the repeal of discriminatory legislation may at least reduce some of the alienation from and anger at the norms, values and practices of white society, which is one cause of Aborigines turning to drink.

Cost

The weekly amount spent on alcohol by the total Aboriginal population was estimated at just over $1500 which was about a quarter of the total weekly income. When I calculated the cost based on the stated consumption of alcohol it came to only $1000 which is probably explained by people sharing alcohol with those who were without money and also by them underestimating their true alcohol intake.

The estimated loss of working days for adult males is shown in Table 25. Since many Aboriginal men were itinerant workers and the older chronic alcoholics found it difficult or undesirable to obtain work, these figures are certainly a gross underestimate of the effect that drinking had on the employment opportunities of Aboriginal men in this area.

Sociological aspects of drinking

In the early stages of a drinking party there was usually much *bonhomie*, good humour, dancing and a display of affection and

Table 25 Estimated loss of working days per year due to drinking in adult Aboriginal males 20 years and older, in 1971 and 1972

Days lost	Number of males	Proportion of males
Nil	64	52.9%
1– 5	15	12.4%
6–10	20	16.5%
11–20	16	13.2%
20+	6	5.0%
Total	121	100.0%

generosity towards children. On the Reserve, children were often seen enjoying themselves around such a group. Before the participants became intoxicated and lost control of their aggressive urges, the children would either be removed by their mothers, or as a result of past experiences, would themselves know when to depart. If a child was present when a fight occurred, he would side with his relatives and later boast that 'my father knocked your father's block off', irrespective of the true results. Children as young as 7 years would play games in which they would imitate some of the older men in their singing, dancing and staggering gait. Although intoxicated fathers often caused family disruption and great anxiety in children, enough of the positive aspects of drinking had been experienced for children to see it as a pleasurable and manly activity.

Experimentation with alcohol began in the middle teens. The first episode of drunkenness was akin to an initiation ceremony. It was certainly an identification with and an emulation of the adult role and was often reinforced by acceptance into the adult group. This desire to identify, copy and be accepted as an adult was best expressed by one 14 year old boy who answered a question about his future plans by saying that he wished to 'get drunk and go to gaol like my father and uncles'.

To be a good 'drinking man' was a partial adaptation to the circumstances confronting most Aborigines. The resultant oblivion was often the only outlet for frustration, aggression, rage and a general feeling of dissatisfaction. Drinking provided one of the few forms of free choice an Aborigine could make. It fulfilled social obligations of hospitality and provided a common purpose to a group. Even the most alienated Aboriginal men developed a decisive step as they strode into town to purchase their liquor and back to the Reserve or the river bank to drink it. Drinking muted the anxiety felt by some Aborigines in the presence of white people and gave them courage to express their views in hotels and at meetings of the Aboriginal Advancement Association. The public bar was a social centre, warm, dry and salubrious in comparison to the housing conditions of most Aborigines. It provided them with an opportunity to be on equal terms with whites.

The giving and receiving of alcohol symbolised mateship and a common purpose in life. To refuse to drink with one's mates was a breach of etiquette of the same order as refusing an invitation to eat with a Bedouin. Refusal was regarded as rejection and betrayal of the group who then stigmatised their former member and left him socially isolated. Since few Aborigines were likely to be accepted into any other group except certain branches of the church, they were loath to risk the wrath or ridicule of their peers. The fear of a prison sentence for breaking a bond to the white man's court hung lightly on them in comparison to the fear of rejection by their friends. These attitudes are illustrated in the following case histories.

Case 1   A male, aged 24 years, was the second of seven children, the youngest four of whom had been taken into the care of the Department of Child Welfare after having been declared 'neglected owing to the chronic alcoholism of both their parents'. The subject began episodic heavy 'binge' drinking at the age of 14 years. He stated on some occasions that he had to conform to group pressures or he would be 'called a woman' by his friends and he said on other occasions that he began drinking because there was nothing else to do. By the age of 21 he was drinking every day and indulging in petty theft to help meet the cost. He had spent all but two months of his twenty-third and twenty-fourth years in gaol for these offences. After each discharge from gaol he would celebrate his arrival back in Bourke by getting drunk with his friends and being arrested again on the same day. After one of these arrests he asked the police to admit him to the regional mental hospital for treatment. This was arranged and he was found to be mentally normal and to function well apart from an inability to assume responsibility. He was noted to be easily led by people with psychopathic personalities in the same ward, black or white. He rejected the idea of a retraining programme and after three months he stated he was cured and wished to be discharged from the hospital. He was met at the railway station by several of his friends and arrested for drunkenness six hours later.

Case 2   A male, aged 51 years, had two alcoholic parents. He was of superior intelligence and displayed a great deal of wit and insight when sober. He began episodic drinking at the age of 15 and this remained his normal drinking pattern until he was nearly 40 years old. His wife drank more than he, but she underwent a religious conversion and stopped. For the last eleven years he had been drunk almost every day and stated he had lost count of the number of times he had been gaoled for drunkenness. He made the claim (well substantiated by reliable witnesses) that when he was away from his mates in another town he did not drink. By this he meant that a flagon of wine would last him for a week instead of four hours. He stated 'If you want to give up drink you have to go where you don't have mates. It is important to me to go with my mates, that's all I've got. If I refused a mate the next time I pick up with him he won't want anything to do with me. He would lend me anything. Now he won't lend me nothing. I'd be sort of insulting him.' When asked why he had just enticed his neighbour to a drinking session knowing that the neighbour faced a long prison sentence the next time he was convicted of disturbing the peace, he replied 'We don't think about it. He is my mate. I want to drink with him. What happens tomorrow? Who knows what happens tomorrow?'

Case 3 A male, aged 30 years, came from a 'drinking family'. His parents, brothers and one sister were all alcoholics. He began drinking at the age of 13 and continued episodic drinking until he was 26 years old, when he lost an eye fighting with a broken beer bottle in a drunken brawl. After that, his drinking increased, and he became violent to his wife and children to such a degree that it produced revulsion even in his closest drinking companions. He stated 'Fighting is like eating. A few Murries get together and have a bit of grog and then they talk fighting. What a good scrapper they are. Then they show each other a few punches and one hits too hard and it's on.' He also claimed that drinking was all that he had. He asked 'What has any blackfellow got? What have the better ones got? A lonely bed in a clean hospital, a blanket on the veranda of a lousy house?' He always became happy, then morose, when drunk. He often threatened suicide, but had never made any attempt at it. After he obtained a glass eye, which improved his appearance, he stopped drinking and took a job. After six weeks he was joined by friends from another town, went on a 'binge', lost his eye and reverted to his former state.

Excluding the 17 subjects who were intoxicated nearly every day, there were two main patterns of drinking. The first tended to occur after work when Aboriginal males drank beer at three of the seven hotels in the town, clearly enjoying the social benefits of drinking without trying to get drunk. In the second form of drinking the aim was to get drunk. The medium used was cheap fortified wine purchased by the flagon and consumed over the space of a few hours by the river bank or on the Bourke Reserve. This pattern has been attributed by the anthropologist Beckett, to a copy of white behaviour in the 19th century (Beckett, 1964), a pattern vividly described as still common in rural Australia (Saint, 1970) and regarded as the extreme form of the 'Anglo-Saxon' pattern of drinking by the English psychiatrists Kessel and Walton (1971). This latter pattern of drinking may also have been the result of the practical necessity for the quick consumption of alcohol in the days of prohibition. The most frequent type of drinking among Aborigines was the periodic 'binge' as described in some of the case histories. Lone drinking did not occur even in chronic alcoholics, except in the case of one man and two women whose drinking was symptomatic of underlying psychiatric distress. One of these women is described in the following case history.

Case 4   A female, aged 34 years, spent seven years of her adolescence in a Child Welfare home, having been declared neglected owing to the alcoholism of her parents. On her release, she obtained a domestic job in an isolated rural area. In her leisure hours she found company by mixing with a hard-drinking group of white itinerant workers. She soon began drinking and was frequently arrested for drunkenness and for assaulting policemen when in such a state. When she married and lived out of town, her drinking ceased except for an occasional 'binge' on her monthly shopping expedition. Because she wished her children to go to school she moved into a house in Bourke. Her husband had difficulty in keeping up the rent payments and she would receive notices of eviction. She always reacted to this firstly by becoming morose and secondly by getting drunk.

The attitudes of women to their husbands' drinking habits

Apart from seven women who observed rigid religious principles, all the other women regarded it as normal for a man to get drunk on a Friday and/or Saturday evening. More frequent drunkenness was not acceptable to them because of the resulting violence and depletion of the family income. When a woman feared for her own, her children's or even her drunk husband's safety, she was forced to turn to the police

154

for help since other Aboriginal men did not intervene on her behalf. The following statements by Aboriginal women illustrate the ambivalent state of mind in which they were placed when their husbands were drunk.

Statement 1   A woman, aged 22 years, said 'I've had to call the police twice. I don't like doing it. They get fined and you go without. It's no use running to another Murrie because if he comes along he's told to keep his nose out of other people's business. So I get the police. Usually he is okay when he's drunk. He loves the kids and cuddles them and they think it's terrific. Sometimes he picks and picks. Once he hit me and my four year old son still hasn't got over it. He keeps telling him: "Daddy, you hit Mummy".'

Statement 2   A woman, aged 31 years, said 'I never call the police to him. He's got a good job and we just lose out if he goes to gaol so I just stand up to him. He's usually so drunk I don't have much trouble.'

Statement 3   A woman, aged 57 years, said 'Whenever he gets drunk he picks up a lump of wood and starts to hit me. I don't like to call the police so I usually stand up to him. The other day he kept hitting me so I picked up the carving knife and warned him I'd put it through him. I told him I'd get put in gaol but it would be worth it. He didn't seem to take much notice so I just let fly. I got him right through the arm. That quietened him down a bit.'

Statement 4   A woman, aged 42 years, said 'The old fella's drinking gets me down. The kids are growing up just like him and just want to drink all the time. I can cope with him most times but about every six months I've got to get on to the drink so I can cope with the old fella.'

Statement 5   A woman, aged 35 years, said 'He goes mad when he's drunk. He was hit on the head with a saucepan when he was young and I guess that damaged his brain. I call the police every time he drinks now, I'm sick of him. My eight year old daughter shakes when he's in the house drunk. She's going to be a nervous wreck like me.'

Statement 6   A woman, aged 33 years, said 'He's been drinking more and more for the last five years. He swims in it. He's drunk every night and he can't remember what he does. He gets stuck into my eldest daughter (she's 15) who keeps out of the house as much as possible. She wants to go to Sydney; she even tried to get herself convicted in court so the Child Welfare would have to send her to a hostel and find her a job in Sydney. He's a rat. If I had my time over again I wouldn't get myself a drunken husband, that's for sure.'

The necessity for wives to call the police as a form of external control added further misunderstanding to the relationships between the police and the Aborigines. The police have learnt, from past experience, that a warning to a drunk Aboriginal male is not effective and so adopt more active measures. If the drunk husband cannot remember the events of the previous evening, he assumes, when he becomes sober, that the police have arrested him in his bed simply to keep the gaol full. To protect herself, the wife never tells him that it was she who sent for the police. Dr Jeremy Beckett, an anthropologist who worked in this area ten years previously, has succinctly summarised the Aboriginal woman's dilemma: 'There is irony indeed in a situation where men, in their endeavour to defy white domination, oblige their own wives to betray them to their enemies' (1964:45).

Not only does the resultant fine and loss of income further deplete the family finances, but the wives of those husbands who are sentenced to a longer period of gaol than the usual 24 to 48 hours, are forced to apply for 'police rations', a procedure designed to remove any shred of dignity that a woman may have had.

Abstinent alcoholics

Ten men and four women who had all been severe alcoholics were now teetotal and had abstained from alcohol for periods ranging from three to 45 years. Half of them had stopped drinking because they were frightened about their health or because they suddenly realised that they 'weren't getting anywhere'. Two of them have moved away from their former companions and lead fairly isolated lives in the town. The others still mix with their former friends but do not drink with them and they are the exception to the rule that an Aborigine cannot give up alcohol and keep his friends. The experience of one of these men is illustrated in the following case:

Case 5 A male, aged 58 years, began drinking with his father and uncles in his late teens. By the age of 30 he was drinking anything he could obtain—chlorodyne, methylated spirits and essence of vanilla. 'I drank to be with my mates. We'd give each other everything. I'd give them my last penny. Then the grog would go to our heads and the old scores would come to the surface and those grievances of five or six weeks ago would be remembered and we'd decide to settle them by fighting. The next day we'd all be mates again. I'd fight over anything. Grog, money, fight over nothing. Who was the best fighter. I got most of my teeth knocked out, a broken jaw, fourteen stitches in my chest from a broken bottle. I spent a lot of money on fines but a lot more on flagons. I had a bit of a job and used to get paid in methylated spirits. I'd have to have a couple of charges[1] before I'd stop shaking each morning. One day when I was about 50 I made up my mind to stop. I had nothing, was getting nowhere, no home, no children (all in the care of the Child Welfare Department). I lived under a tree. So I twisted[2]. Some guys get religion and twist but I twisted myself. I'm not religious. I never go to church. I go to the brothers (Pentecostal). I like their services.' He has tried unsuccessfully to pass his experiences across to his sons. His relationships with them are close when they are sober but when they are drunk he would not let them into his house.

The remaining seven problem drinkers ceased drinking in 1959 following an almost instantaneous religious conversion after listening to a visiting Pentecostal evangelist. They maintained their abstinence from alcohol by adopting a rigid religious observance as a defence against the temptations offered by their former companions. Their membership of a religious body also made them a member of a new supporting peer group. The following case histories are of two such people.

Case 6   A male, aged 55 years, is a large, impressive, self-educated and gentle man who used to be a professional fighter. He came from a non-drinking family. When he first came to Bourke in 1940 he stated that few of the young people used to drink. They amused themselves by competing against each other in athletic pursuits. 'The drink came in gradually. The old people must take much of the blame for that. They were after the young fellas' cheques when they came in off the properties. They made them "captains"[3].' He began drinking as a release from frustration—in his words 'from the frustration of being a black man, through not being able to go into a pub, of being looked down upon because I was black, of being afraid of going into white people's clubs or white people's homes. You drink to feel important. When you are sober you're nothing. You're not even second class. When you drink you're important. They [the Aborigines] know who the steady workers are. They're around like leeches. You're out in the bush and

1. A 'charge' is vernacular for a drink.
2. 'To twist' is vernacular for going straight, the opposite to being crooked.
3. Captain—the person who was buying the drinks.

you're not going to waste your money. Three or four drinks and you're handing it out. Same fellow when he's sober mightn't even give you a cigarette. I had three stages, happy and important, mad, and flat out to it. When I was mad I looked for a fight. I'd fight about anything. If you had a grudge or if you just didn't like someone, you'd pick a fight. When I gave it up [drinking], I figured that if my mates wouldn't let me, then they weren't really mates. Some of them try to pick a fight with you when you drop out but I guess they weren't game with me.'

He had a period of religious upbringing when he was a child and when a Pentecostal-type preacher came to Bourke in 1959, he underwent an instantaneous conversion and has not drunk a drop of alcohol or smoked a cigarette from that day.

He would not go into a hotel, insisting that he was frightened that the smell of alcohol would set him drinking again. He was intolerant of anyone who was drunk, and rigidly reminded everyone that he was the pastor of his own church group and had to observe strict religious practices.

Case 7 A woman, married to the subject of Case 2, was aged 52 and had been brought up in a hard-drinking family. She began heavy drinking in her late teens and preferred to get drunk on straight rum and whisky. 'When the flagon came out I bloody near died. I knew I'd had enough but I couldn't stop. I had hangovers and blackouts and the horrors but I still couldn't stop. You'll laugh at me but one day I asked God to help me and He did. Of course, having the responsibility of the children helped.' (She adopted six children after she stopped drinking.)

In their survey of the Melbourne suburb of Prahran, Rankin and Wilkinson (1971) found only seven recovered problem drinkers (0.4% of the adults surveyed), while the corresponding figure for Bourke Aboriginal adults was 14 (5.5%). In Bourke only one white problem drinker was found who was now teetotal. This indicates that far from their being 'the hopeless drunks' of the dominant white stereotype, the prognosis for sobriety in Aboriginal problem drinkers was better than that for whites. Before the advent of 'citizens rights' Beckett (1964) described the drinking habits of Aborigines in a community not far from Bourke and he reported them as saying that if they were allowed into hotels they would drink socially, and to some extent this appears to have happened.

Other circumstances which were widely observed by myself and

Table 26 Percentage of moderately heavy and heavy drinkers among Bourke Aborigines compared with other surveys of white Australians

Place	Grams of alcohol per day				Percentage of problem drinkers	
	41–80		>80			
	M	F	M	F	M	F
Hayfield[1]	28.2[2]	1.8			8.9	0.8
Prahran[3]	11.3	1.2	7.4	1.1	5.6	1.2
Canberra[4]	10.6	0.2	1.4	0		
Bourke	13.7	4.0	53.2	3.2	31.4	3.0

1. Krupinski et al., 1970, for a Victorian country town.
2. Also includes all those drinking more than 80 g of alcohol per day.
3. Rankin and Wilkinson, 1971, for an inner Melbourne suburb.
4. Hennessy et al., 1973.

Aboriginal informants to reduce the frequency and amount of drinking were full employment through government relief grants and moving from the Bourke Reserve into an adequate house. All of those who took an active interest in the affairs of the Aboriginal Advancement Association and the six Aborigines who formed a team building houses for the Association, all drank less than formerly. Also, increased contact and drinking with white helpers began to change the style of drinking from finishing the bottle to milder social habits.

Comparison with other studies

The prevalence of both heavy drinking and problem drinkers in Bourke Aboriginal men is far greater than that recorded in other recent studies of white populations in Australia (*see* Table 26). This too, was true of Bourke (a hard drinking town) and in a survey of his general practice in Bourke in 1968, Dr Coolican recorded that 8% of Aborigines and only 3% of whites were treated for alcoholism (Coolican, 1973).

Bourke Aboriginal women drank relatively little and if one allows for under-reporting by white women in those studies performed solely by interviews, it is probable that heavy and/or problem drinking in Bourke women differed little from that found in the other studies.

Treatment

Attempts at treatment through admission to hospital, individual and group therapy, Alcoholics Anonymous and the prescription of

Antabuse[1] were all unsuccessful. Community education on the health hazards of alcohol fell on ground rendered infertile by the low priority that physical well-being occupied in the needs of Aborigines, coming after food, money, social acceptance and sex.

In this community, drinking was due more to group psychosocial pressures rather than to individual psychological need. Because of this any logical approach aimed at diminishing the alcohol problem needs to be community-directed, and to influence the norms of peer groups rather than those of individuals. Heavy alcohol intake was a partially adaptive response to the life problems of Aborigines and, until other available solutions are accessible, they will continue to drink in excess.

The frequency of alcoholism has been shown to increase in times of stress and during the Industrial Revolution in England 'alcohol became for many the only recourse from the miseries inflicted by dire poverty' (Kessel and Walton, 1971). The situation of Aborigines is in many ways similar and, just as improvement in the living conditions of the English reduced the prevalence of alcoholism, an early but optimistic indication from this study is that helping Aborigines to fulfil their felt needs has reduced some of their social unhappiness, enhanced the self-image of some individuals and set a climate for the development of less damaging drinking patterns.

Analgesics

In the first half of 1971 I called at each Aboriginal dwelling and asked if I could see all the medicines, tablets and 'headache powders' kept in the house. If I found any analgesics, I asked the spokeswoman for that household how many she had taken in the last 24 hours, and whether she had seen anyone else in the household take a powder or a tablet in that time.

I found a total of 142 separate containers of analgesics in 68 of the 92 households. Twenty-four packets were unopened. Forty-eight women had taken at least one analgesic that day and had seen a further 26 women and 40 men in the same household do likewise. Thus, on the day their household was surveyed 45% of the women and 26% of the men over the age of 15 years were known to have consumed at least one analgesic preparation.

1. A drug which by preventing the metabolism of alcohol makes the recipient violently ill.

After further close contact with the Aboriginal community and from checking my observations with key Aboriginal informants, it was apparent that this was a considerable underestimate of the usual pattern. I asked one key female informant if she would believe that one half of the Aboriginal women in the town took an analgesic powder every day. She replied that I was surely wrong since nearly all the women that she knew were taking more than one powder every day. The number of analgesics taken by women on the day of the survey ranged from one to 24. Nine women had taken twelve or more powders, and the remaining analgesic consumers averaged just over three powders that day. I did not make a direct count for men but information I obtained from them at a later date showed them to take only one or two powders a day. The pattern of analgesic consumption differed between men and women. Men took the powders to relieve the symptoms of hangovers, headaches and toothache. Women also took analgesics for the latter two reasons but more usually because they felt 'low'. Almost two-thirds of the women who took analgesic powders did so as soon as they awoke to help them 'get going' in the morning. They also took a powder as a form of tension release after any argument or other emotional upset. All these women were conscious of their dependence on analgesic powders but none had any knowledge of the potential dangers of the habit. The following case histories serve to illustrate the views and practices of some of the women in the community who were addicted to analgesics. Their statements were recorded verbatim from or in relation to the people dependent on their use.

Case 1   I obtained the history of a female, aged 54, from her daughter, aged 32, who was also an analgesic addict. The daughter said 'She has taken Bex every day as long as I can ever remember. If she can't find one she gets awful cranky. She'll walk all around the Reserve to get a Bex. She'll have the whole family walking from house to house to find her one. She takes about a packet [12 powders] a day. After she's had one she calms down.'

Case 2   A female, aged 47, said 'I started after my first baby. Now I just take three a day, sometimes six. I never take a whole packet. I like Vincent's better than Bex. If I wake up in the night I have one, or when I wake up in the morning. If I see them somewhere I always take one.

Case 3   A female, aged 27, said 'I take a packet every day. If I see one, I can't stop myself. I've got to have one. I'm a real drug addict.' When I asked whether she would get out of bed at night to borrow analgesics if she had run out she replied 'No, I'm scared of the dark. I'd send the kids round to friends to get some.' 'And if they didn't have any?' 'They always got 'em.'

Analgesics were purchased as part of the groceries in cafes and stores and rarely in the two pharmacies. The two most common powders contained aspirin, salicylamide and caffeine, and aspirin, phenacetin and caffeine. The former preparation was regarded as having 'more kick' than the latter and did contain slightly more caffeine (168 mg compared to 145 mg). Women, but not men, exhibited brand loyalty and when in need would go to some inconvenience and even to the expense of a taxi ride to obtain their preferred powder, even when the other brand was readily available.

Two doctors who were investigating the effect of analgesic consumption on pregnant women in Sydney, identified a group of mothers who started each morning with an analgesic powder. Like Aboriginal women in Bourke, the majority of these mothers had a parent who was also dependent on the same analgesic powder. The two researchers suggested that it is the caffeine in the analgesic preparation which leads to the habituation (Collins and Turner, 1973). It is also possible that the restlessness experienced as a result of the withdrawal of phenacetin may have contributed to perpetuating the analgesic habit.

The side-effects associated with prolonged analgesic use were apparently few. Two women had a duodenal ulcer, and a further two had iron-deficiency anaemia. I did not arrange radiological studies to detect the type of kidney damage associated with analgesic abuse, but it is possible that prolonged analgesic consumption may have contributed to the high incidence of recurrent urinary tract infections which I discussed in chapter 3.

Psychological distress and analgesic consumption

A correlation was made between those who had taken an analgesic on the day of the survey and who were regular analgesic takers, and those later diagnosed as having psychiatric illness (*see* chapter 5). In both men and women those diagnosed as psychiatric patients consumed significantly more analgesics than the other people surveyed (*see* Table 27). Most of the male users were diagnosed as having personality

Table 27 Psychiatric disorder and regular analgesic consumption by sex

Regular analgesic takers	Numbers of males (a)			Numbers of females (b)		
	Psychiatric disorder	No psychiatric disorder	Total	Psychiatric disorder	No psychiatric disorder	Total
No	17	99	116	5	85	90
Yes	36	4	40	38	36	74
Total	53	103	156	43	121	164

(a) Relationship of sufferers from psychiatric disorder and analgesic takers: χ^3 on 1 d.f. = 71.951, P = <0.001.

(b) Relationship of sufferers from psychiatric disorder and analgesic takers: χ^2 on 1 d.f. = 41.691, P = <0.001.

disorders and took analgesics to help relieve the physical effects of alcohol 'binges'. The most common psychiatric diagnoses in female users were anxiety and depression and analgesics were taken to help alleviate the associated symptoms.

The results of epidemiological studies and sales figures in Australia suggest that the consumption of analgesics has become part of the coping repertoire of large numbers of white Australians. Surveys in the eastern states of Australia have found up to 13% of men and 19% of women are frequent or regular users of analgesics. The authors of one of these surveys estimated that 'about 10% of the population of Queensland and perhaps northern New South Wales were taking aspirin daily'. They also found that the highest ingestion of analgesics occurred in those with the lowest occupational ranking (Gillies and Skyring, 1972).

The role of analgesics

In many ways analgesic powders occupied a similar role in the lives of the women to that of alcohol in the lives of the men. Analgesic powders were an essential ingredient in the pattern of Aboriginal life in this community. They were used as one of the first methods of treatment for all illnesses. Sick infants were often given small doses of the powder on the end of a spoon. Asking for an analgesic powder was a way of communicating physical or psychological distress and giving it was the beginning of solace over that condition.

As with alcohol abuse the logical approach of preventive medicine should be in initiating major pieces of social engineering to relieve the misery, anxiety and unhappiness that underlies much of the 'dis-ease' of the Aboriginal analgesic consumer. These programmes are slow, difficult and the results uncertain.

In the meantime, a sympathetic education programme on the potential ill-effects of these analgesics may help to reduce their consumption.

It was a hopeful sign in Bourke when one smallgoods shop started to sell single powders at two or three cents each. The owner told me that this was due to the demand by Aboriginal customers who stated that if they had a whole packet they would take them, and that they no longer wished to do this as I had told them that too many powders was a cause of kidney trouble.

Chapter 7
Some child rearing practices and their effect on attitudes, behaviour and health

A knowledge of the child rearing patterns of a community or sub-culture is essential in understanding the attitudes and behaviour of people in that community. At the same time it is necessary to remember that there are wide individual variations so that neither the patterns themselves nor a knowledge of the manner in which they operate are necessarily causal to the behaviour of any particular individual. My purpose in this chapter is to make some observations on the effects of child rearing practices on the health, behaviour and attitudes of Aboriginal children and young adults in Bourke.

Infant feeding

Although there was a common sentiment in all age groups that breast feeding was more desirable than bottle feeding, only 71 of the 128 women interviewed had breast fed their last child. The average duration of those who did breast feed was 9.4 months, with a range from one to 36 months. The reasons given for not breast feeding were — no milk (43 women); easier to bottle feed (7 women) and because of medical or nursing advice (7 women). Most mothers seemed to have an 'all or nothing' approach to breast feeding and did not persevere if there was not a quick and ready flow of milk. There was a general lack of understanding of the role of complementary feeding while waiting for the development of an adequate supply of breast milk. This common sentiment was expressed by one mother who said, 'If you haven't got it, you haven't got it'. Another factor which contributed to a preference for bottle feeding was the fear amongst mothers that their children were not getting enough breast milk because they could not tell exactly how much the child had taken. Five mothers mentioned that they had previously had their children weighed after a test feed and this showed that the child was not getting enough milk.

It is probable that the previous nursing practice of making a decision on breast feeding after a single test feeding and weighing, had

Plate 21 The hazards of bottle feeding without facilities for hygienic preparation showing pathogenic organisms from the milk and teat growing on a blood agar plate

contributed to the belief, in some Aboriginal women, that they did not have enough milk. Seven women under the age of 24 had refused to even contemplate breast feeding, even when they had a plentiful supply of breast milk. They stated that they felt 'shamed' to expose their breasts in public when the child needed a feed. Obtaining privacy was a very real difficulty in the overcrowded conditions of most Aboriginal households. Many young mothers tried to continue with either work or their adolescent development almost as if they had not had children. With these women breast feeding was an inconvenience, especially when the responsibility for rearing the child had been turned over to its maternal grandmother. It is also probable that their failure to suckle their infants inhibited the further development of normal caring, maternal behaviour. The older women did not have the same reticence as the younger ones, and breast fed their children quite happily in the midst of any social gathering. For all age groups breast feeding was on demand and the breast was used extensively to comfort a crying child.

The bottle was given partly according to the demands of the child, and partly on whether a filled or partially-filled bottle was readily available. In the early months the bottle was given with the child cradled in the mother's arms. When the child could support the bottle himself, the amount of body contact then depended upon the mood or commitments of the mother, father or older female siblings. Children who were difficult feeders were almost certain candidates for frequent hospitalisation, since their mothers either assumed that they had had enough milk or lost patience in trying to feed them.

Bottle feeding is known to predispose infants to gastroenteritis, and in the twelve months from September 1971 to August 1972, 35% of all hospital admissions of Aboriginal children under the age of 5 years were due to this infection. The bottle shown in Plate 21 together with the organisms cultured from it was a typical example of those commonly used to feed Aboriginal children in this area. Under the conditions of Reserve living, with its lack of refrigeration and cooking facilities, hygienic preparation of an infant bottle was a difficult procedure.

Weaning

Information was obtained from 121 mothers. Fifty-six had introduced solid food by the age of six months, 47 by the age of nine months, and the remaining 18 by the age of twelve months. It was my impression that weaning took place earlier in those children who had been difficult to breast or bottle feed. The foods most commonly used for weaning were 'smashed potatoes and pumpkin'. Proprietary baby foods in tins or jars were regarded by mothers as being good foods for babies. Their use was governed by how much money was available in the household at a given time. Forty-five mothers claimed to have given vitamin supplements to their children, but in practice this was a spasmodic occurrence and when I surveyed their 92 households in 1971, I found only three bottles of vitamin drops.

Toilet training

The parents' approach to toilet training was entirely casual. The majority of small children wore napkins only when they were taken to town or to hospital, and the rest of the time they defaecated at random about the Reserve or in the areas surrounding their houses. A pot was a foreign implement, even in those few households which were predominantly white-orientated. Children were usually dry by the age of two and had control of their bowels between the ages of two and three years. Soiling by children after the age of three years was virtually non-existent, but accidents producing wet pants were quite common. These were regarded as normal and produced no reproof from parents or anxiety in the children. Even when they had attained bowel control, children on the Reserve were encouraged to use the bush, since their mothers felt that this was hygienically safer than to use the poorly maintained toilet facilities which were available.

Childhood behaviour, experiences and attitudes

The three common factors running through nearly all the experiences of Aboriginal children in this community from infancy to adolescence, were those of inconsistency, unpredictability, and a conflict of values with the dominant white society.

The amount of body contact, fondling, smoothing and stimulation received by an infant depended upon the moods and pre-occupations of his parents to a much greater degree than was apparent in working-class white people in the same town. A baby might be cuddled and played with all day by his parents and older brothers and sisters, only to be left crying for several hours on the following day while his mother played bingo.

Pre-school children were usually treated with indulgence, occasionally threatened, but rarely punished. Older children were more subject to the vagaries of their fathers' moods and his state of inebriety. Misdemeanours which were usually ignored were then punished with a degree of violence hardly comprehensible to the child. Since the control of behaviour was nearly always punitive and lacked verbal reasoning, children often failed to develop those internalised controls necessary to cope with the demands of white society.

Because of over-crowding, children were aware of and accepted sex as a natural act long before they reached puberty. It was hardly consistent with their previous experience and understanding when the fathers of about 10% of the girls reacted so punitively to their pubescent sexual explorations that they sought refuge by running away from home.

Materialistic and affective rewards were also unpredictable to the child and depended upon the mood of the father and the availability of money. When he felt expansive, the father would take his sons fishing or hunting and talk to them of old times, and of his prowess as a hunter, boxer or worker. When he was angry, a father expressed his feelings by telling his children to 'Git!'.

Separation   Separation from their families was a common occurrence in the early life history of Aboriginal children in this area. Between the ages of 5 and 14 years 34% of the 320 adult males and females interviewed had experienced the absence of one parent for more than five years. Absence of both parents for the same time period was recorded in 5% of males and 7% of females.

During the period that I was resident in Bourke the main causes of separation were due to the father pursuing itinerant work on grazing, fruit and cotton growing properties, and lesser periods spent in gaol, usually as a result of drunkenness. Ten boys and fifteen girls under school leaving age were also separated from their families by admission to either gaol or reformatories. The most common cause of separation, however, was hospitalisation. A survey of admissions of children under the age of five years to the Bourke District Hospital showed that 72% of children were admitted on at least one occasion in the twelve months under survey (1971–1972). Of these, 16% were admitted on more than four occasions. Some records were available from the Royal Far West Children's Health Scheme and these showed that there were at least 31 children under the age of 13 years (approximately 10% of that

169

age group) who had each spent a mean time of 188 days in Sydney hospitals.

There is well documented psychiatric evidence that such excessive and prolonged separation of children from their parents does interfere with their future capacity to form meaningful relationships with other people (Bowlby, 1951; Maddison and Raphael, 1971). It is also likely that these long hospital sojourns contributed to the feelings of helplessness and passivity so common in Bourke Aborigines.

The most extreme examples of this alienation were seen in young adults who had spent a major part of their childhood in government institutions. I found three men and six women who had spent most of their youth in Child Welfare Institutions after having been declared neglected because their parents were chronic alcoholics. They were still having a reaction to 'being pushed around all their life'. They responded aggressively to any real or imagined personal slight, and could not abide supervision of even the most benign form in the work situation. Their declared ethos in life was to be 'free to do what I like'.

All of them now had fairly good relationships with their parents and held no grudge against them. Only one of the six women seemed to have developed any mothering instinct. The children of the others were repeatedly hospitalised. These six women had borne 17 live children. Five had died before the age of one year, four had already been declared Wards of the State, and one had been adopted out through the Child Welfare Department. Although the birth-rate amongst these women was half that of the Bourke average for Aborigines, the mortality rate of their children was almost five times the average. They all declared in retrospect that they were angry at being separated from their parents, and although none would have heard the adage that a bad parent is better than a good institution, their testimony and life style would add weight to the correctness of this cliche.

Discrimination   No account of child rearing practices in this community would be complete without reference to the over-riding feelings of exclusion and inferiority of Aboriginal adults in relation to their white neighbours. These attitudes are observed by and passed across to Aboriginal children at an early age, and reinforced by direct experience. My wife observed the three year old son of a bank manager tell a four year old Aboriginal girl to go away because she smelt. The white mother was embarrassed by this incident and physically chastised her son, saying that she had taught him never to say such hings. She then turned to the other white people present and added, 'But they do, you know'. It is not surprising that at the beginning of each year white children in pre-school were reluctant to hold hands with Aboriginal children and that at primary school there was almost no mixing between Aboriginal and white children outside the classroom.

It is probable that the discrimination to which an Aboriginal child is subject long before his school years also has an effect in cementing the type of behaviour which is expected of a second-class black person. While working in India, the psychiatrist, Carstairs (1957) described how members of a lower Indian caste introjected both the image of behaviour appropriate to them and the image of behaviour of a higher caste which would be inappropriate to them. Similar observations of the effect of being excluded from the dominant society with its resultant problems of identity and of personal worth have been made in America by another psychiatrist, Brody (1966).

The strongest influence on a child's behaviour was adherence to the norms of the peer group to which he belonged. The fear of being ridiculed or shamed by one's peers led to the proscription of any individual initiative which would result in one Aboriginal child doing better than another. In this way, under-achievement was valued as a method of conformity.

A first year High School girl was discovered to have broken into her classroom after school hours. She had correctly completed a set of sums which had been left on a blackboard for discussion on the following day. Her peer group had so derided her for this deviation towards the white norm, and by implication, a rejection of her peer group norm, that she had broken into the school in order to rub out her 'shame' from the blackboard.

Job expectation of parents and children Most of the mothers and a few of the upwardly mobile fathers wished to see their children stay at school. Two fathers expressed the view that, 'I've been a bum all my life. I was born a "down-and-out" and I'll die a "down-and-out", but my boy's going away to school. If he stays here he'll end up just like me.' This view was probably more prevalent than was admitted to me. All of the first six families who left Bourke for Newcastle as part of a family resettlement programme[1] did so mainly because they felt their

1. The family resettlement programme is an experiment to assist Aboriginal families in areas of low employment to resettle into centres offering better opportunities.

children would have a better chance in life in a large city. Despite this, most fathers did not see why their children should get an education and pointed out defensively, that they themselves had 'done all right' without one.

I twice surveyed all children aged 10 to 14 years about their job expectations. Of the 58 boys, twenty-two wanted to be mechanics, twelve jockeys or boxers, four pilots and one a doctor. Three children said they wanted to make money, three said, quite seriously, that they wanted to be drunks, and thirteen always replied that they did not know.

Girls had even less definite views, with ten aspiring to be nurses, six secretaries and three wanted to work in a factory. Thirty-three of the girls had no particular ambitions and did not know what they might do. That their expectations were rather stereotyped was in keeping with the limited physical horizons of children in Bourke. At the time of this survey, there was no television and even those homes which owned a radio could only obtain good transmission at night.

The expectations of most of the children were quite realistic. This was in keeping with a similar survey in a fairly well integrated Aboriginal community in Queensland where children aspired to higher status jobs than their fathers, but less than 6% conceived of jobs higher than rank 4 on the Congalton scale of occupational status[1] eg. a post office clerk or a storekeeper (Gough *et al.*, 1970). These findings reminded me of the statement by the anthropologist Margaret Mead, 'The fact that a man is born a prince or a nobleman cannot ensure nobility of character and behaviour, but the status of the slave, serf, or commoner is an effective deterrent to the play of ambition and aspiration in most societies' (1965:248).

The conflict of values between the middle-class way of life advocated at primary school and the values of the adults in their lives to whom they had ties of admiration and family affection, were best expressed by a 9 year old boy on the Bourke Reserve who, when asked what he might do when he left school, said, 'I'm going to be the biggest drunk on the Bourke Reserve'. This was understandable in terms of the life-style of his father and uncles. A half-hour later he sought me out and added, 'and if I'm not going to be the biggest drunk on the Bourke

---

1. This is a commonly used scale which divides people into seven social classes on the basis of occupational prestige and income.

172

Reserve I'm going to put my money in the Rural Bank and live up town'. He then turned to his mother and stated, 'And if I live up town I'm not even going to come and visit you in this dump'. At the age of nine he apparently recognised that he had choices. By the time he left school the need to conform with his peer group would be paramount.

Summary

It is difficult to speculate about the effect of child rearing practices on the attitudes and behaviour of Aboriginal people. Nevertheless I think it reasonable to suggest, that the inconsistency and lack of predictability of emotional relationships with parents were partly responsible for the hostile and over-sensitive attitudes exhibited by many Aboriginal people in this community. This was accentuated by early experiences of racial discrimination which contributed to the widespread feeling of a lack of personal worth.

Chapter 8
Housing and health

Housing is no abstract social and political problem, but
an extension of a man's personality. . . . A house is a
concrete symbol of what the person is worth.

Clark, 1965:32-33

Any attempt to improve the total health of Bourke Aborigines must
take into consideration the deleterious effects of their sub-standard
housing conditions.

In June 1971 there were 730 Aboriginal people who occupied 92
dwellings in Bourke, an average of 7.9 people per dwelling. At the same
time there were 4399 whites who occupied 1160 dwellings in the
Bourke Shire, an average of 3.8 people per dwelling (Commonwealth
Bureau of Census and Statistics 1971). Taking into account the fact that
approximately one-half of all Aboriginal dwellings were less than
18.5 square metres in area, it was apparent that Aboriginal people lived
under conditions of gross over-crowding in comparison with the white
population. There were six different types of housing available to
Aborigines in Bourke and these comprised:

Transitional houses

There were eight houses which were built between 1964 and 1965 by
the now defunct N.S.W. Aboriginal Welfare Board. They were the first
houses built for Aboriginal people and so housed some of the first
families to move off the Bourke Reserve. They were small three-
bedroomed dwellings with a narrow front verandah (*see* Plate 22), with
adequate furniture, all had refrigerators and all were sewered.
Protection against flying insects was generally absent. The average
number of people per house was 13.4 or 4.5 persons per bedroom.

Half of the tenants regarded the houses as comfortable, and half as
uncomfortable depending on the number of people sharing the house.
Rent was cheap, averaging $4.15 a week with electricity at $2.13 a
week.

Homes for Aborigines (H.F.A.)

There were nine of these houses which were virtually identical to a normal N.S.W. Housing Commission house. Most houses had rerigerators and adequate furniture. Insect protection was poor but all enants regarded the houses as comfortable or acceptable. The mean number of people to each was 9.1 with 2.8 persons to each bedroom. Rent was subsidised by the N.S.W. Department of Child and Social Welfare and averaged $9.40 a week with an extra $2.40 for electricity.

Housing Commission homes (H.C.)

There were ten normal Housing Commission homes for which Aboriginal people had competed with the white population. Half of hese houses had very scanty furniture but all had refrigerators. Fly-wiring was adequate in half of the houses. The people regarded the houses as comfortable or as acceptable. There were 7.1 people per house or 2.2 people per bedroom. The rent averaged $12.40 a week and the cost of electricity averaged $2.14 a week.

Plate 22   One of the eight 'transitional houses' built in Bourke between 1964 and 1965.

Privately owned or mortgaged

There were twelve houses in this group which were inhabited by the most acculturated Aboriginals in Bourke. Half of these people had never had reserve or mission experience, their parents having been people independent of government or church welfare agencies. All the houses were refrigerated and adequately furnished. Only half of the houses had adequate fly-wiring and all except one family regarded their house as comfortable. There was an average of 7.8 people per dwelling with 3.2 people per bedroom. Payments in rates averaged $3.75 a week, and electricity was $2.00 a week. On the whole these houses were generally noticeable because of their well kept appearance and especially because they were virtually the only Aboriginal homes in Bourke to have a lawn and a garden.

Privately rented houses

There were twenty-one such houses being rented by people for whom not enough H.C. or H.F.A. homes were available. In general, the houses were decrepit. Included in this group of houses were shanty-type accommodation for which the inhabitants paid rent to cover rates on the land they were using. Only half the people living in these privately rented houses had lived on reserves and preferred even the most inferior accommodation to a reserve situation. Two-thirds of these houses had refrigerators and adequate furniture but less than a third had any flying insect protection. A third of the houses were not sewered and five were without electricity. Two-thirds of the tenants regarded these houses as uncomfortable. There was an average of 7.4 people per house and 2.8 people per bedroom. Even though the rent averaged $10.40 a week there was a range of $10.00 to $30.00 per week. Electricity also ranged from $1.00 to $8.00 a week. One house of 83.5 square metres had 28 people living in it. The only cooking facility was a single hot-plate. There was no sewerage, little furniture and no fly-wiring. The house had been condemned by the Shire Health Inspector but this family was obliged to pay $18.00 a week for it. The family paying $30.00 a week rent were regarded as bad risk tenants simply because they were Aborigines. The male head of this family had worked on one property for 18 years and had he come from a non-Aboriginal family would have certainly been regarded as being a desirable tenant.

Plate 23   Better type of housing on the Bourke Reserve.

Plate 24   Cooking facilities on the Bourke Reserve.

The Bourke Reserve

There were thirty-one shanty dwellings on the Bourke Reserve and one on private property on the opposite bank of the river. They were all made of wood, corrugated iron and straightened-out petrol cans. Some were of a single room but the majority exhibited some ingenuity in making them into sturdy structures (Plate 23). Thirteen had a separate place outside in the open air for cooking and eating (Plate 24). There was no sewerage or electricity and only one family had purchased a kerosene refrigerator. Each dwelling had a tap close by but nearly all the taps were surrounded by a pool of mud (Plate 25). All the dwellings had earthen floors and in wet weather the whole Reserve became little than a swamp (Plate 26). There was a communal wash-house and ablutions block with hot water, but only for those who rose earliest in the mornings (Plate 27). Furniture was totally inadequate in ten of the homes and most of it had come from rubbish tips. Beds were in short supply with less than half as many beds as there were people (Plate 28). This was brought home to me while I was treating a thirteen year old boy with an infection of his left leg. When I asked him if it was causing him a great deal of pain, he replied, 'only when my sister kicks it in bed'.

There were 7.4 people in each dwelling or an average of five people per room. The mean size for a dwelling was 13.5 square metres. Despite this, six families claimed to be comfortable, nine regarded their accommodation as acceptable, and sixteen of them as uncomfortable. Nine of the families had lived in a house previously, but only two had lived in houses in Bourke itself and had returned to the Reserve because of difficulties in keeping up with rental payments.

Health and housing—a year in the life of an overcrowded family

An illustration of the effects of close living can be obtained by describing a year in the life of one of the most overcrowded of families as seen from the records that I kept in my capacity as their general practitioner. During the period of November 1971, to the end of October 1972, this family had 47 different people living in the same house for a period of more than one month. The highest number of people living in the three-bedroomed house at any one time was 36. Table 28 illustrates the number of people together with the number of

Plate 25 Drinking water facilities on the Bourke Reserve.

Plate 26 Swamp conditions on Bourke Reserve after rain.

Table 28 The effects of overcrowding: disease in one household with a maximum of 47 people over a twelve-month period

Disease category	Number of people affected	Number of doctor consultation
Respiratory	23	78
Gastrointestinal	27	53
Skin	27	32
Psychiatric (nerves)	13	31
Intestinal parasites	15	24
Other infective disorders	14	17
Ear	6	11
Dental	7	10
Other miscellaneous disorders	5	9
Kidney or urinal tract	3	7
Total	43	272

doctor consultations for each broad disease category. In this household there were 272 separate doctor consultations which is an average of 5.8 doctor consultations per person per year. Most of the disease episodes

180

were of an infective nature spread by the conditions of close living and poor sanitation experienced by this particular family. In addition, other conditions of propinquity and sanitation such as louse infestation of the hair and fungal infections of the skin were endemic in the family.

Having only one toilet to 36 people meant that many of the children were poorly toilet trained and that the indiscriminate defaecation about the yard contributed to the spread of intestinal infections and infestations. This, combined with the inadequate fly screening was an added factor in the spread of disease. Much of the skin disease arose from infected sand-fly and mosquito bites.

Interpersonal problems

All consultations in this family for 'nerves' were precipitated by family arguments. There was little doubt that the overcrowding, the noise and the difficulty in obtaining enough sleep made a large contribution to family disharmony. The dominant person in this family was the grandmother. From her point of view, the worst thing about the overcrowding was the noise. She attributed this to making her so nervy, 'It's not nice.living like this, but I'm not going to let my family live under a tree'. One of her daughters stated 'It's so noisy, you can't get any rest. There's no room for the children to play and arguments flare up over nothing. There is no privacy in this house.' This daughter had refused to breast feed both her children because of a lack of privacy. 'I won't breast feed my children with everybody looking at me.' This undoubtedly contributed to their recurrent gastrointestinal infections.

Another daughter obtained a prestigious job in the town but her punctuality and attendance did not meet with the expectations of her employer leading to friction and unhappiness in her job. This girl was extremely fastidious in her appearance and with 36 people trying to get into the same bathroom, she was not often at the head of the queue. There was a similar difficulty in washing her uniform and having it dried and clean for the next day's work. The reason for her being late was that if her appearance was not acceptable to her, she preferred not to go to work where she would be 'shamed' by being regarded as 'a dirty Aborigine'.

Although the family used in this example had the greatest number of people under the one roof, there were many other families especially on the Bourke Reserve who had a greater density of people to each

Plate 27   Toilet facilities on the Reserve were totally inadequate and constituted a health hazard.

Plate 28 Beds were in short supply.

dwelling unit. This same family was one of the more acculturated and integrated Aboriginal families in the Bourke area. Their general health status was good in comparison with the rest of the Bourke Aboriginal population.

Social health and morale

Perhaps the worst aspect about the quality of housing was that Aboriginal people lived under conditions of social disrespect both from themselves and from the population at large. A man who lives in a corrugated iron humpy thinks of himself as a makeshift person. His feeling that he is 'the lowest of the low' is daily reinforced by his physical surroundings and the knowledge that the kangaroos in the park have better accommodation than he does. When a woman on the Reserve says 'I'm not going to live in this shit all my life' she means that she knows that she lives in a virtual rubbish dump and she identifies in this way. Her living conditions confirm in her the self-derogatory view that has been internalised over the years by her socialisation process and the attitudes of the majority culture.

183

The overcrowding and noise combined with the lack of bed
contributed to poor sleep with resultant irritability and arguments. The
lack of privacy led children to an early knowledge of the facts of life
and contributed to early sexual experimentation with early preg
nancies. Even in those dwellings with electricity there was neither
space nor opportunity for a child to do his homework should he be so
motivated. The noise, the arguments, the flies and mosquitoes, the cold
or the heat, the rain and the mud all encouraged the male members o
the household to escape to the more salubrious atmosphere of the pub

If homelessness is regarded as a physical housing condition in which
the inhabitants cannot lead a normal family life, then the majority o
Aboriginal people in Bourke must be regarded as being homeless.

The provision of housing for Aborigines
History and legal status of Reserve housing

The history of the Bourke Reserve prior to 1946 has been mentioned in
chapter 1. From 1946 to 1969 the Reserve was leased from the Western
Lands Department to the Aboriginal Welfare Board. In 1969 the
Aboriginal Welfare Board was dissolved and its responsibilitie
assumed by the Department of Child Welfare and Social Welfare and
Directorate of Aboriginal Welfare was set up according to the
Aborigines Act of New South Wales 1969. Under this Act, Aborigina
reserves are regarded as public places 'to facilitate the administration o
the law' (Department of Child Welfare and Social Welfare bookle
1969:5). Social drinking and bad language are not allowed in a publi
place. These two misdemeanours are the most common cause fo
Aboriginal people appearing in court in Bourke. Similarly, dwelling
on reserves have no legal status and can be entered without a warrant
The most feverish activity that occurred on the Bourke Reserve prior to
1971 was the building of fences around each shanty under the mistaken
belief that this would turn them into a legal building into which th
police could not enter without a warrant. The powerlessness of peopl
who live in reserve conditions extends to lack of ownership of
dwelling which an individual person has built. If his family should
move out of the dwelling for any reason, even to pursue seasonal work
then according to the Department of Child Welfare and Social Welfare
any other Aboriginal family can move into this dwelling. If there are n
other Aboriginal families using the dwelling, then it has to be pulled

down. Although this policy was not strictly enforced it did serve as another reminder to an Aboriginal that his day-to-day life was subject to controls not applied to white Australians unless they were residents of Her Majesty's prisons or other official institutions such as leprosariums or mental hospitals.

Aboriginal housing

In the eight year period between 1964 and 1971, seventeen houses had been built specifically for Aboriginal people. Eight of these were transitional houses which were meant to be low rental homes from which people would graduate to a Housing Commission house when their standard of living improved. By 1974, none of the people who had originally shifted into these houses had moved to a better style of home. In addition there were another ten families living in Housing Commission homes of the normal kind for which they had competed with white people. Including this latter group, 27 houses had been made available to Aboriginal people in Bourke over an eight year period. During that same eight year period 340 births were registered in the Aboriginal community.

It is obvious from these figures that the provision of public housing was not even keeping up with the normal rate of increase of the population, let alone catching up with the leeway in the need for adequate housing.

Housing Commission

Because the Housing Commission is always chronically short of funds it cannot keep pace with the demand for low rental housing. From its point of view, the multi-problem family (that is, often unemployed, with large numbers of children, chronic sickness and with male members who are frequently drunk) turns out to be unrewarding and problem tenants who are better avoided.

It has been Housing Commission policy to assimilate Aboriginal people into the white community. A circular, signed by the Under Secretary of the Department of Child Welfare and Social Welfare and the Secretary of the Housing Commission of New South Wales, noted the disparity of rent on reserves (ie. reserves with houses) or their equivalents, to rent in a town. Their solution was to increase the rent on reserves so that it approximated to that of houses in the towns. It was presumed that this would encourage Aborigines to move into the white

185

community thus aiding assimilation (Department of Child Welfare and Social Welfare housing policy 9.1.70). There is little doubt that this plan was evolved with the best of intentions. It does however display a lack of understanding of Aboriginal life styles as well as the situation of white prejudice in most rural towns. It reveals a grossly unrealistic view of the Housing Commission's ability to supply the necessary number of houses for this assimilation policy to be feasible. Above all, it is based on a decision made without adequate consultation with Aboriginal people.

In chapter 5, I recorded that 74% of all Aboriginal women with an anxiety and/or depressive state came from houses with two white neighbours. This of course does not imply causality. It only demonstrates a statistical association between having white neighbours and having complaints of psychiatric discomfort. It is possible that many of these women were more anxious as part of their desire for upward social mobility. Nine of the women however were definite in attributing their symptoms to the time of moving from the Reserve to the new Housing Commission homes. Since they lived in a state of virtual siege by their white neighbours who did not want them, and since they became isolated to a degree from their relatives and friends on the Reserve, it was not a great wonder that symptoms of anxiety or depression should manifest themselves at this time. One man took a Housing Commission house between the town detective and the Child Welfare Officer. During this time his ten year old son was sent to a reform school for stealing. The behaviour of the father gradually became more and more apprehensive to the extent that he would not move from his house. When he eventually shifted to an area that he found more secure much of his anxious behaviour disappeared. I could find no evidence that any Aboriginal family had even begun to be assimilated into the white community as a result of their living in a white neighbourhood. Even the most acculturated family who had spent six years in a Housing Commission house and who were assimilationist in their outlook, were still isolated from their neighbours and found that any minor mishaps such as a stone on the roof or a broken window were blamed on their children.

Housing Commission houses have in the past been difficult to acquire because of their short supply. In many cases Aboriginal people had been discouraged by the long wait for a house. Several families believed that they had been on a waiting list for Housing Commission homes for longer than five years. A check revealed that their names had never been on such a list. In some cases this was apparently due to subjective and arbitrary behaviour by white authorities who had taken it upon themselves to decide who was and who was not suitable for a house. There were virtually no completely literate members of the Aboriginal population and so they were forced to rely upon designated white officials to complete their application forms. The economist Frances Lovejoy (1970), had written a step-by-step information sheet for Aborigines who wished to apply for housing. This was given to Bourke Aborigines but it was only of help to those few with a high degree of literacy.

When socially responsible people such as medical practitioners are not alive to the nuances of behaviour resulting from cultural differences it is expecting a lot of Housing Commission and Child Welfare employees to have these sensitivities. The employees of the Housing Commission have to start work at times which are not convenient to housewives. They do however need to be more sensitive in their behaviour than this:

He just walked in at eight o'clock and said that the house wasn't tidy and that I had better get it cleaned up. I would like to see how many white people's houses are clean at eight o'clock in the morning.

The mother who made this statement displayed a deep hurt. She had ten children and was making a great effort to keep her place clean. She was so particular about this that she would specify a suitable time for the doctor to visit a sick child so she could be sure that the house was tidy. These officials were not ogres. In general they were God-fearing, church-going pillars of the community who belonged to at least one service organisation in the town in which they lived. They may have been concerned with helping Aborigines but in general they did not have, nor were they taught to have, that sensitivity which would enable them to get a glimpse of life from the viewpoint of Aborigines. Many inhabitants of Housing Commission houses had a real feeling of being harassed. I have personally been examining a patient in a bedroom of a newly occupied Housing Commission house when an official came in and asked to see a reputed hole in the floor. Although he admitted to never having seen a hole in the floor of an Aboriginal dwelling in that town, local rumour was enough to make him believe that such a thing had happened.

187

It was extremely easy for people without a knowledge of the workings of the Housing Commission, or of their right of tenure, to be harassed and in their confusion to adopt the only solution that they knew and flee from the harassing body. The following letter best expresses the state of mind of a woman in fear of eviction from her house when in fact the Housing Commission would have had to go through many more steps before she could have been legally evicted.

To Doctor Camaien

Sir my husbane & I are in a bit of trouble with the Housing Commissioner as we owe him the amount of $77 dollars as we cant raise the money until my Husbane get payed on Saturday but Mr. — the Housing Commission said he cant wait until then he said if we havent got the money in at the office today he will take us to Court tomorrow and put us out of our house. So my husbane & I was wondering if we could borrow that amount of money of you and he will pay you the money back as we wouldnt like to get put out of our home as we havent got another place to move into we would be very thankful if you could loan us the money. I know its a large sum of money to borrow as we tryed everywhere & couldnt get it any where from Mrs. —

I have no knowledge of what the Housing Commission officer really said to this woman. My aim is to convey what this particular tenant understood of what was happening in this particular situation. All this led to an insecurity of tenure which was expressed by the lack of care taken of the outside environment of most of the houses and the frequent comment: 'Why should I look after the lawn, I might get kicked out tomorrow'.

Rental

The best and cheapest houses were those of the N.S.W. Housing Commission, especially those which were subsidised by the Federal and State Governments. The rents on these, as low as they were, could be exorbitant for an Aboriginal family, especially if they were having difficulty in understanding the budgetary requirements of the dominant Australian society. A family may have managed to pay the weekly or fortnightly rent only to be defeated by the quarterly electricity bill. There was a rental rebate for those unemployed or for those paying more than 20% of their weekly income. The catch in this was that it was determined by the Housing Commission officers and that people had to apply for the rebate. Many Aboriginal people regarded rent as money that was down the drain. It was of course possible to buy Housing Commission houses and also the houses for Aborigines with repayments determined over a 45 year period, but in 1971 there was only one family doing this.

Furniture and facilities

Some people living in Housing Commission houses regarded them as badly designed for Aboriginal people. 'Look at the joint, it's got no verandah and no fireplace, a guy could suffocate in here.'

Although it was theoretically possible to obtain up to $500 in furniture loans from the Department of Child Welfare, in practice these loans were either difficult to get or took many months from the time of application to the time of being granted. Whatever the reason, most families moving into Housing Commission houses had an almost total lack of furniture. The psychological impetus to changing one's life style was often missed because of this. Similarly many women moved into houses for the first time without having any idea of how to use the new facilities. When a family was not sure how to use an electric stove and were frightened of it, they were likely to leave the stove unused and go out into the back yard and cook over an open fire as they had done while on the Bourke Reserve. Occasionally stoves were regarded as electric heaters and left on all day and all night. This practice was not correlated with the subsequent enormous electricity bill. One story that was related with gusto by most white people in Bourke was that of an Aboriginal woman who put an electric heater in the bath to heat her water. Nearly everyone found this a hilarious indication of the low intelligence of Aboriginal people. I came across few whites who stopped to think of what an indictment this story really was of the lack of understanding and helpfulness of the white population.

In the last five years (1972–1976) it has become easier for Aboriginal people to get houses. However, as long as Aboriginal people feel harassed and insecure by living amongst people who do not want them, with gadgets that they do not know how to use, and with a rental that they find difficulty in paying, it is doubtful that the Housing Commission will really be fulfilling anywhere near the housing needs of this minority group. At present, there is even the possibility that Housing Commission policy is unwittingly contributing to mental ill-health and discomfort, particularly of women who are living in houses isolated from their peers. It may be asking a lot of a State Housing

Commission to make allowances for a style of life that 'is not in keeping with the middle-class values of the housing societies' (Jones, 1972:199). However, if the Housing Commission wishes to be more successful than it has been in aiding Aboriginal people, then it needs to inculcate in its employees more of the philosophy of the social worker and less of that of the rent collector.

In this chapter I have shown that most Aborigines in Bourke lived in housing conditions which prevented them from leading a normal family life and they could therefore be regarded as homeless. The deficiency in the number, type, quality and administration of housing contributed to the poor morale of Bourke Aborigines, as well as being a physical, psychological and social health hazard. Any health professional concerned with the promotion of health and not simply with the alleviation of disease episodes needs to exert his or her influence in providing Aboriginal people with help in satisfying their housing needs. One such programme is described in chapter 15. Housing is not a panacea for the ills of Aborigines but it is one of the factors which many Aborigines see as essential to improving their self-esteem.

Chapter 9
The health care services: cultural chasm and chaos

I have already referred to the poor state of health of Bourke Aborigines and related it to the cultural disintegration of their community, their low socio-economic status, some of their child rearing practices, and to the grossly inadequate condition of their dwellings. A further factor in their ill health is their lack of ease with and therefore their reluctance to use the health services that are theoretically available. Medical and nursing services alone will not alleviate the bulk of ill health in a community like that of the Bourke Aborigines, but the absence or poor utilisation of such services will increase the severity and length of many of their disease episodes. In this chapter I examine just how effective and efficient the existing health services were in providing for the health and cultural needs of Bourke Aborigines.

Existing services

In 1971 and 1972 there were 65 health personnel beside myself, resident in the town of Bourke who were concerned to various degrees in the health care of Aborigines. In addition to the doctors, dentists and pharmacists who were in effect autonomous, the other health personnel were responsible to six different organisations (*see* Table 29). There were also ten visiting consultants representing the specialities of general medicine, paediatrics, dermatology, psychiatry, ophthalmology, otorhinolaryngology, orthopaedics and gynaecology. Their visits occurred at two to four monthly intervals and lasted from one to four days. A team of specialists from the Royal Far West Children's Health Scheme also made one visit to Bourke each year.

It is probable that Bourke was better endowed with health services than any other rural town in Australia with a comparable population.

In addition to the services already documented, those Aborigines and whites who lived in rural Bourke could obtain the services of two Bush Nursing Sisters and in one area the Royal Flying Doctor Service.

Table 29 Health personnel resident in Bourke 1971 and 1972

Employing body	Personnel	Main place of work
Autonomous	2 general practitioners 2 dentists 2 pharmacists	2 surgeries 2 surgeries 2 pharmacies
N.S.W. Hospitals Commission (Sydney) and Hospital Board (Bourke)	1 chief executive 1 matron 16 State registered nursing sisters 24 nursing aides 1 radiologist 1 pathology technician 1 physiotherapist	District hospital

N.S.W. Department of Health (Sydney)	1 community health
	    nursing sister
	1 health inspector
		Child Welfare and Social
		    Services office
		    Shire Chambers

University of N.S.W.	1 Aboriginal health aide 1 medical research fellow	Bourke Aboriginal Reserve
Voluntary organisations:		
St John's Ambulance Association of N.S.W. (Sydney)	4 full-time officers	Bourke Ambulance Centre
Royal Far West Children's Health Scheme (Sydney)	1 infant welfare nursing sister	Royal Far West Centre
Sisters of Charity (Calcutta)	5 nuns 1 mothercraft nurse	St Vincent de Paul Centre

The effectiveness of the health service

One method of assessing the effectiveness of a health service is to apply the criteria of 'death, disease, discomfort, disability and dissatisfaction' (Last, 1970).

Death

I have already discussed the high infant mortality rates and pointed out that in almost two-thirds of these infants the nature of their illnesses and the age at which they died, suggested that the seeking of early medical care would have been successful in saving these children (*see* chapter 3). At the same time I found no evidence to suggest that any Aboriginal adults had died from not having sought medical advice.

Disease and discomfort

This too has been discussed in chapters 3 and 5 where I found that over 70% of all Bourke Aborigines had diseases or disorders which could be expected to respond to conventional medical therapy.

Disability

In the three years, 1970, 1971 and 1972, an average of 14.6% of the Aboriginal population was admitted to hospital each year for reasons other than childbirth. Many had multiple admissions so that the overall admission rate per year was 85.3 per 100 of the population. Aboriginal people spent 6613 days per 1000 of population per year in hospital and white people 3040 days per 1000 of population per year.

The most common causes for admission were respiratory disease in adults and children and gastroenteritis in children. The higher incidence of hospitalisation applied particularly to Aboriginal children under the age of 10 years who were responsible for 20.6% of all admissions and 16% of the total bed occupancy of the hospital. Their expected admission rate based on the total population figure was 6.8% per annum.

In the 12 months from September 1971 to August 1972, 72% of all Aboriginal children under the age of 5 years were admitted to hospital compared with 15% of all white children of the same age. The mean number of admissions per head of population in this age group during this period was 2.0 for Aboriginal and 0.22 for whites.

Between 1964 and 1969, 17 Aboriginal children under the age of 8 months were transferred by air on 28 occasions to teaching hospitals in Sydney. Twenty-four of these evacuations were for failure to thrive. During the same period, six white children in the same age group were transferred, only one of whom was suffering from a poor nutritional state. At least 31 children had attended the Royal Far West Children's Health Scheme Hospital at Manly on the coast between 1962 and 1972. Five had orthopaedic disease and they each spent an average of 523 days in hospital. The remaining 26 had ear, eye and gastrointestinal disease. They had 46 admissions and their average total stay was 26 days. Their average age was 6.3 years.

Although nearly all Aboriginal people attended the hospital outpatient department and not the doctors' surgeries for their medical consultations, the average number of attendances per month in 1971 and 1972 was 73. Forty-five per cent of these patients were admitted to hospital.

Dissatisfaction

With the exception of antenatal visits (average number 5.7 per pregnancy) the failure of most Aborigines to utilise the services available at an early stage of illness was due to their expressed dissatisfaction with these services. This also applied to preventive services so that in 1971 and 1972 no Aboriginal child completed a course of prophylactic immunisation with triple antigen except for two families who were immunised as an emergency procedure after contact with a case of whooping-cough. Similarly, few children had received Sabin vaccine until after a case of poliomyelitis had occurred. In the six month period from October 1970 to March 1971 only one Aboriginal mother in the town of Bourke was attending the infant health centre.

There was also a lack of demand for or referral to specialised services with only 21 (1.7%) of all specialist consultations in the period 1970 to 1972 being for Aborigines who had been referred through the usual channels. Aboriginal attendances for physiotherapy in the same period accounted for only 3.9% of the total treatment episodes.

Insurance status

At the time of this survey, 25 Aboriginal families were enrolled in a medical and hospital benefit fund. Of these fourteen were enrolled through a group scheme at their place of employment and eight were known to have let their membership lapse on changing or ceasing to work for that particular employer. A further twenty families were covered by the pensioner medical scheme and one was covered by the Repatriation Department Medical Scheme.

In 1972, 30% of Aborigines had medical and hospital cover of some sort. I obtained a rough estimate of comparable figures for white people in the town from data on 157 consecutive consultations by the white patients of one doctor, of whom 82% had either insurance, pensioner or Repatriation Department cover.

Twenty-nine families were members of the District Ambulance

Service, and fourteen of them had been enrolled through their employers.

It was my strong impression that membership of a medical benefit fund did not influence patient's consulting behaviour and that they still tended to use the outpatient department of the hospital. On the other hand pensioners appeared to go to the doctors' surgeries.

Pharmaceutical services

There were two pharmacies in Bourke. Both shops had fully extended bulldog clips containing unpaid bills for prescriptions dispensed to Aborigines in good faith in the years 1968 to 1970. Both pharmacies believed that about a quarter of all prescribed medicines were never collected. In order to test this impression, both pharmacies agreed to record the date of writing of the prescription, the date of receiving the prescription and the date of collection of the pharmaceutical goods for all prescriptions written by me over selected periods of one week in each of the months of May, June and July, in 1971.[1]

There were 114 prescriptions. All were delivered to the pharmacies within 24 hours of being written. The pharmaceuticals prescribed in 28 (24.6%) prescriptions were not collected within a 48 hour period after the medical consultation. The goods prescribed in twelve were collected on the third day, and thirteen were collected over a period ranging from four to thirteen days after the medical consultation. In only three cases were the goods never collected.

I interviewed all the Aborigines who had not collected their medicines within 48 hours of their medical consultation. The main reason they gave was having to wait until money became available either on pay day or through other sources.

One of the children whose prescription was never collected had a father who had recently become unemployed and who was in the three-week waiting period for Social Service payments. He stated that he had no money available for medicines. One week after the original consultation with that child, I was summoned from a picture theatre to re-examine the child because his mother had discovered maggots in the discharge from his ear and was concerned that they would eat her child's brain. This anecdote is included because it illustrates what can happen to the indigent who cannot or does not get needed medicine,

1. I wish to thank Mr Bill Crothers and Mr John Maroulis for their co-operation in this as well as in many other matters.

195

and also because it illustrates the necessity for repeated consultations when the original plan of action is not implemented.

When the prescription fee was 50 cents, both pharmacies philosophically accepted the bad debts which sometimes resulted in filling prescriptions in the good faith that settlement would be made. When the prescription fee was increased to one dollar in November 1971 they became more concerned since they were now incurring a personal loss due to the lower subsidy they received from the Commonwealth Department of Health. Although most Aborigines would have been entitled to benefits under the subsidised Health Benefits Scheme, only one patient was able to produce an entitlement card in 1972.

Now the prescription fee has risen to two dollars and this, not the doctor's fee, is the major obstacle for most Aborigines who seek medical help.

The law of inverse care

It is apparent that, although there were ample health service theoretically available to the Aboriginal people, they were mainly being used only when an illness reached such a stage of severity that hospitalisation was indicated. In the town of Bourke the 'inverse care law' applied, with those in greatest need getting the least care (Hart, 1971).

The major reasons for the ineffectiveness of health care for this Aboriginal population were, first, the cultural chasm between the providers and the potential consumers of health care, and secondly, the inefficiency of the health delivery services themselves.

The cultural chasm

Accessibility to medical care is one of the prime essentials in the provision of an adequate health care system. This refers not only to geographical but also to cultural proximity. Culture is the way of life of a people and is 'the sum total of the customs, beliefs, attitudes, values goals, laws, traditions and moral codes of the people' (King, 1966).

In New South Wales most of the medical care obtained by Aborigines was given in an honorary capacity. The doctors who acted as 'honoraries' mirrored to some extent the spectrum of their fellow men. The majority worked as efficiently as their training and capabilities allowed, and expected an adequate recompense for their labour. They complained that Aborigines did not join a medical benefit fund or even utilise the subsidised medical system. They maintained that Aboriginal people had no concept of time, were tardy in bringing their children to be seen in the early stages of an illness and were demanding of medical care outside the normal consulting hours.

Aborigines on the other hand, had learnt to live from day to day. It is unrealistic to expect them to insure against tomorrow. Even if most Aboriginal people were entitled to receive the full subsidised medical benefit, not one had ever made permanent use of this system, owing either to ignorance of it or to lack of that degree of education necessary to master its intricacies.

To the Aborigines a doctor is a wealthy man, and they did not see why he should worry about being paid when the obvious primary concern is the sick person in front of him. Aboriginal mothers are no less anxious than white mothers about illness in their children. Since they also had a fear of evil spirits that inhabited the camp at night, it is only natural for them to become more worried about illness at this time and to seek out the doctor.

Well, I get worried in the night, and sometimes I think the baby will die. Sometimes I'm not worried, but my husband is. There's plenty of cars around, then, so I can get a ride up to the doctor's.

In general, Aborigines in this area also had a different view of disease which is almost the opposite to the usual reaction found in whites. Quite severe injury produced little reaction of anxiety from them, but a common cold with a headache is hardly able to be tolerated.

To wake a doctor in the night hardly warrants an apology—'After all, it only took him five minutes to see me'. To explain that there may be several other such five-minute periods throughout the night is not regarded as an acceptable argument and is met with the irrefutable logic of, 'That's O.K., Doc., but it wasn't me who woke you the other times, was it?'

The more anxious members of the Aboriginal community, especially the women, often prefer the anxiety of having a sick child to facing the possible wrath of a doctor who considers he has been unnecessarily disturbed. They give the child an aspirin powder and hope he will get better. If he does not, they then have to face the censure of the doctor for not seeking medical attention earlier.

Similar cultural difficulties apply to their relationships with paramedical personnel—which lead the latter to express various degrees of intolerance. These usually take the form of,

197

> We are sick to death of the D. family. They never come to see the kid. Mother does not care about him. They just dump the child here so they can go out and enjoy themselves. When we want to get the child out of hospital the parents won't come and get him.

Although the quality of inpatient care in the hospital was not influenced by the patient's ethnic origin, the judgmental intolerance of white staff was sometimes expressed by the quality of anger and harshness in their voices.

An Aboriginal mother, Mrs D., did not like to visit her child because,

> He cries so much, I just go and peep at him so he doesn't see me. I don't like putting the children in hospital but if they are sick you've got to.

That she was causing inconvenience and irritation to the staff was also not lost on an Aboriginal mother. If a child died it was always regarded by hospital staff as due to the iniquity of the mother and never to the lack of skill of the medical and nursing staff. The feelings of guilt that all mothers had on these occasions were accentuated by the disapproval of all the white authority figures who became concerned in the matter.

The District Ambulance Service was largely self-supporting and the financial loss incurred in 1971 was mainly attributed to carrying 242 Aborigines, 20 500 km. In a report published by the *Western Herald*, 8 October 1971, the President of the Bourke District Ambulance Service stated:

> I think you should know that of these people [Aborigines] only about five per cent were subscribers [that is, in Bourke and Brewarrina] and only about one per cent of the non-subscribers paid for their transport. So if we work this out at the rate of 30 cents per mile, it means we lost about $3692.

In a materialistic society such as Australia, the basic economic facts were that, consciously or not, individuals or organisations which are even partially self-supporting, will tend to exclude, or at best to begrudge their services to, non-paying customers, especially when they are fully extended in caring for their paying customers.

In the case of pharmaceutical goods it is ironic that should a pharmacist out of altruism or conscience provide medicine without receiving the prescribed fee, he can in theory be prosecuted for it (National Health Act, 1953).

It is apparent that neither the medical and nursing staff nor the Aborigines had much insight into each other's conceptual world. The health personnel under discussion all exhibited that degree of conscientiousness and concern found in most people who deal with the ick. The majority, however, were lacking in that breadth of world view which enables a person to respect, to understand and to empathise with another person from a community with a different way of life. This attitude was illustrated by the frequent complaint that 'The Aborigines aren't grateful for what we do for them'. Aboriginal Australians and white Australians will, one hopes, one day improve their cultural understanding. In the meantime, it should be possible for those who are the products of our tertiary educational institutions to achieve it first.

The mix of health services

A basic essential to the adequate delivery of health care is the continuity of care between the various parts of the health system. Figure 5 shows the lines of communication between those agencies concerned with the health care of Aborigines at a district level.

Liaison between the personnel of these organisations was rudimentary and was mainly concerned with individual illness episodes and not with preventive or promotive health planning. One major cause of this poor communication was that in Bourke itself each of the thirteen people or organisations most concerned with health services were housed in thirteen separate buildings in the town.

An example of the local fragmentation of health services was epitomised by the division of labour and responsibility for the immunisation of children. Triple antigen was the responsibility of local government, but was performed by the staff of the district hospital. Sabin vaccine was distributed at the shire chambers by the health inspector. Measles vaccine was kept by the health inspector and made available to medical practitioners who requested it for administration in their surgeries. B.C.G. immunisation against tuberculosis was the responsibility of the community health nursing sister and german measles immunisation was administered in the schools by a visiting doctor from the regional health department in Bathurst.

Lack of co-ordination between the Sydney based headquarters of some of these organisations, also contributed to the general confusion and duplication of services. One notable example was the arrival in Bourke of two separate and unconnected teams of children's specialists within three days of each other. The team which came last, virtually duplicated the work of the one which had arrived earlier.

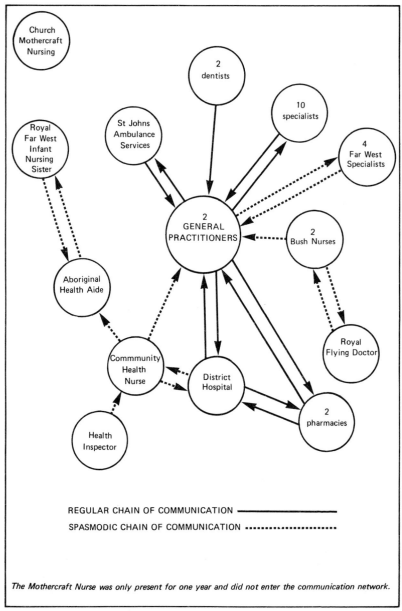

Within the figure:

- Church Mothercraft Nursing
- 2 dentists
- 10 specialists
- St Johns Ambulance Services
- 4 Far West Specialists
- Royal Far West Infant Nursing Sister
- 2 GENERAL PRACTITIONERS
- 2 Bush Nurses
- Aboriginal Health Aide
- Commmunity Health Nurse
- District Hospital
- Royal Flying Doctor
- Health Inspector
- 2 pharmacies

REGULAR CHAIN OF COMMUNICATION ————

SPASMODIC CHAIN OF COMMUNICATION ••••••••••••••••••••

The Mothercraft Nurse was only present for one year and did not enter the communication network.

Figure 5   Communication network of health personnel at district level, Bourke, 1972.

Red tape

Much of the health care of Aboriginal people especially those who lived in outlying areas, was met by nursing sisters who travelled from Bourke. One infant health sister would not immunise any isolated children because she was not insured against mishap by her employing body, and a community health nurse would not administer antibiotics for obviously infected injuries because this was not approved by her central office. Under conditions where no other convenient health care was available, such examples of administrative rigidity diminished not only the real value of these people, but also their value as perceived by their patients.

There was an implicit attitude that health services were run for the benefit of Aborigines but that they were conducted at times and places convenient to the providers of these services. Therefore they were poorly utilised. The hospital outpatient clinic for Aborigines was run at 9.00 am which was the most inconvenient time of the day for a mother with several school children.

To turn up to the outpatients at 9 am means getting all the children ready for school, and then taking a taxi. The taxi fee is $1.40 return to the Reserve. The outpatient's visit cost 50c now. If I say I haven't got it, I don't get charged, but I don't like saying I haven't got it. The lady on the desk looks at me like I'm some sort of nuisance.

In effect the Aboriginal patient was put in the position of having to lose status in return for treatment.

Immunisation clinics took place at monthly intervals and mothers requesting triple antigen for their children on non-clinic days were often told that 'Immunisation clinics are on the first Friday of each month'. Children discharged from the local or Sydney hospitals received no immediate follow-up care unless their mothers sought a medical consultation. It follows naturally from such attitudes, that those children who required frequent hospital admissions were simply regarded as the unfortunate products of incompetent mothers and never as the unfortunate products of an unorganised health system.

The lack of evaluation of services

Any organisation (or person) which lacks a valid method of assessing and auditing whether the work it is doing is leading to an effective end result runs the risk of perpetuating its mistakes. When the situation arose, as in Bourke, that the health personnel were isolated from each other and were receiving varying degrees of support from their organisations which in turn had different philosophies and aims, it was not surprising that personal insecurities should have occurred. Insecurity led in turn to defensiveness and to a cementing of the accustomed modes of delivering health care.

Community and infant health nursing personnel in this shire had a large area to cover. Their commitment to travelling tended to become inflexible and limit their availability and effectiveness in that 'time spent travelling is not time spent working' (McPherson, 1972). The effectiveness of these personnel needs to be assessed in terms other than kilometres travelled and babies weighed.

The lack of epidemiological and sometimes commonsense knowledge of the important health needs of the Aboriginal community, led to each individual health worker formulating his or her own hypotheses on what health services were needed. These opinions often reflected those conditions with which the health worker was familiar from previous experience, but which were not necessarily relevant to this community. In the Bourke Aboriginal community measles was a recurrent cause of severe illness in young children, while tuberculosis was almost non-existent. A lack of awareness of this led to a greater emphasis on preventive treatment against tuberculosis than on prevention of measles. Similarly, public health measures stressed conditions such as hydatid disease (of which there was one known case in the district) to the relative neglect of potentially more essential factors such as immunisation against diphtheria, whooping cough and poliomyelitis and the frightful toilet facilities on the Bourke Reserve.

Felt needs of Aborigines

Perhaps the greatest lack of direction was due to the lack of consultation with Aborigines about their felt needs and their opinions about the sort of health care that they might want and therefore be prepared to help organise. At all levels Aborigines were regarded both directly and by implication as passive objects who were expected to accept the results of any planning decision which was thought would be of benefit to their health status. There was a serious lack of appreciation of consumerism as essential to an effective health service.

Using data from Dr Lickiss and the social scientist, Dr Charles Rowley and reinforced by his own observations, Dr Peter Moodie (1973) has found a similar under-utilisation of health services for relatively similar cultural and financial reasons as described in Bourke.

There are undoubtedly areas in which real health care for Aborigines is as good as that available for whites, but from reports made to me by part-Aborigines from a wide variety of areas of the southern half of Australia, these areas would not seem to be numerous. Even under optimal general practice conditions in Bourke, Aborigines were noted to refrain from seeking preventive care and to be more reticent when attending the doctor, so that an average consultation took only two-fifths of the time taken for a white patient (Coolican, 1973).

In summary then, the high rates of infant mortality, general illness and hospitalisation in Aborigines were evidence of the lack of effectiveness of both preventive, early diagnostic and treatment services. This was even more obvious when compared with the data available on white people in the same area. Despite the large number of people and organisations involved with the health of Aborigines, cultural and material obstacles prevented their effective utilisation. The fact that health services were unorganised, unco-ordinated and leaderless also contributed to the inadequate coverage of the health needs of the Aboriginal population.

The question for health planners is how to overcome these obstacles so that existing knowledge and existing services can be brought to bear on this and similar semi-urbanised rural Aboriginal communities. The health professions are very short of objectively verified success stories in their attempts to reduce the ill health and discomfort so prevalent amongst Aborigines. Experiments in health care delivery as applicable to such specific circumstances are needed in order to find solutions to these problems.

Chapter 10
Changing the patterns of health care delivery

I have shown that a major cause of the severity of disease episodes in Bourke Aborigines was the relative inaccessibility of the existing health services. This was the result of the personal and social distance between the providers and the potential consumers of health care and was compounded by the lack of economic power of the Aboriginal patient. A further circumstance which interfered with the adequate delivery of health care was the absence of direction, cohesion and leadership among the various health professionals concerned with providing health services. Any attempt by me to use medicine as a spearhead for further social change was dependent on my ability to narrow the cultural gap in the doctor-individual patient relationship. Similarly the adherence of Bourke Aborigines to the results of my medical intervention depended to a large extent on my ability to leave behind me a health care system committed to providing more rationalised services that were more in tune with the cultural, geographical and economic needs of the Aboriginal community.

Individual services

Time and place

Two of the reasons why Aborigines made poor use of the medical services were that these were generally available at times which were inconvenient to them and at places not readily available to people without transport. I corrected this by running clinics at times and at places regarded by a majority of Aborigines as suitable. This entailed working in the wash-house on the Bourke Reserve which, because of its broken doors, leaking taps, frequently blocked drains and resultant wet floor, lacked either the adequate privacy or hygiene necessary for more intimate consultations and medical procedures. It was however a place of familiarity and therefore security for Aboriginal people and as the clinic became firmly established various of its physical defects were spontaneously improved by some of the users.

I also used my car as a consulting room for people who stopped me in the street and if necessary provided them with essential drugs from a supply I kept in the car boot. In addition I paid a daily visit to the bingo game where many Aborigines passed the afternoon and where people who would not attend the hospital or my clinic could conveniently seek advice.

Economic availability

A lack of money caused Aborigines to delay seeking medical consultation in two ways. In the first place they had to rely on the charity of the doctor and many were disinclined to ask for this outside of the honorary hour allocated at the hospital each morning. In most cases it precluded attending a doctor's surgery. Secondly and perhaps of greater concern at times, was the lack of the taxi fare to the hospital. However, the credit system was such that these two reasons should not have been of major importance. Even so, I was concerned with breaking as many of the barriers to seeking early medical advice as were possible. Because I was funded by a research grant from the New South Wales Institute of Psychiatry I was able to provide all services without recompense. After I had been in Bourke for about a year I did send accounts to Aborigines who belonged to a medical benefit fund, partly for my own benefit, partly out of a desire to educate people in the use of such funds and partly because those in a fund obtained an obviously increased self regard through (what they saw as) returning a previous favour.

Cultural accessibility of services

Although the geographic and economic factors described contributed to the inefficient use of those health services which were in theory available, by far the most important obstacle was the lack of reciprocal understanding between the white providers of health care and these particular dark consumers. This was a similar situation to the one between the housing authorities and the Aboriginal residents.

My first step was to personalise the individual doctor-patient relationship by offering Aborigines the choice of one doctor instead of the pot luck of whomsoever had been rostered as honorary hospital outpatient doctor for the week. My second step was to try to humanise the consultation process by providing adequate time for the patient to form some relationship with me. Even when the number of patients made this impossible I still tried to avoid practising 'conveyor belt' medicine.

Many mothers were depressed about the repeated hospitalisations of their children and felt guilty over their inability to prevent these sickness episodes. This guilt was accentuated, probably inadvertently, by most of the white doctors, nurses and welfare workers whose judgemental approach was another burden an Aboriginal mother had to bear at a time of crisis for one of her children. It was important that I, at least, broke this non-empathic cycle because apart from humanitarian considerations the fear of being 'roust upon'[1] was the single most powerful reason for a mother to postpone taking a sick child to the doctor.

Aboriginal people in Bourke had learnt to be wary of white people from whom most had suffered discrimination, apathy and lack of respect all of their lives. This even applied to the few whites whom they apparently trusted. Any unavoidable or inconsistent action was likely to be pounced upon to prove that such a white was no different from any of his race. They were particularly sensitive to any suggestion that the medical care they received was in any way inferior to that given to white people. One classic example was of two mothers who threw away two bottles of Abbocillin[2] I had given them for their children because they thought it was an inferior penicillin made especially for Aborigines.

To maintain credibility I went to great lengths to make my actions both consistent and congruous to my Aboriginal patients and their relatives. This sometimes led to conflict with the medical norms under which I was accustomed to function. One such example occurred when an Aboriginal mother asked me to take over the care of her hospitalised child from another doctor who was particularly sensitive about breaches of medical etiquette. The mother regarded it as an obvious lack of concern when I tried to explain how the workings of medical ethics constrained me from directly following her wishes. This situation is difficult enough when both patient and doctor are middle class white Australians. Instructing a diffident Aboriginal mother to make the request to the other doctor was at that time asking her to

1. Vernacular for upbraid.
2. An oral penicillin mixture manufactured by the pharmaceutical firm of Abbotts Pty. Ltd.

perform an act of exceptional gallantry. In the end she and her very large family were only convinced of my sincerity when I had intervened on their behalf.

Being concerned about sick Aborigines, especially children, was not enough in itself. The concern had to be transmitted to Aborigines so they could see that I was providing the best service of which I was capable, and at the same standard as I treated white children. There was something of the self-fulfilling prophecy in this expression of concern in that it indicated an acceptance of an Aboriginal as the equal of a white. If he was equal he was entitled and expected to demand medical care whenever he needed it.

It was my aim to encourage this demand both as a means of treating disease in its earliest stages and also as a means of ensuring that medical consumer demand became an accepted form of patient behaviour which would persist after I had departed.

Punctuality

Another aspect of consistency and credibility which I felt was important was to be punctual. Punctuality was one example of the double standard used by whites to judge Aborigines as unreliable. Aborigines were expected to be punctual but not doctors or nurses. I made a strict principle of it as a means of proving my reliability. If I had arranged to make a house call at 2.00 pm, I made it at 2.00 pm. At first my chances of finding anyone at home were small but I would always leave some indication that I had been. After the third or fourth time of always keeping my side of an appointment the Aboriginal people began to regard my word as meaningful and it became exceptional for most of them not to be equally punctual.

Aboriginal women also complained about the lack of consideration shown to them by white authority figures who visited their houses at inconvenient times (often in the early morning school rush) and who, finding the house less than spotless, criticised their housekeeping abilities (see chapter 8). In my first year in Bourke I never entered an Aboriginal home, even when asked to make a house call to a sick member of the family, without asking when I should come. Most Aboriginal women, like many white women, did not like being caught unawares with an untidy house. Such courtesies will seem commonplace to those with any degree of empathy who may feel that I am labouring the obvious. The point is that receiving this basic respect from a white was a rare experience for Aboriginal women and was part of the sum total of factors which went into shaping a mutually beneficial doctor-patient relationship.

Health education

Bourke Aborigines were most receptive to health education just after they had recovered from an illness. The doctor who was given credit for the cure was most likely to be heeded at this time. In the same way, providing effective primary care resulted in confidence not only in the doctor's diagnostic skills, but in his general health knowledge. I tried to capitalise on these circumstances by incorporating an element of preventive and educative experience into as many consultations as proved possible. I was careful to avoid any suggestion that an individual mother's health or child rearing practices were dirty or that ill health in a child was due to neglect by the mother. By removing the fear of blame I was better able to establish dialogue with Aboriginal people which in turn allowed me to work from what was real to Aborigines at that moment to something new. In this way I was able to bring about some modification of existing medical beliefs and behaviour.

For example, anaemia and worms were already common concepts before I arrived in Bourke. This was due to a study conducted by a former doctor in Bourke which had a large educational component since he asked the Aboriginal mothers to assess if they or their children were infested with worms (Coolican, 1973). Some of the parents of Aboriginal children who were discovered to have parasitic infestations of the bowel were shown the 'worms' under a microscope. This helped enlarge their understanding of the effects of these parasites. In particular the rapidly moving *Giardia lamblia* captured their imagination and they called them 'motor boats'. The reality of having several hundred thousand of these inside the gut of many of their children led to these parents initiating a discussion at an A.A.A. meeting about measures which could be undertaken to rid the area of this intestinal parasite. This eventually resulted in action from the shire health surveyor in trying to reduce the moist soil hazard on the Reserve. Of comparable importance was the increased awareness by Aboriginal mothers of their children's stools, and their increased request for investigation and treatment of probable *Giardia lamblia* infestation. This at least gave the gut of these children some weeks' respite from a heavy load of protozoal parasites.

Running ears were a common ailment in Aboriginal children. Every time I treated a child with such an ear I gently stressed that I regarded an earache as important enough to treat at any hour of the day or night since early treatment would probably prevent a perforation of the eardrum. After 18 months in Bourke I did see a child at 3 am with an unperforated acute middle ear infection and my enthusiastic response was enough to reinforce the idea that I really did want to practise what I preached. This medical intervention did not prevent middle ear disease but it did have an appreciable effect on reducing the seriousness and chronicity of ear disease in Bourke Aboriginal children.

It would be false to claim that I made enormous steps in the field of health education. However, perceptible change occurred in the response of many Aborigines to recognising or querying possible illness and then seeking early medical advice about it. Aboriginal people frequently initiated discussion with me about the illnesses which caused them most worry. These were sick children, diarrhoea, earache and running ears, immunisation and diabetes. They also tested out vague ideas that they had heard to see if I was in agreement with them. One particular example was a family consultation, which turned into a spirited debate about the pros and cons of oranges. The husband maintained that oranges were necessary to keep his children well while the wife was even more certain that oranges were a potent cause of diarrhoea. We purchased some oranges from a nearby orchard and conducted a 'clinical trial' which alleviated the wife's fears. She was later heard to tell other women that 'an orange a day keeps the doctor away'.

When I first began to treat Bourke Aborigines they expected to receive a medicine, especially an antibiotic, for each episode of illness. I was reluctant to prescribe these drugs when I thought they were not medically indicated and this led to some Aborigines bypassing me in favour of a more compliant doctor. On the other hand, their lack of confidence in the contraceptive pill was as strong as their faith in penicillin. After my competence as a doctor was accepted by Aborigines I was able to use the educational opportunities of the medical consultation to slowly change these attitudes and practices. I was even able to influence Aboriginal women to decrease their consumption of analgesic powders (*see* chapter 6).

Co-ordinating health services

I saw my role as providing the time, the concern, the status and the medical authority to attempt to make the health care services more effective in fulfilling the health needs of Bourke Aborigines.

The various health services to Aborigines in Bourke were like a series of small planes all flying without the aid of good maps. The health workers lacked both diagnostic skills and directional aids. I attempted to remedy each defect through information and discussion about my medical findings. Their increased awareness of the real health needs of Aborigines was the impetus for some health professionals to change the method and direction of some of their services. The Matron and Chief Executive Officer of the Bourke District Hospital liaised with Aboriginal field officers to organise immunisation services at the A.A.A. community centre. The Community Health Nursing Sister, a Royal Far West Infant Health Sister, an Aboriginal health aide and the Aboriginal field officer co-operated in immunising all susceptible children against measles many months before measles vaccine became routinely available through the N.S.W Department of Health. The Royal Far West Infant Health Sister, Sr Loreen Boyd, was motivated to start a clinic in the wash-house of the Bourke Aboriginal Reserve and this increased the number of Aboriginal infants seen by her organisation in Bourke from one to over 100 per month. The Matron and the Chief Executive Officer of the District Hospital persuaded the hospital board to create the position of community sister to extend the role of the hospital outside its four walls. The first appointee Sr Marge Payton showed an inherent understanding and respect of the culture of Bourke Aborigines which made her work an outstanding success. The Chief Executive Officer of the District Hospital Mr John Bissett, and I, devised a plan for rationalising all the health services at the local level through adapting the hospital to a community health centre. We wrote an article crystallising our new ideas which Mr Bissett submitted to the newly formed New South Wales Health Commission which promised support for our proposals (Kamien and Bissett, 1974).

Having initiated change, my role became one of supporting the people who had made the changes. This meant feeding back information on improvements in health such as a decrease in hospitalisation periods which had resulted from their innovations. I also provided a measure of indirect feedback by passing on this information to the executive officers of their employing organisations. I was careful to express an understanding commiseration with them when some central administrative body had rejected their proposed changes and I tried to bolster their resolve to fight their battle another day.

The other form of support I provided was purely medical but it made the life of nursing sisters much easier. For instance I would attend the latter part of the clinic run by the Infant Health Sister and see any children she felt needed my attention or whose parents wished to see me. There was thus no problem in finding a doctor or in admitting those who required it to hospital. I also supplied and gave community and infant nursing sisters the sanction to provide medicines to those consulting them. This loosened the administrative restrictions which limited their potential effectiveness.

Integration and continuity

The unco-ordinated intervention by the various health agencies had two results. In the first place the usual medical channels were by-passed by a type of well-meaning but unnecessary service in which children were repeatedly taken to Sydney for treatment which was available in Bourke. On their return to Bourke these children often lacked continuity of treatment and follow-up for their particular illness and in some cases this was responsible for the failure of operations such as reconstruction of the ear-drum, which had been performed (*see* chapter 3).

I have always believed in the concept of a patient having a general practitioner who would take an overall view of his patient's needs. In Bourke I was the general practitioner to most of the Aborigines and regarded it as my responsibility to regulate the activities of other doctors and nurses attending them. This enabled my patients to enter the broader health care system when they needed to, or not to enter it when they did not need to. In the former case I was in a position to discover patients who needed referral to specialists with the result that the proportion of the total consultations made by Aborigines to specialists visiting Bourke increased from 1.7 % in 1970–1971 to 19.8 % in 1972. I also provided the necessary information to such organisations

211

as the Royal Far West Children's Health Scheme to allow the redeploying of their visiting specialist health teams to areas of need This reduced the confusion resulting from the duplication of specialist services in Bourke. A further co-ordination of services was obtained through bringing some members of the Aboriginal community into meaningful contact with the senior staff of the District Hospital.

The most effective catalyst in co-ordinating some of the health services was Mrs Gladys Currie, a 42 year old Aboriginal woman who worked as a part-time health aide. Although she lacked any medical training and was not literate, her innate intelligence was such that she provided valuable help to her own people and to other white health workers in Bourke. She was able to detect illness and insist that the sick seek attention at any hour. She performed minor first aid procedures, helped organise immunisation clinics and ensured that forgetful patients were reminded to keep their appointments with visiting specialists. Perhaps even more useful was the central position she occupied amongst those who delivered health care. In theory she was responsible to me and was paid out of funds made available to the Human Ecology of the Arid Zone Project through the Department of Aboriginal Affairs. In practice she worked with the community health sister and the infant health sister. She was a common denominator in integrating many of our efforts.

The doctor and the delivery of health care

The realities of the present day health care of Aborigines have been accurately summed up by a general practitioner who provided medical care to Aborigines in the far west of New South Wales for 22 years.

The medical care of the rural Aborigines has, in New South Wales, ever been the private charity of the general practitioner. Their state of health reflects the interest of the doctor and those who work with him in hospitals, towns and villages, have in the care of the poorest of the poor. An interested doctor has good results, a disinterested one a high mortality. (Coolican, 1974:127)

Dr Coolican would doubtless agree that an interested doctor is not enough. In order to make any immediate effective impact on the health of Aborigines they need more than the services of a busy, usually overworked, general practitioner. They require a doctor concerned with preventive and promotive medicine who is attuned to their cultural attitudes and accepting of their resultant behaviour, and who

212

is flexible enough to provide a service that will fit these cultural patterns and will meet the felt health needs of an Aboriginal community. If, for example, a large proportion of Aboriginal men find the pub a place of comfort, and they choose it as the place in which to have a consultation, the doctor can accept this or else he can tell them to come to his surgery on the following day. In the former case he will form contact with them from which he can extend his role. In the latter circumstance he will be seen to be rejecting potential patients whom he knows (and they know that he knows) will not go to the surgery.

In Bourke, Aborigines needed to have available to them a doctor with whom they could have a comfortable, trusting and ongoing relationship. They needed a doctor who was available and who did not belittle them in return for the charity of his treatment. This need has been expressed by other Aboriginal communities and has resulted in the development of Aboriginal medical services in places that have abundant medical resources such as Sydney, Brisbane and Perth. The need for special medical services for Aborigines has been argued by Gordon Briscoe, one of the initiators of the Sydney Aboriginal Medical Service.

> To impose one sort of health programme on an area that works in another is futile. Equally futile is the provision of a health service which fails to meet the day to day needs of the consumer and which fails to be modified to the demands of the consumer in this case the Aboriginal community in Redfern. (Briscoe, 1974:170)

One expected result of the rising political awareness of Aborigines will be for them to demand better quality and greater quantity of medical care. They are unlikely to accept anything less than what is available to white people.

Is a doctor in an Aboriginal community a 'technological misfit'?

The authors of a recent paper describing a hospital-based experiment in health care among 2000 Navajos in Northern Arizona have shown that the type of medical technology that one doctor can apply to one patient at a time, had little effect on the overall incidence of disease in the population (McDermott et al., 1972).

The theme of the Navajo experiment has been taken up by Dr P. M. Moodie, who stated that,

... the likelihood of improvement in Aboriginal health, over a period of, say, five years, by a great expansion of highly skilled and motivated personnel and the best of 'bricks and mortar' facilities for medical technology is small. (Moodie, 1973:270)

There is little doubt that where the real health problems of a community are those of preventive medicine, then the doctor to whom patients are brought for the application of a technological set of procedures is a 'misfit', in relation to the real health needs of Aborigines. If there is any doubt about this it is quickly dispelled by reading the descriptions of health services to Aborigines in the Northern Territory (Hamilton, 1974; Tatz, 1974). Moodie (1974) has classified disease conditions into three groups according to whether they are resistant, partially resistant or amenable to control by medical technology. In the former group are respiratory and gastro-intestinal infections, accidents, malnutrition and behaviour disorders, each of which is a major cause of severe illness and, excluding the last cause, mortality in Aboriginal children. It is true that medical technology cannot prevent these diseases. It is equally true that if the technology is applied early enough in any of the above diseases then the mortality rates drop and the severity and duration of the illnesses are diminished. It is this ability to effectively treat or relieve the ill in the here and now that gives the doctor his status and his relative power in nearly all societies. It also gives him his position of influence for preventive and other forms of developmental medicine. McDermott *et al.* (1972) applied an essentially hospital-based service to the problems of the Navajo Indians. The hospital was staffed by recently graduated and disease-oriented resident physicians (Adair and Deuschle, 1970). This service was found to be wanting. It is I believe a mistake to quote his conclusions out of their total context in order to imply that a doctor has but a minor part to play in the delivery of health care to Aborigines.

Alternative methods of delivery of health care to Aborigines

The alternative methods of delivering and improving health care to Aboriginal communities in most areas of Australia are through registered nurses, community health nursing sisters, health centres, health educators and subsidising private practitioners for treating Aborigines.

Registered nurses and community health nurses

At present registered nurses and community health sisters provide much of the care available to Aboriginal people in rural Australia. They are responsible to their employing organisations which are usually geographically and culturally remote, and without the support of a local participating doctor, their task is almost impossible and without an associated doctor's diagnostic guidance may on occasions lack relevance to the real health problems of the community among whom they work. Although the present shortage of medical manpower allows for no other logistic possibility, it is incongruous and unfair to ask those with the least and often the most rigid medical training to cope unaided with the illnesses of those who have the worst health status in Australia.

The role of the community nurse has been sensitively defined by Nancy Frith at 'Coasttown'. Despite having the guidance and the ready availability of at least two university-based doctors in Sydney, she agrees that her role would have been more satisfying and the services to her clients more efficient had she had the ready support of a resident doctor who was committed to both treating Aborigines and to forming a team with her (Frith *et al.*, 1974; Frith, 1975, pers. comm.). Similar sentiments were expressed to Professor John Cawte by many settlement nurses during his survey of eight Pitjantjatjara communities in Central Australia (Cawte, 1973).

In Bourke, Aborigines were used to the conventional Western medical system of attending a doctor for their health needs. They did not prove amenable to accepting nursing care for their illness episodes unless it was tied to a readily accessible and obviously co-operating doctor. Community health nurses were also officially responsible for the promotion of good health practices. Health education was a slow process even when applied with the greatest skill. Without being tied to a component of treatment it did not seem that members of the Bourke Aboriginal community were much influenced by such an approach.

Fee for service

In the year 1974 the New South Wales Government introduced a fee to private general practitioners for each service they rendered to an Aborigine. A year later this became part of the Medibank scheme. In Bourke this has made health care more accessible since Aborigines now

215

consult the doctor of their choice in his surgery. This is a necessary interim measure and is an improvement over taking 'pot luck' at 9 am in the hospital. The fee for service makes the doctors happier, but it does not make much of an impact on the real health needs of Aborigines. Most country general practitioners are fully extended by the white demands for medical attention. Even those who are sympathetic to Aborigines and who wish to help them often find that their services are dominated by the more verbal white Australians. Enlarging their case load simply means that they can give less time to each illness episode in a patient and that their care remains oriented towards illness and not to prevention. An assessment of a similar scheme, the New York Medicaid Program, commented on the lack of professional commitment to a subsidised health service:

Enrolling the poor and paying for their care is one thing, improving either the quality or the availability and accessibility of care is another. (Roghmann *et al.,* 1971:1056)

The doctor as co-ordinator

It is not my intention to exalt the role of the social medical practitioner by setting him up in an elitist position *vis-à-vis* other health professionals who work in the field of Aboriginal health. Many of these latter have training and personal qualities often lacking in doctors. At the same time I have no intention of taking the fashionable but unevaluated position of assuming that since Australian doctors lack the necessary training to deal with the health of under-developed people they should be replaced by community health nurses, health aides and social workers. In theory all those concerned with health care should supplement and complement each other in such a way that each can make the maximum contribution according to their skills. This viewpoint is hardly original and has been advocated by several doctors amongst whom are the N.S.W. Director of Child and Maternal Health (Douglas, 1973) and a regional medical officer in north-west Australia (Spargo, 1975).

In practice this co-ordination of health services and their various employees is lacking because of the absence of clear aims arising from a lack of local leadership. It would require a remarkable non-medical health worker to provide the focus around which the other health personnel in a town would organise.

My view of the importance of a doctor oriented towards the practice of social medicine is purely pragmatic. In areas such as Bourke with an Aboriginal population of over 500 people, the doctor is the only person in the health team who is, by Hippocratic Oath, responsible for the medical care of an individual patient, who can diagnose the health situation of individuals and communities, provide immediate comprehensive health care, and who has the legal authority to prescribe for it, as well as the status to influence the acceptance of his prescription.

The competent practitioner of social medicine is a resource person who reinforces the competence of the other health professionals. He (or she) provides some of the data and the leadership to help them identify their role, clarify their tasks, evaluate their effectiveness (as they evaluate his) and if necessary helps them formulate alternative strategies of action. The role of such a doctor is to provide non-authoritarian assistance to his fellow health workers so that all can reach a consensus of who does what, when and to whom. This should enhance both the quality and the continuity of health care to an Aboriginal community.

This type of medical intervention was fairly successful in Bourke despite my lacking a mandate to attempt it from most of the central administrations of the various Bourke health workers. When the N.S.W. Health Commission rationalises and decentralises its health services, and the role of the community practitioner of social medicine is legitimised, co-ordination of the health services at a local level should hopefully be even more successful.

Concluding remarks

People should have access to care where and when they need it. The distribution of health services and resources should be consistent with those modern concepts of equity that hold all people equally entitled to such comprehensive health care as they may need. (New South Wales Department of Health, 1972:4)

In this section I have argued that if the medical profession and the health departments wish to apply the recommendations of their advisers to the improvement of the health of Aboriginal people, they have to provide for culturally attuned health personnel who have available to them the skill, the knowledge, the direction and the leadership relevant to their stated goals. It has been my experience that the only person who can make an immediate contribution to fulfilling all these requirements is an interested doctor who can apply the principles of medical sociology and psychology to both Aboriginal patients and to white health professionals who work with them.

This doctor has three short term objectives. The first is to improve the health of Aborigines in his area by providing them with accessible and continuous preventive and curative medical care. The second objective is to co-ordinate the various health personnel and the organisations to which they belong into a co-operative whole so that their services are relevant and empathic to the needs of their Aboriginal patients. The third objective is to assist Aborigines to change their reticent behaviour in asking for medical help to becoming active and demanding consumers of health care so that they can develop the initiative to enter into, find their way about and make full use of the health services available in their town or suburb.

When these three objectives have been attained the work of this doctor is done. To a degree these aims have been fulfilled in Bourke in that the health status of the Aborigines, although still far from good, has improved; the responsibility for co-ordinating and delivering health services to Aborigines has been accepted by the executive staff of the Bourke District Hospital who are in meaningful contact with the elected Aboriginal leaders and the two Aboriginal health aides; and the Aborigines are taking an active interest in their health problems and are coming for medical and nursing attention at an earlier stage of an illness episode than was formerly the case.

Medical services alone will not permanently influence the health status of Aborigines in the absence of adequate nutrition, housing, sanitation and the other factors which contribute to host resistance such as the relative equality of opportunity, power and citizenship open to most white Australians. At the same time one of the preconditions necessary for change to occur is an immediate improvement in their poor health status which contributes to their low morale. By providing and organising effective health care in an atmosphere which enhances the dignity of the recipient, the doctor to an Aboriginal community is supplying a key to one of the doors that Aborigines need help to open if they are to achieve their aspirations to a better quality of life.

Chapter 11
Family planning

The aim (of family planning) should be a personal service suited to the needs of the individual, and available to all who want to avoid pregnancy. At this time, there is no better example of preventive medicine.

Russell, 1972:310

In chapter 1, I reported that the birth rate for Aborigines in the Bourke Shire between 1964 and 1971 was 61 per 1000 and for the town of Bourke itself it was 71 per 1000. These are amongst the highest birth rates ever recorded in the world. These early, closely spaced and often unwanted pregnancies were a perpetuating factor in the despondency and chronic weariness of many Aboriginal women. Any programme of social medicine aimed at helping Bourke Aboriginal women to improve their health, and the health of their children, would be incomplete without providing them with ready access to family planning. In order to give help that was adequate, it was necessary to have an understanding of the attitudes and beliefs of the Aborigines in Bourke to family planning practices.

Attitudes to family planning

In September 1970, I administered the following semi-structured interview to 34 fertile women who had at least one child and whom I saw in the course of a general medical practice consultation. These 34 women represented a 25% sample of Bourke Aboriginal women aged between 15 and 44 years.

Contraceptive attitude questionnaire

1. Do you know that white women have ways of not having babies?
2. Which of these methods do you know?
3. How did you find out?
4. If you wanted to stop having babies either for ever or just for a while, which method would you use?
5. Why would you use that method?
6. Have you ever used anything to stop having babies?

219

Plate 29 Aboriginal women in Bourke used to have one of the highest birth rates in the world.

7. What does your husband think about planning the number of babies that you are to have?
8. Do you know any of the 'old ways' of not having a baby?
9. Are there any people here who know how to get rid of a baby once it has started?
10. Do you know of any ways to get rid of a baby once it has started?
11. What do you think of getting rid of a baby once it has started?
12. How many times do you need to have intercourse to make a child?
13. How does a child result?
14. What do you think is the best number of children to have in a family?
15. What do you think is the best space of time to have between children?
16. When is the best time to consult a doctor after you get pregnant?
17. Have you heard of anything happening to women who are on (a) the Pill; (b) the loop or the ring; (c) who have had an operation?

Of the 34 women interviewed only one claimed that she had never heard about contraception. Thirty-two women had heard about the Pill, 23 about tubal ligation, and 12 about intrauterine devices. Although 30 of the women interviewed were of the Catholic faith, only two had a vague knowledge about the 'safe period'. All the women denied any knowledge of coitus interruptus. This finding is in conflict with the findings of the anthropologist Calley, who reported that coitus interruptus was the only form of birth control in Aboriginal people in the northern part of New South Wales (Calley, 1956). None of the interviewees claimed any knowledge about the Dutch cap, or the condom and the total lack of use of both these methods and the diaphragm was substantiated by both the pharmacies in the town.

After living three years in this community, I became aware of two other methods of contraception. One was abstinence engineered by the woman, who encouraged her husband to become paralytically drunk each evening. The other involved both partners, with the husband informing the wife just before ejaculation, when she would tense her pelvic floor muscles in the belief that this would prevent the entry of spermatozoa.

At the time of this survey only one of the 34 women questioned was currently taking the Pill and three other women had previously taken it.

Most of the available knowledge had come from relatives and friends and this accounted for the high level of misinformation about the side-effects of different contraceptive methods. Only three women had gained their knowledge from magazines, another three from doctors and one from a nursing sister in a hospital. Anecdotal beliefs about the Pill and the intrauterine device (I.U.D.) were common. Seven women believed that the Pill caused thrombosis of the legs, three that it caused cancer, five that it caused deformities in babies and five that 'it made you ill', while one woman had the conviction that if she took it 'she would go to hell'. Three women stated that the I.U.D. could get lost and 'wander into your stomach and cause you to bleed to death'. A further two women believed that the I.U.D. would cause cancer of the womb.

Tubal ligation was also the subject of some misinformation. Thirteen women thought this to be a temporary procedure, stating that if they wished to have another child, they could get their tubes untied. Eight women likened the procedure to a minor operation like a tooth extraction and only two realised that a woman would have to stay in hospital for longer than one day after the operation.

Knowledge about the physiology of conception was limited with only eight women having any real understanding of it. This was a reflection of low educational standards and of a total lack of sex education in the schools of the area. Twenty-two women stated that one experience of intercourse could produce a baby and seven were not sure. One woman stressed that intercourse twice in the same day would produce twins.

There was no real knowledge about any traditional method of contraception or abortion similar to that described by Professor Cawte in Aborigines on Mornington Island (Cawte, 1969). However, nine women did claim some knowledge of how to cause an abortion. Five mentioned the use of Epsom salts, and three spoke of the effects of an analgesic powder which had to be taken in a large dose, one woman adding that the same analgesic powder had to be used per vaginum as well as being taken by mouth. Only two women were in favour of the idea of abortion and five were undecided. The other 27 were strongly against termination of pregnancy and expressed abhorrence of the idea.

In eleven cases the number of children had exceeded the number that the mother now thought to be ideal. Each of these families had an extra four children above their stated ideal number. Nearly all the women regarded two years as the best interval of time between each child.

In answer to the question about which method they would use if they wished to stop having babies, 23 women said they favoured the Pill, two preferred the loop and one preferred tubal ligation. The remaining eight women stated that they did not believe in contraception. Of those who favoured the Pill, 20 said that it was the simplest method, and four stressed that it did not involve vaginal examination. Only two women were in favour of an I.U.D., one because she thought that she would forget to take the Pill, and the other because she believed that 'the Pill kills you or makes you terribly sick'. Only one woman preferred tubal ligation because she wanted 'something forever'.

Eighteen of the wives were certain of their husbands being in favour of family planning, and five were equally certain that their husbands would be against it. The remaining eleven women had no idea of what their husbands' views on the matter would be. I interviewed the eighteen husbands whose wives claimed were in favour of birth control. I explained the operation of vasectomy, but the response in nearly every case was so hostile that I thought it best not to broach the subject any further at that stage.

At the end of this survey I was fairly sure that eight women were enthusiastic about the prospect of a Family Planning Service, eight rejected it and eighteen were undecided as to whether they would use it or not. Among those who wanted or thought they would want the Pill if they were going to seek to plan their families, the fear of complications far outweighed the religious objections to the acceptance of this contraceptive technique. Overall, I felt confident that a Family Planning Service was warranted and that special care would have to be taken to correct the inaccurate beliefs held by the majority of Aboriginal women in Bourke about the most effective methods of contraception. This survey also indicated that initially at least, the responsibility for the contraceptive technique would rest with the female partner.

The provision of family planning

I told the eight women who had expressed an eagerness for family planning that the Pill would be provided, without cost, to anyone who was interested. Apart from an initial brief history taking and the recording of blood pressure and weight, I did not insist on further examination. Since most requests came in the course of my research or general practice activities and the consultations took place in a car, alternatives were not practical. When the opportunity arose I subsequently completed a physical examination at the district hospital.

Although I organised film shows about family planning I tried to avoid active proselytism. I also made every attempt to provide the

223

service with a minimum of fuss and inconvenience for the patients and I avoided criticising any woman who mislaid her pills or forgot to take them. As added insurance a middle-aged Aboriginal woman who was working as a health aide, kept several packets of the Pill in her home on the Reserve for those people who ran out of supplies.

A year after the inception of this Family Planning Service I made a request to the Family Planning Association in New South Wales to participate by setting up a clinic in the Bourke District Hospital to ensure that a Family Planning Service would be available after I left Bourke. This clinic was staffed by two part-time nursing sisters paid by the Family Planning Association of New South Wales. I acted as the medical officer to the clinic, which was open at regular times twice a month, and offered both the Pill and the I.U.D. as the two methods of contraception.

The acceptance of this Family Planning Service was better than I had anticipated after the attitude survey. Thirty-three months after the family planning service began, 79 women had sought contraceptive advice. This comprised 50% of the female population aged 15 to 44 years in the Bourke district and 53% of those potentially fertile. Their ages ranged from 15 years to 43 years and the number of their live children was from none to 14.

Eight women who requested the Pill never used it because of opposition by their husbands or their church. Of the remaining 71 initial acceptors, 50 have either continued with family planning practices or have returned to them after a planned pregnancy. This has led to a fall in the Bourke Aboriginal birth rate from 71 per 1000 between 1964 and 1971 to 35 per 1000 in 1972, 25 per 1000 in 1973, 33 per 1000 in 1974, 32 per 1000 in 1975 and 43 per 1000 in 1976.

The most common reasons for women seeking family planning advice were: enough children (32 cases); a desire to space their pregnancies (13 cases); economic difficulties and poor housing (11 cases); and eight women wanted no more children while their present ones were always sick. The other reasons given were problems with their husbands or regret at never having had a pregnancy-free period in their later teens to enjoy themselves. Three girls without children wished to complete their School Certificate studies.

In 32 cases the person who was most immediately concerned with influencing a woman to seek contraceptive advice was a close relative or friend who was already using a method of family planning. A further

30 women made up their minds after discussion with me or with Mrs Pat Cameron, the pathology technician at the hospital, who was a trusted confidante. Four women made their own decision without or against outside advice and the remaining women were influenced by their husbands, an officer of the Department of Child Welfare and Social Welfare or nursing staff from either the district hospital or the Family Planning Association.

When I first began to prescribe the Pill, I encountered some scepticism from a variety of health professionals about the likelihood of Aboriginal women remembering to take it. Ten women did admit to missing the occasional pill and a few were initially confused about the method of taking it. The main reason for this was a combination of too hurried an explanation by me together with advice from relatives who had some knowledge of the 21-day Pill. Some women also experimented with the dose and regularity of pill-taking in order to bring on their periods to make sure they were not pregnant. The use of the continuously taken 28-day packet, together with adequate follow-up, resolved any further mathematical confusion. Since there were only four unwanted pregnancies among the Pill takers, it must be regarded as a fairly successful method of contraception. Three of these women became pregnant when they were unable to renew their supplies while in another state. Two of them (both aged 21 years) did attend a doctor's surgery to get a prescription for the Pill, but were refused on the grounds that they were too young. They had omitted to tell the doctor that they already had nine children between them.

The I.U.D. was equally successful despite two pregnancies which ended in spontaneous abortions. The women's confidence in it grew to such an extent that this method became as acceptable as the Pill and for those who did not wish to have any further children it is now the favoured method.

The known complications of the Pill and the I.U.D. were accentuated by the high frequency of diabetes mellitus, elevated levels of blood fats, anaemia, genital tract infection and migraine found in the women of this community. (These side-effects are more fully described in an article in the *Medical Journal of Australia* [Kamien, 1975]). Although the side-effects were inconvenient they were rarely severe enough to contraindicate the use of the Pill or the I.U.D. and in a non-directive, readily available and personalised service they did not influence the overall acceptance of family planning by Aboriginal women.

Social and psychological factors in the acceptance or rejection of family planning

It is apparent from what I have already described that half of the fertile Aboriginal women in Bourke welcomed access to family planning. Even so, many Aborigines were suspicious of it and tended to see it as the white man's newest attempt at the genocide of their race. Consequently this medical service was the most likely to be misunderstood and to cause offence to Aborigines. It was essential to understand and to pay constant attention to the social and psychological factors which influenced the acceptance or the rejection of the family planning service which I was providing.

The family

Family ties in Aboriginal people are very strong. Most Aborigines in Bourke knew more about the life and doings of a third cousin in Darwin than many white Australians knew about a brother in the same town. The family represents the only security an Aborigine is likely to know in present-day rural white Australia. Children are the means of continuing the family and are highly valued. Male children are not obviously more prized than females. However, if a woman has many children of one sex she will keep trying to have at least one child of a different sex. Should a child die, the mother will try to have another.

When a couple have formed a liaison which they regard as likely to be permanent, they cement this relationship by having a child. If a woman has not become pregnant within six months, she becomes worried and seeks medical advice. This desire for a child applies to couples who may have numerous children from previous liaisons, even when the woman may be reaching the end of her reproductive life. In Bourke, this was one of the most common reasons for a planned pregnancy.

Given the value placed upon children, it is absolutely necessary to impart the message that family planning means what it says and is not to stop people having children permanently, unless that is their wish.

In this community, if a woman had no ambivalence about family planning, then she would almost surely practise a form of contraception with success. The younger women welcomed family planning as a means of spacing their family and were less keen than their mothers to have a large family. Some women did like to perpetuate a family norm. One client with seven children became pregnant and

226

was thought to have had a Pill failure. She was one of eight children, her sister had eight children and she had decided that eight was the number that she wanted.

Adolescent girls often reject contraception despite positive advice from their mothers. In many cases this appeared to be a form of rebellion against maternal control.

Even among young children there is 'shame' (embarrassment) about exposing their bodies. Teenagers swimming in the local pool often wear a shirt over their bathing costumes. Whether this is a result of former beliefs or of missionary involvement is not clear. Definitely this uneasiness about their bodies extends to a vaginal examination, and many seeking family planning were eager to avoid this if possible. With further acceptance of family planning practices, this reticence diminished. This reluctance towards vaginal examination may have been a local phenomenon since it was not found by a gynaecologist in a similar population only 100 kms away (D. Blackledge, 1973, pers. comm.). However it is more likely that a visiting gynaecologist sees a self selecting sample of women since those who choose to consult him expect to have a vaginal examination. Medical studies have shown a positive correlation between cancer of the cervix and low socio-economic status. I found two cancers of the cervix in women of child-bearing age in this community in 1972. Any attitudes which militate against the taking of cervical smears need to be explored, but not at the risk of destroying a Family Planning Service.

Aboriginal males regard children as a mark of virility. A man is often heard to taunt those with fewer children about their poor performance. By the time he has had six children, he has generally proved his virility to his own and his community's satisfaction. A few men still are not satisfied after a dozen positive proofs. The Aboriginal male also takes intense pride in the prowess of his children in those things important to his way of life. Whether he is dominant and supporting, or is a more shadowy figure in the running of his family, he usually has a strong power of veto. If a Family Planning Service tends to concentrate on the female and appears to usurp the male right of decision-making in this area, he invariably exercises his veto. Neglect of the husband in regard to both his views and his knowledge of contraception often leads him to resist family planning.

Some men regard the taking of oral contraceptives by their wives as in some way emasculating. During a time of argument when the wife is further questioning the dominant status of the male, there have been four incidents in which the husband has retaliated by burning his wife's pills. Two husbands were happy for their wives to be taking the Pill or to have a tubal ligation, but not to have an intrauterine device inserted. They were fearful of having a small foreign body inserted into their wives and regarded this as an infringement of their wives' privacy and their own territorial rights. Possessiveness and sexual jealousy are a norm in both sexes in this community and approximate the behaviour of the tribal Aboriginal male to any hurt or suspicion of infidelity of a spouse.

In white society this degree of jealousy would be regarded as pathological. Contraception, by preventing the natural result of an infidelity, adds further to a husband's suspicion and may be a cause of his preventing his wife from participating in family planning.

One man whose wife had heard about vasectomy sought to have this operation. In view of the predominant male attitudes on virility, and because he did not really want it, I left the family to come to a different conclusion about a method of birth control. At this time vasectomy would be a psychologically hazardous procedure in this community. After I left Bourke, this man had a vasectomy. His subsequent ambivalence about the procedure has done nothing to alter my above stated view.

The community viewpoint

The feeling that family planning was some form of genocide was expressed by such questions as 'Do you give the Pill to the whites as well?' and 'Do white women take the Pill?' In the early days of family planning some male members of the community questioned which government department was employing me to cut down the number of Aborigines. They asked if this was because the government could no longer afford to make Child Endowment payments. This is a quite important source of regular income to many large Aboriginal families.

The effect of religion

Sixty-five per cent of the women of child-bearing age in this community professed the Roman Catholic religion and all were aware of their church's proscription of the type of family planning methods that were being offered. However, 80% of the acceptors of family planning were Catholic. Dr Hurst (1970), also found that religious teachings were not very important in determining the method of birth control used by white women in an industrial rural area in Victoria. Active opposition to family planning by a segment of the Catholic church appeared to be ineffective if a woman had a desire to plan her children. There were a few women who were influenced not to participate in family planning, but no efforts were made by the Catholic church to teach them the rhythm method if they wished to try to plan their families. Religious beliefs tended to upset a woman's conscience rather than prevent her from practising family planning. Considerable guilt feelings, however, were aroused in practising Catholics, especially when they believed they were no longer entitled to attend church or confession.

Communication

Dissemination of communication for successful family planning proceeds at several levels. In the beginning, the family planning field worker needs to communicate that he or she can offer a service. Husband and wife then need to discuss their feelings about accepting contraception. Early acceptors must then communicate their experience to other potential acceptors.

In this community, communication occurred from myself as a doctor to eight women who expressed a desire to stop having children. At first I was assisted by an officer of the Department of Child Welfare and Social Welfare who was concerned with the well-being of Aboriginal women and children. He displayed too much zeal in publicising the new service, which was then seen as a compulsory measure to be resisted.

When none of the predicted dire effects of the Pill eventuated, relatives of the original acceptors began asking for contraceptive advice. The main avenue of communication has been through relatives and friends. Workers conducting an experiment in communicating family planning availability in Taichung, Taiwan, came to the conclusion that the most powerful means of communication was 'by informal diffusion processes' (Fawcett, 1970). Family planning acceptors tended to come from interrelated families. Relatives also tended to choose the same method of contraception. Conversely there were large, stable families in which all the members rejected family planning. The communication process extended to relatives in other country towns, making the inception of family planning there a more easy process.

The approval of those people with influence in the community was obtained by explaining to them the aim of family planning. Two

229

Aboriginal health aides, both middle-aged women, began to be of considerable help in the communication process. 'Community education is best done for the people by the people. There is no credibility gap' (Hutton, 1971).

Some husbands and wives communicated poorly, especially about such matters as planning children. I found it necessary to set up an informal information network amongst the men themselves. This was achieved by frequent discussion groups and resulted in considerable success.

Film-going is an established pattern of behaviour in this community. Suitable films seemed to produce an increase in knowledge about the physiology and anatomy of conception, but they did not influence the actual acceptance rates. After the first showing of family planning films, both sexes requested that future films be shown to segregated audiences.

It may be expected that women who are anxious and depressed and who have adopted a fatalistic acceptance of their life's circumstances will not bother to seek family planning advice. However, in this community twice as many women with diagnosed psychiatric illness accepted family planning as rejected it.

The application of social medicine

It is not enough to provide the possibility of family planning as one method of professing an interest in the welfare of Aboriginal people. This Aboriginal community was quick to sense any impatience or exasperation on my part and equally quick to reject any attempt by me to force my views. In the first months of the Family Planning Service, six women to whom I gave the Pill did not take it. It later turned out that one of the factors responsible was that my approach was too directive. An Australian social worker, Ms Jennifer Burden, has discussed the reluctance of Aboriginal women with an interest in family planning to consult their doctor. The main reasons were embarrassment about discussing 'women's business' with a strange male doctor, their lack of ease in a clinical surgery setting and their extreme sensitivity to being rebuffed or judged by the medical profession (Burden, 1971a).

As I showed in chapter 9, it is difficult for many Australian people to understand a culture very different from their own. This applies equally to medical and nursing personnel. A doctor working closely with a community of Aborigines not only is in a position to learn those beliefs and attitudes that influence acceptance or rejection of family planning, but also has the expertise to apply this knowledge. Should a woman require an I.U.D., he can insert it at the appropriate time and avoid the situation described by Burden (1971b) in the north-west of South Australia, in which the patient is scared away by a long waiting time. Being part of the informal network system, this doctor is also in a position to provide information and to correct misconceptions about family planning practice in the community such as occurred in June 1971, when a well publicised multiple pregnancy in Sydney was misinterpreted as being the normal occurrence among women who stopped taking the Pill to have another child.

In a small community, failure of the Pill or the I.U.D. for whatever reason produces anxiety in other women practising family planning. Four pregnancies occurred in women with an I.U.D. As I was almost part of the Aboriginal community, it was possible for me to explain and have accepted that the fault lay in the technique of supplying the I.U.D. and not with that particular contraceptive device itself. One of these women even requested that another I.U.D. be inserted, but this time by a gynaecologist. A similar situation exists in this community as that described in white Australian women who were more influenced by their doctors than by adverse publicity about the Pill in the media (Bertuch and Leeton, 1971).

Tubal ligation warrants special consideration in relation to the role of the 'social medical specialist'. There is a body of medical opinion which maintains that this is the best form of family planning for Aboriginal women. There are some racial overtones in this, in that it is an expression of a castration attitude to a minority group, and of a paternalistic attitude implying that Aboriginal women are not capable of managing any other method. Other doctors hold the view that, since the life expectancy of Aboriginal women is less than the Australian norm, tubal ligation is indicated at a younger age than would normally be considered for white Australians.

A doctor with knowledge of both communities should be able to assess the degree of persuasion involved in an Aboriginal woman opting for tubal ligation and the likelihood that she will later regret her decision. In some instances the patient does not realise that the operation is permanent. In some cases she is ambivalent about having more children, and in others she may have an unstable relationship

231

with her husband. If the relationship breaks up and she forms a new liaison, she will almost certainly wish to have another child. All these circumstances are reasons for discouraging a woman from having a tubal ligation. Admittedly it is sometimes difficult, for those without this knowledge of the patient and her community, to see why I will discourage a 35 year old woman with seven children and an unstable home relationship from having a tubal ligation, and yet will arrange one for a 30 year old woman with five children who has a very stable family life.

Traditional Western family planning services

A typical course of events in family planning after the appointment of a medical director is described by an American doctor B. Berelson (1969:341):

He begins by designating family planning as a health service, to be administered through the existing network, and/or by setting up family planning clinics whenever possible. The approaches typically fail and slowly the responsible officials come to realise that more vigorous efforts are needed in the form of special staff, materials, and supplies, and in ways to reach people rather than waiting for them to come in.

Hospitals and doctors' surgeries are often places where Aboriginal women are ill at ease or even unwelcome. Difficulties arise when medical practitioners are not familiar with the ways of a different ethnic group, as was illustrated in this community when two already pregnant women mistakenly had an I.U.D. inserted. Consequently, the Aboriginal people will try to avoid these places. Also women without transport, with one or more children to carry, do not lightly undertake a walk of more than 6 km.

The official Family Planning Clinic was totally ineffective for eight months, until its two part-time nursing sisters extended their services outside the confines of the hospital and outpatient department. After 21 months the clinic was still not a success, even when I was in attendance. Because it was held on only two occasions a month, the Aboriginal women had to fit in with the convenience of the clinic rather than the other way about. Consequently, only two new acceptors had resulted through the single efforts of its nursing personnel. A survey in Britain showed that the number of women who found family planning clinics the most helpful source of advice declined from 12% in 1968 to 9% in 1970. This led the author to suggest that it was time to re-examine the functioning of the traditional Western type of family planning clinic (Cartwright, 1970). If this is true of the British population, and if this study is in any way representative of other Aboriginal communities, then it is obvious that the traditional Western family planning clinic as found in Australia will need to make major adaptations in the delivery of its services, if it hopes to increase its acceptability to rural Aboriginal women. In the last two years the official Family Planning Service has been more effective as its paid, part-time nurse has learnt to pay attention to many of the cultural factors mentioned in this chapter.

The social psychology of an Aboriginal community will vary according to its beliefs, practices and degree of acculturation. Therefore it may be expected that providing a Family Planning Service to predominantly traditional communities will pose additional problems to those that I have described. For example, some Antagarinja women have been reported to 'associate the I.U.D. with the damaging magical effect of the small, illness-causing sticks which have the power to move throughout the body. No amount of anatomical knowledge can overcome the belief that such bodies have this magical property' (Ellis, 1972:8). However, if those providing the Family Planning Service observe the basic tenet of social medicine of trying to gear the service according to the understanding, viewpoint and health needs of the Aboriginal client group—they are more likely to be successful than if they provide the same services as those used by middle-class white Australians.

Family planning is but one rung in the ladder which needs to be provided to help Aboriginal people to achieve a health status similar to that of white Australians. The method of delivering this form of health care to this minority group is all-important. In a group whose dominant frustration is powerlessness, family planning can represent either an increased control over their circumstances, or, if badly handled, a further increase in their lack of power. It is important for the success of family planning and for the progress of the community that contraception is seen to be a method of control, not a method of being controlled.

233

Chapter 12

The doctor as an agent of social change: a retrospective view of what I tried to be

Our healing gift to the weak is the capacity for self help. We must learn how to impart to them the technical, social and political skills which would enable them to get bread, human dignity, freedom and strength by their own efforts.
Hoffer, 1964:13

The initial credibility of a change agent rests on his ability to achieve rapid improvement in some aspects of his client's lives. The real challenge for a change agent is to initiate and support changes which will result in a long term improvement in the overall condition of his client community.

Social change and those wanting to initiate it are part of the history of mankind. Much of this change has been haphazard and has resulted in unnecessary human suffering. Increasing awareness of the dangers of haphazard change has led social scientists to look for ways of enabling social change to occur with as much benefit and as little harm or discomfort as possible to those involved in the change process. The central philosophy behind this new discipline of 'planned change' is based on the value judgement that social intervention to help socially, economically and culturally deprived communities to solve their own problems and so exert control over their own fate, is preferable to a *laissez-faire* policy of non-interference and survival of the fittest.

Planned change is a behavioural science in that it attempts to understand and to systematise the process by which change occurs and it is also an applied science in that it tries to put this acquired knowledge into practice. This is a relatively new discipline so that there are still many theories, techniques and methods of approaching it. These theories are based on assumptions about the causes of human behaviour and draw heavily on a wide variety of disciplines ranging from psychology and anthropology to sociology and economics.

'Planned change' is used by some writers as a generic term for any deliberate effort to alter the behaviour and function of a social system.

This may concern change in individuals, the ecological setting in which individuals live and work, change in knowledge, social control, and change through confrontation and political activity.

Other writers prefer to use the term 'planned change' more restrictively to describe the process of a collaborative and co-operative relationship between a change agent and a client system (Goodenough, 1963: Bennis, Benne and Chin, 1970; Freire, 1972). The definition most applicable to what I attempted at Bourke is that,

Planned change is change which derives from a purposeful decision to effect improvements in a personality system or social system and which is achieved with the help of professional guidance. (Lippitt *et al.*, 1958:vi)

The particular form of planned change and social intervention that I was most concerned with in Bourke was that of community development. This has been defined as any process which 'encourages, educates, influences or helps people to become actively involved in meeting some of their own needs' (Batten, 1965:vii). It is based on the assumption that all people no matter how backward, depressed or disintegrated, have needs whose fulfilment is beyond their resources and that if opportunity and 'know how' are provided in terms acceptable to them, they can begin to fulfil their needs and shape their own destiny. At the same time I must stress that community development is not a religion and does not attempt to convert people to a certain way of thinking or acting.

Before embarking on any process of change, a change agent should know something of the community with which he will work and also something of the opinions and knowledge held by those who have gone before him or who are doing similar work. Different workers of course stress differing methods for achieving improvement in the social condition of Aborigines.

Their views range from developing an Aboriginal sense of identity to engaging in programmes of political action. Whatever their proposed strategies most white Australians who work with Aborigines have, after 200 years learned that what most Aborigines want is not assimilation or integration but the same right of choice held as an ideal by the majority white culture—the right of independence and self determination. This right has been expressed by the political scientist Dr Charles Rowley, as 'the right of free men to make their own decisions, within an acceptable framework of the law applicable to all' (1966:345). Similar sentiments on self determination were expressed by the anthropologist, Jeremy Long (1970), as 'the independence from being managed' and by the president of the Aborigines' Progressive Association in Sydney, the late Mr Bert Groves, as 'the end of paternalism' (1966:187). Self determination is an end-goal composed of an aggregation of smaller components, and Aborigines and those who work with them are beginning to take a more comprehensive view of these multiple needs. These needs include the development of an Aboriginal identity, economic independence, educational parity with and political participation in the affairs of the wider Australian society. Without them Aborigines in Australia will never have what one research worker from the Centre for Research into Aboriginal Affairs at Monash University sums up as a 'share of the wealth and a piece of the action' (Lippmann, 1970:88).

The path to self determination is a formidable obstacle course and at present Aborigines lack many of the skills needed to traverse it. To sustain them in their struggle they will need interested and skilled white (and Aboriginal) helpers who will operate with them at the face to face grass roots level.

Assisting change is not an easy occupation especially with a people who lack such skills as literacy, mechanical and financial expertise and whose social order is so fragmented that it is hard to find out what they want and even harder to get consensus on how they will go about it. My challenge and my charter under the Human Ecology of the Arid Zone Project was to explore ways of extending my role as a doctor to that of a change agent.

Change agents

The first European contact with Aborigines in western New South Wales in 1829, began a process of change from their long-established tribal life which grew apace with the advent of missionaries about 1880, and officers of the Aborigines Protection Board, which was established by the colonial government of New South Wales in 1883.

In retrospect the methods of those first white agents of change were authoritarian and paternalistic, their strategies involving too much stick and too little carrot. The process of acculturation began with superficial changes in Aboriginal life brought about by their adoption of some of the Europeans' material goods. Deeper changes were wrought by those of a religious nature and those who denigrated Aborigines as being constitutionally inferior to whites.

Such changes were haphazard and created strains and tensions in the Aboriginal community. A basic difference between myself as a modern change agent and those whites who had been responsible for change in the past was that my efforts at change were conscious and planned, and collaborative rather than coercive. Authoritarianism was replaced by participative, consultative decision-making and indoctrination by information.

The term 'change agent' in modern social science refers to a person who works with a client system in order to apply knowledge to the problems confronting them. My work as such a change agent in Bourke also cast me in another role defined in modern social science as a 'community developer', in that I assisted the community to develop towards its own chosen goal. My aim was to produce a capacity for self-help within the community with which I worked.

Tactics

There are many models of community organisation practice which a change agent can follow. With individuals, families, social groups, organisations and the Aboriginal community as a whole I tried to work in three main ways. The first was to develop problem-solving skills, the second to implement specific programmes of change and the third was to act as an advocate and negotiator with legislators and administrators who had influence over, or whose actions affected, the felt needs of the Bourke Aboriginal community.

I assisted Aborigines in developing problem-solving skills in the following ways. The first was by acting as a resource person in human relations groups with the aim of developing those interpersonal skills necessary to resolve personality clashes among potential Aboriginal leaders. The second method was to stimulate rational discussion and planning by presenting and co-ordinating data that had been collected either by myself or by Aborigines. This method led to Aborigines taking action over a variety of issues ranging from the poor immunisation status of their children to the remanding in gaol of children awaiting trial for petty offences. The third way was by acting as the bridge by which Aborigines could come into meaningful social contact with some interested or sympathetic white people such as school teachers and visiting university students. This contact played a considerable part in broadening the horizons and the knowledge of many Aboriginal people and proved to be an important factor in helping them to develop the skills they needed to begin to solve some of their problems.

The second main way in which I worked was to help Aborigines implement specific programmes. This entailed planning, running and consolidating services such as adult education, sporting and social activities, a community bus and a housing project.

My third role was as an advocate for the Aboriginal people. I made representations on their behalf or together with them to various administrative, political and charitable bodies. In this way I was able to help the A.A.A. to obtain money for their housing co-operative from the Federal government, the funds for dental and medical expenses from the State government, and the salaries of the elected Aboriginal field officers from the Australian Freedom From Hunger Campaign. I also acted as a publicity officer for the Bourke Aborigines by mentioning their needs to various organisations which were, or would in the future, be likely to be in a position to help them. One such example was keeping the Chairman of the Aboriginal Legal Service (Professor J. H. Wootten) informed about the legal needs of Bourke Aborigines. This was one of the factors that eventually resulted in Bourke Aborigines obtaining the services of a lawyer.

My role as advocate was important in that it enabled the Bourke Aboriginal leaders to see that not only was I on their side but that I was firmly committed to act on decisions which they had reached at their committee meetings, even when I had held a contrary opinion.

In most cases I worked in each of these three roles simultaneously. For example, my function with regard to housing was to encourage discussion by Bourke Aborigines about whether or not they wanted houses and if they did so, what they might do to get them. When more than half the community indicated that they wanted housing I helped find an architect and builder and the finance that was needed. When the Shire Council first deferred and then rejected an application to build the first house I was able to allay the fears of the Shire President and to obtain a rescission of a previous order pending an appearance of the architect and myself before the Shire Council on behalf of the A.A.A. This resulted in permission to build the first house.

Directive or nondirective help?

My aim as a change agent and community developer was to enable the Bourke Aborigines themselves to analyse their predicament, to point

238

out ways in which they could realise their felt needs and to encourage and support them in overcoming obstacles which arose in the fulfilling of these needs. I tried always to remember that my job was to help the community and their leaders to be the controlling body and that I was a participant helper and not a director. In short, my aim was to assist them by pointing out the alternative ways of achieving their chosen goals and the known degrees of ease or difficulty of each alternative and leaving it to the individual Aborigine or Aboriginal group to choose which way he or they would take.

When I first went to Bourke I did take the initiative in beginning the process of change but after the A.A.A. became operational and there was some impetus towards change I slowly became less and less the initiator of ideas or actions. I also made a conscious effort to avoid being manipulative except when I thought that my taking no initiative would be construed by my clients either in the present or in the future as being apathetic or irresponsible. For instance, when a group of Aboriginal people planning housing decided to incorporate a wood stove into the plans of their new houses simply because they had not experienced any other type of cooking apparatus, I thought it in their interests to leave the planning options open until some of them had gained experience with gas and electric stoves. This particular decision was justified when the occupants of the first three homes stated that they were glad they had an electric and not a wood stove.

Another circumstance in which I felt that a more active role was indicated was when the Aboriginal leaders became demanding and dependent because they were confused about their roles or were losing face with their peers over their inability to deliver promised goods or services. One newly elected field officer reported to me at 9 am each day to receive instructions for his day's work. To tell him that he was now his own boss would have been callous in that it would have exacerbated his already high level of anxiety. I provided a mildly directive programme for the first two months until he had begun to find his own feet. On other occasions I would try to intervene to help the Aboriginal leaders keep their promises. This sometimes meant activating the leaders by bolstering their confidence in themselves and sometimes through taking short cuts by making a direct approach to the white people or organisations which were causing delays. One such event occurred in 1971 when the committee of the A.A.A. reported to their members that they would further their efforts to obtain housing

239

by arranging a meeting with the N.S.W. Minister for Child Welfare and Social Services when he visited Bourke. When they were not granted an appointment, a small number of their peers taunted them by taking the view that this proved how unimportant and ineffective they really were. In order to disprove this view, I solicited the support of a sympathetic local politician who obtained the required interview for them. I was careful to explain to the Aboriginal leaders that this was the way white society sometimes worked.

This active role had its dangers and often put me into a double-bind situation. If I responded I was often accused by the Aborigines of always interfering. If I did not respond then I was 'white-anting' the Aborigines and, as they said, 'letting them drown in the mud hole which I had dug'. In the particular example I have just quoted the meeting with the minister went so badly that the Aboriginal delegation thought it would have been better not to have had it at all. They not unnaturally blamed me for arranging it.

Supporting change

The *leit-motiv* running through all the models of change agentry that I tried was the provision of emotional support for my clients. The emerging leaders were among the most vulnerable of Bourke Aborigines since they were prone to attack by their peers, by white authority figures and by each other. These anxieties were compounded by uncertainty over their role and how to play it (*see* chapter 14).

My responsibility as the person who initiated change, was to support them until they developed the confidence and the skill to support each other and to act by themselves. I tried to counter the pessimism and criticism of some of their Aboriginal peers by focusing as much attention on their achievements as on the reasons for their failures.

I also tried to make myself available to them as both a person and as a friend. I was particularly concerned that I did not give off any cues such as 'I am a busy doctor' which would nullify my supportive intentions. The two elected field officers and myself also met for lunch for two hours every Monday for a period of two years. We each took it in turns both to provide the lunch and select the venue. We would discuss how things were going, how we felt about it and why there were resistances to change and a lack of involvement of certain key members of the Aboriginal community. We also analysed what had happened at the previous meeting of the A.A.A. if one had occurred and we paid particular attention to why certain members who had come with the intention of having their say about some contentious issue were not given the opportunity to participate. These Monday luncheon meetings developed into mutually enjoyable occasions which we missed only because of absence from Bourke. (Extracts from the verbatim comments by Aboriginal leaders at these meetings are recorded in chapter 14.) As the Aboriginal field officers gained in confidence our consultations became a two-way process, with the field officers giving me better insight into my errors and blind spots. This mutual support process has continued since my departure by means of interstate visits, letters and telephone calls. The psychological presence of a departed change agent as a source of support is a well known phenomenon (Lippitt, 1958).

Partly because of personal contact with me and partly because there was a research project taking place in Bourke, a large number of interested whites and other Aboriginal groups have paid periodic visits to Bourke. Their acceptance and sometimes praise of the efforts of the Aborigines, especially their leaders, often provided a form of indirect support and gave a small impetus to their continuing efforts towards change.

The majority culture

A change agent who works with any Aboriginal community in Australia cannot ignore the white *milieu* in which his client community lives. The sensitivity which the change agent intuitively or by learning, displays to the Aboriginal client population also needs to be exhibited to the white population. After all, individual whites have their views and values of Aborigines to which they are entitled, no matter how disagreeable these may be to the change agent.

It serves no purpose to label unsympathetic whites as 'sick' as a means of explaining their racial prejudices. It is wise for the change agent not to threaten the self esteem of members of the majority culture even when they are threatening his, or to close irrevocably the doors of communication with them by taking the unrealistic and partisan view that Aborigines are always in the right. On occasions, however, this may prove to be impossible without risking a loss of congruence with the client group.

Congruence

My first experience of this situation occurred when the A.A.A. voted to complain to the N.S.W. Minister for Child Welfare and Social Services about an officer of his Department whom they alleged had mis-appropriated the pensions of three Aborigines. I thought this highly unlikely, but it was important at that time for the A.A.A. to flex its muscles by making its own decisions. It was equally important to me to be seen by Aborigines as being on their side and not as a disguised arm of established authority, so I did not oppose their action.

When he received a querying letter from the Minister, the welfare officer was furious at what he regarded as my perfidious behaviour. I pointed out that although we were (or had been) friends he did not tell me what decisions were reached at meetings of the Freemasons and Rotarians of which he was a member. Conversely I did not feel I should inform him about decisions reached at meetings of the A.A.A. I made it clear that I was available to help both black and white, but that in any conflict of interests between the two, my first loyalty would be to the Aborigines.

The role I tried to play and the one which came most naturally to me resembled that of a fairly partisan member of a political party. My allegiance was to that party but at the same time I was aware that not all of the policies and opinions of opponents to my party were false or wrong. It was really a matter of standing up and being counted, so that both the Aborigines and the whites knew where I stood. It was another means of being congruent. Apparently some white people appreciated this and I was told by the then Matron of the Bourke District Hospital, Mrs Pat Baker, that one of my traits she appreciated was that although I was 'so obviously on the blacks' side, white people were able to communicate with me because I did not see the blacks as all white'.

A cross-cultural interpreter

One of my roles as a change agent was to translate and explain Aboriginal feelings to those who were insulated by office or by culture from Aborigines, yet whose decisions had a great influence upon them. An example of such a role is the part I played in helping two Aboriginal women obtain a smallgoods shop. The price asked of them seemed rather high, so I advised them to have the shop independently valued. This resulted in a reduction in the asking price by fifty per cent. They entered into negotiations with a bank manager who thought they had lost interest when they failed to keep an appointment. What had in fact happened was characteristic: they had a meeting with the bank manager at 12.30 pm. He had to break off for another appointment at

1 pm and because their business had not been completed he suggested another meeting at 4.30 pm. This was misconstrued by the Aboriginal ladies as being 'told to get lost'. I was able to rectify this misunderstanding. After the money to purchase the shop had been available for four months and the legal requirements necessary to take possession had not been fulfilled, I told the two women how to motivate the lawyer concerned. Twelve months after taking over the shop they complained of a lack of help from the man hired to assist them with their accounting. I found out that he felt they thought he was interfering. The shop has since run adequately and with profit. It is probable that without my simple role as a cultural interpreter it would never have begun.

Another role I was given by the Aborigines was that of official interpreter at meetings with potential white helpers and government officials. Besides differences in concept of the same work, there were vast differences in vocabulary between Aborigines and educated whites. As one Aboriginal activist, Mr Wally Byers, stated, 'We need you as a translator, the Gubs don't understand us very well. Maybe we use slang. And they use big words which get us lost. You'd be more use as a translator than running all your sly schemes behind our back.'

Medical students

Another and very important part of my role as a cross-cultural interpreter was to try to influence the potential doctor-change agents of the future. Few Australian doctors have shown an interest in practising in distant rural areas, and even fewer have been much concerned with anything more than the immediate health problems of Aboriginal patients presenting to them. This is partly due to the scant exposure received by medical students to the practice of medicine outside the hospital situation and partly to a lack of awareness among many medical educators that a knowledge of social pathology is as much a basic necessity in the armament of doctors as is a mastery of the basic elements of physical pathology and psychopathology. If future doctors are going to exert any influence on the improvement of man's social condition, as distinct from treating his episodes of illness, they will have to recognise that an understanding of the strategy of initiating social change is as much a tool in the therapeutic equipment of a doctor who works with communities as is his knowledge of medicine when dealing with individuals.

243

During 1971 and 1972 I conducted a pilot study to test the value of having medical students work with me in the Bourke Aboriginal community. Fourteen students spent between two and five weeks in Bourke. I evaluated their subjective experiences by asking each student to write a letter stating what he expected from his stay before he came, and to complete another letter two to four months after he had left, expressing views on his experience. I later met most of the students at periods ranging from two to thirty months after their stay and recorded further comments on their experiences.

Only three of the students chose to come to Bourke because they were particularly interested in or curious about Aboriginal people. One wanted to know about the conditions of life of Aborigines. Another wanted to know what medical conditions were peculiar to Aborigines and the third wished to see how a doctor from a 'progressed society' went about bringing medical care to a less progressed society'. The other students were more interested in getting practical experience outside of a large teaching hospital.

It was an irony that the only one who had any real knowledge of the anthropology and history of the Australian Aborigines was a visiting English student from Birmingham.

Although the students commented on having had a wide exposure to Aboriginal problems through newspapers and television, all exhibited various degrees of incredulity at what they found by direct experience. The general tenor of feeling is perhaps expressed best in the words of one student,

It's unbelievable! I was unaware that such attitudes prevailed in our country and in our State. It astounded me. I've read about Aborigines, heard about their conditions and seen them on TV, but I never realised before how shot to bits they were. People in Sydney just don't realise what goes on, or else they turn a blind eye to it.

Nearly all the medical students came from middle-class backgrounds, and nearly all found it difficult to relate to Aboriginal people. When they first arrived in Bourke, most expressed the view that the condition of the Aboriginal people was simply a manifestation of their 'laziness and drunkenness'. This 'Protestant ethic' view of life was conditioned by the attitude of the dominant society in the town and also by the students' competitive middle-class backgrounds. One student was present when a child was taken into the custody of the Department of Child Welfare and was amazed at the total lack of reaction by the parents. He could not make up his mind whether this was a response of callous indifference or of total despair.

However, by the end of the elective term all students had at least the beginning of an understanding of how a group's culture and norms could affect its way of life. They had begun to learn the culture concept of behaviour. Those students able to form relationships with Aboriginal people commented on how gratifying it was to them to be accepted, particularly by Aboriginal children. They began to question the dominant society's views on Aborigines and found: 'Some whites are very "one-eyed". Their ideas of what should be done either to or for Aborigines are both unrealistic and unpleasant.'

One student commented, 'This is the first time I have seen patients as members of a particular group with particular codes and customs'. Another was 'profoundly moved by the plight of the Aborigines in Australian society'. Yet another student, perhaps with more insight than most, came to a realisation that, 'the Aborigine was being used for selfish ends by a host of people, including medical and social research workers'.

Nearly all students remarked about the vast amount of physical pathology which they saw in Aboriginal people and three commented that there was nothing in the medical course about diseases which might be found in an Aboriginal population.

In addition to coming to grips with health problems, many students developed insight into the difficulties of the delivery of health care to Aboriginal people and several students were highly critical of the general health care of Aborigines. One student saw two Aboriginal children who had just returned from medical care in Sydney and expressed almost total incredulity that their state of health was so bad one week after specialist medical attention. This one experience showed him that the large city hospital had but a small part to play in alleviating the poor state of health of most Aborigines.

Another student regarded his experience of health care for Aborigines as the approach to the health care needs of any oppressed minority group. He felt that what he had learned in a remote country area applied equally well to dealing with any minority group anywhere.

Not only was there real insight into the magnitude of the social and medical problems of Aboriginal people in Bourke, but also in the entire State, and there was a general questioning: 'What can be done by people at our level of training to meet the demands of Aborigines, and to bring them medical care in the way that they want? Or, is the medical student, so poorly trained, better than nothing?'

245

Only time will tell if this undergraduate experience has any effect on stimulating those future doctors to work in areas with large Aboriginal populations. Even if they do not, their new found insights should serve them well in their contacts with people from other deprived or developing communities. One of the students (now Dr Christopher Halloway) should have the last word since he has summed up the importance of giving medical students (and other students in the health field) the opportunity to broaden the scope of their education:

To talk through with you the problems you were experiencing in dealing with the total health care of a group of individuals was for me a highlight of my education, not as a sterile medico, but as a professional and a responsible citizen. You don't have all the answers, but I am indebted to you for acquainting me with a few of the questions. After all, medical students are perhaps a bit like the Bourke Aboriginal group in being slow to be directive about what they want because they don't know the questions they should be asking—thank you for giving me the time to start to question off my own bat.

Government bureaucracy

The increased involvement of the Australian Government since the election of the Labor Party to office in November 1972 in Aboriginal development, made it a significant agent of social change. However it sometimes took considerable effort to remember that the bureaucrats in the Office (later the Department) of Aboriginal Affairs did share a common interest with me in helping Aborigines.

An understanding by the change agent and his clients of the difficulties encountered by public servants may have made us less critical. A reciprocal understanding by bureaucrats of the difficulties and frustrations of those working at the grass roots and the loss of psychological impetus caused by lengthy delays to decisions and to allocating funds is perhaps even more important.

One of my omissions was my lack of concern in getting real central government involvement in the changes which were occurring in Bourke. At the time the effort needed to penetrate the armour of 'business, overwork, under-staffing and changes in staffing' in the Department of Aboriginal Affairs did not seem to me to be a worthwhile use of my energies. I preferred to remain at a peripheral level and to try to co-ordinate the sometimes contradictory actions of the different Commonwealth, State and Local Government bodies. For instance, it was the policy of the N.S.W. Department of Child Welfare and Social Welfare to gradually close down the Bourke Reserve. At the same time the Bourke Shire was obtaining money to build a permanent road

246

around the Reserve and was opposing the A.A.A.'s building project in the town. This lack of co-ordination between different agencies would appear to be widespread and to have improved little, if at all, in the last ten years (Gale, 1966). Ideally the change agent and his clients need to be partners with government in deciding what needs to be done to get the maximum effective change.

The sanctioning committee

The intention of uniting organisations which profess to have a common interest in Aboriginal progress is a logical development. I explored the idea of having a group of influential white citizens in the town who would give their sanction and support to both the Aborigines and myself in our efforts towards change. Most of the 'influential citizens' however were not ready for this role. Firstly I was viewed with some suspicion in that I had not been supported by the other doctors in the town. I was a psychiatrist and my role was new and not well defined (*see* chapter 13). Most of the influential whites had very definite views about the capabilities of Aborigines and their place in society. At that time I regarded these as fixed enough to be beyond my capacity to change. However my main reason for letting this idea lapse was that the information I provided to white citizens was then used against or misrepresented to Aborigines. The idea thus backfired in two ways. Firstly I was seen by Aborigines as being on the side of whites, and secondly people on the sanctioning committee were using their information to hinder rather than to help change.

A change agent and his Aboriginal client community cannot ignore the presence of the white community and its leaders. Ideally they should be partners with government at all levels in deciding what needs to be done to get maximum effective change. This means involving governments by information, by lobbying, by pressure and by all the other political means used by reputable white organisations.

Government has the material resources and the change agent and those of his clients involved in change, the grass root human resources. At present neither can succeed very effectively without the help of the other.

Public relations and the press

Given the underlying mistrust of newcomers to Bourke, the derogatory views held about Aborigines, and the informal grapevine as the source of most information, it could only be expected that I, my motives and

247

my clients would be the subject of many false rumours (*see* chapter 2, pp. 80-81. This was especially marked during a period of rural recession when nearly all whites in the town believed that Aborigines were receiving a host of social services and educational benefits denied to them. Many also believed that I could obtain Housing Commission homes at will for my Aboriginal friends. I thought it important to counter all the false rumours that I heard with a brief statement of fact. I also encouraged the A.A.A. to correct false statements in the press through writing to the editor of the paper concerned. Such measures did not stop these rumours but they did have enough of a braking effect to prevent them from escalating totally out of control. A spin-off from the Aborigines' letters to the editor was a small gain in pride, expressed by the invariable but still tentative comment from A.A.A. members of 'Well that told 'em didn't it?'

I was aware that one aspect of working within the majority culture had to be to let the whites know what I and my Aboriginal clients were trying to do and what was actually happening. It was obvious that this would best occur through an informal diffusion process primed by general everyday conversation. However, in the three years I spent in Bourke only two whites ever asked me what I 'was on about'. Since I did not wish to 'button hole' and bore people, I was left with the choice of talking to service and church clubs and writing bulletins for the local press. Neither of these tactics achieved more than a temporary cessation of rumour.

Writing to or speaking to the press was also a potentially hazardous procedure. On one occasion a medical reporter who had interviewed me wrote a most benign and laudatory article about Bourke Aborigines and their achievements (the *West Australian* 29 March 1971). The article was syndicated around Australia and finished up as a single paragraph in the *Australian Workers' Newsletter* which one Bourke Aborigine read. He decided it was derogatory and called a meeting of the A.A.A. to discuss what I had said. This meeting got out of hand and was the most fiery I have ever attended with those present almost equally split between those who trusted and supported me and those who wanted me to cease my activities in Bourke. The rift was fairly quickly healed with no visible resultant scars. However, the original article achieved no purpose other than giving me and my university some publicity without furthering the cause of the project in any apparent way.

I was left with the view that a change agent should, in theory, try to allay white apprehension about his work with Aborigines, but that trying to use the news media to that end is likely to achieve little at the risk of jeopardising a lot.

So far in this chapter I have described the role I tried to play in developing problem solving behaviour amongst Aborigines and in fostering leadership, followership and organisation in their community in order to diminish the degree of powerlessness that contributed so largely to their apathy, alienation, maladaptive behaviour and unhappiness. The success of such a planned intervention is crucially dependent upon the personal qualities and attitudes of the change agent. In the remaining part of this chapter I will discuss the qualities that I would look for in choosing a change agent to work with Aboriginal communities like the one at Bourke. This is done with the benefit of hindsight on my own experiences in Bourke, observation of would-be 'change-agents' at work in the same town and attendance at two workshops for advisers to Aboriginal communities.

The qualities and attitudes needed to facilitate change

A successful change agent cannot, by definition, be a person of conservative outlook. The quality I am thinking of has nothing to do with socialist politics, but the term 'moderately radical' comes to mind. The change agent is likely to be a divergent thinker and must be liberally minded, committed to the philosophical concept of social justice for all men. He must respect his clients as equal human beings and recognise their fundamental right to choose their own way of life so that he will not try to manipulate them or interfere with their freedom to enlarge their own personalities and abilities. In addition to this respect for his clients, a change agent should have a capacity for friendship and a willingness to make himself available to them. (This must, however, be tempered with caution: in Bourke I had to learn to avoid arousing resentment by being thought to pay more attention to one person or one group than another.) These attitudes that a change agent needs to exhibit to his clients to facilitate change are the same as those which the American psychotherapist Carl Rogers has found to be essential for a teacher to facilitate learning:

I think of it as prizing the learner, prizing his feelings, his opinions, his person. It is a caring for the learner, but a non-possessive caring. It is an acceptance of this other individual as a separate person, having worth in his own right. It is a basic trust—a belief that this other person is somehow fundamentally trustworthy. (Rogers, 1969:109)

A change agent with this respect and concern for his clients can learn by his experience to cultivate another necessary quality—a sensitivity to the feelings of individual clients and to the client community, to do what Rogers has described as 'understanding another person's reactions from the inside' (1969:111). In my case, I had to learn how the world and my attempts to make it better seemed to Bourke Aborigines.

In the case of a doctor change agent, he should know a little about a lot and have a broad view of health such as an awareness of the effects upon his Aboriginal clients of overcrowding, subnutrition, unemployment, over zealous law enforcement and other socio-economic problems as well as the maladaptive effects that men and women can have upon each other.

Attitudes to self—insight

The change agent needs to be aware of the strong and weak points which he brings to his work, and to have insight into his own prejudices and value judgements. He must have defined his objectives in order to make sure that they are compatible with those of his clients. He needs to consider how much he is motivated by altruism and how much by self interest. How much is he there to help and how much to 'do' research and write papers? How much is he using the Aborigines and their situation for his own personal advancement? It is important that the change agent ask himself who is to benefit from his intervention: himself, his clients, or both. An honest and clear analysis of this question will enable the change agent to set realistic limits on the amount of time that he is prepared to give to his clients and on the amount of privacy he needs to further his own aims and to preserve his own and his family's well-being. (It is a point which does not go unnoticed by the Aborigines, either. In 1972 I heard two social scientists address a group of Bourke Aborigines about their work in a way that gave the impression that Aborigines were merely experimental data to them. A spokesman for the A.A.A. quickly sensed this and told the visitors 'Well, I don't know what you are doing here, but it sure isn't to help us'.)

It was fairly obvious to Bourke Aborigines that I was trying to do something positive about their ill health. It was equally puzzling to them to understand why. I explained that our relationship was to our mutual benefit. They would get better medical care and I would write about what happened and get a better job when I went back to a university. I am not sure that the concept of writing a thesis had any

250

meaning to them but the idea that I was working with them for some gain to myself made my motivation understandable at least to some of their leaders.

Emotional security

The change agent who works with Aborigines in rural Australia needs a high degree of emotional security. Not only does he need to cope with his own anxieties as he learns about a new role, but he must tolerate and handle the antagonism, derision, exclusion and the lowered status that is accorded him by those members of the white majority culture particularly prejudiced against Aborigines. The secure person will be able to recognise and place in perspective just where his position and his primary discipline lie in the scheme of things. He will be able to accept that he is simply one cog, even if a large cog, in a complex wheel of change. In the case of a doctor, he needs to be secure enough to work in a health team with other health personnel or to face active consumerism among his patients without feeling threatened. The team approach is necessary to maximise the effectiveness of delivering health care, and encouraging the consumer rights of patients ensures community participation and a strong voice in the sort of health services that they want.

For those change agents who are married, the most important factor in their emotional security is their relationship with their spouse. An already harassed change agent whose wife is excessively demanding or dependent, or who dislikes living in the area in which he works, will have to be an unusually resilient person to survive and to succeed.

I was fortunate in that my wife adjusted quickly to life in Bourke (despite accommodation problems), and could quite happily have settled there. Her life view tends more to pessimism than to optimism and at first she was sceptical of my chances of bringing about any improvement in the life of Bourke Aborigines. This gave way to a guarded optimism when the A.A.A. was at the height of its activities. Her pessimism about the outcome of my endeavours returned when I was not immediately replaced by another doctor. This was not because she doubted the ability of the Aborigines to continue to effect changes for the better, but because she could see little change in the attitudes of whites towards Aborigines.

My wife exhibits varying degrees of diffidence in company and so does not push herself upon other people. As a result she remained interested, but not deeply involved with Aboriginal people. At the

251

same time she did attend many of the A.A.A. meetings and also came to a residential Human Relations Group at Armidale. When invited, she visited Aboriginal women on the Bourke Reserve or in town houses and she later returned the invitation. On one occasion she became concerned that our 2 year old daughter who went with her would get ringworm which was then rife amongst children on the Reserve. To avoid giving offence to the Aboriginal mothers she did not interfere with our child's play habits. However, she did get upset when our daughter developed the ringworm rash.

Few Aboriginal men ever completely relaxed their guard in her presence and although they would call in on business or simply to chat, only a handful ever got around to addressing my wife by her first name even when she pointed out how uncomfortable this was for her. She entered the mainstream of white life in the town and participated in tennis, physical education and crochet clubs. Because of this and also because she was not intimately involved in all that I did, she was not regarded by whites as a party to my misguided behaviour. Her temperament enabled her to fall naturally into the role of a mediator between our family and the white female community. White women would complain to her about the iniquities of the Aborigines and those who tried to give them ideas 'above their station'.

Her position in the town was summed up by one influential white, who after telling me in short four-letter words what he thought of me and 'my nigger loving ways' excluded my wife from his vituperations by saying, 'But your wife—she's a lady'.

Other attitudes and qualities in the ideal change agent

The change agent needs the attitudes of the student in order to learn from his clients and also from his experience on the job, the qualities of the academic to research the areas of need to find the means to supply those needs and the qualities of the teacher to help people from the client community to learn new skills. He needs to be something of a psychotherapist to help him to actively listen to what he is being told and to sense what he is not being told, and to be able to act as a non-directive counsellor. A psychiatric outlook, although not necessarily a psychiatric training, is a helpful attribute in bringing a therapeutic approach to the anxieties of the client group and their emergent leaders. It also assists in recognising, analysing and helping the changing affective relationships which a client community will have with the change agent.

At the beginning of my stay I was treated with distrust. This was followed by a period of testing, sparring and identification. The latter even took a physical form when three of the Aboriginal leaders grew beards identical in shape to mine. For my part, I experienced periods of frustration, exasperation and anger with Bourke Aborigines. It was only after attending the Bourke Court of Petty Sessions for the first time that I began to identify with them.

The change agent needs to be something of a diplomat to help him consult with those whose influence or actions impinge upon his client community and he sometimes needs the pragmatism of the politician when consultation has proved futile. To these abilities must be added that of the chess player in that he must continually monitor what is happening, why and where each move may lead. The ability to be a community chess player will also provide a degree of self protection for the change agent if he can learn to analyse the reasons for resistance, and sometimes recognise its value, rather than simply emote against the people who resist.

A further skill of considerable importance for a change agent in an Aboriginal community is a sense of time and timing. The change agent needs the patience and the understanding not to rush his clients faster than they can comfortably and safely proceed. At the same time he needs to know when his job is done. The change agent who does not know when to terminate his guidance is not only inhibiting the maturation and growth of his clients but risks the fate that can befall a parent who fails to recognise when a grown child wishes to be independent.

The qualities and attitudes which inhibit change

Having drawn attention to some of the qualities desirable in a change agent, it is equally important to mention some of those which may predispose to his failure.

The authoritarian person who has a great desire to manage and organise people can be as inhibiting to Aboriginal development and self-determination as were the majority of government officers whose dicta were so skilfully ignored by Aborigines in the past. Missionaries and those who wish to make others into images of themselves or to conform to some other idealised norm, are in their way authoritarian and are often trying to fulfil their own felt needs rather than those of the Aborigines.

253

White people wishing to expiate some sense of deep inner guilt about what whites have collectively done to Aborigines are often unsuitable in that their Achilles' heel shows and lays them open to manipulation by their Aboriginal clients. Such manipulation is not a bad thing in itself, but it inhibits the formation of the most desirable relationship between change agent and clients. Similarly the emotionally insecure or maladjusted who have difficulty in coping with their own peer groups are often not satisfactory change agents, particularly when they are looking to their work to give meaning to their lives and hoping, as a secondary benefit, to solve their own problems by solving the problems of others. These people, the guilty and the insecure, have a need to be indispensable which is contrary to one of the tacit understandings of change agentry—that the change agent should be working to make himself dispensable.

The change agent who seeks publicity for himself is likely to arouse the antagonism of both his client community and the whites with whom he and they must live. Both may object to his seeking fame. Even where his motives are purely to further the interests of his clients, he runs the risk of being misunderstood, both by his clients and the white community. The dangers of being misreported only increase that risk. On the other hand, the opportunist who seeks publicity for himself by jumping on the Aboriginal bandwagon to make the most of it while it lasts is unlikely to deceive Aboriginal people for very long.

There was a view strongly supported in some church circles in Bourke that people of like skin would gel and so it would be a good idea for other dark skinned people to help Aborigines. This may be true when the helpers are other Aborigines, but it is not true for all dark skinned people. Indians, reared in a culture where society is stratified according to a socio-religious caste system, made poor change agents in Bourke because they tended to regard the Aborigines as being lower than the lowest caste of India, which did not help in the battle to change the Aborigines' long-standing view of themselves as 'the lowest of the low'.

Commitment and congruence

It must be admitted that a prospective change agent who possessed all the virtues and none of the disadvantages I have described above would be a paragon of rare virtue. Exhaustive use of those criteria in the selection of change agents would make recruitment extremely difficult. A more realistic approach is to recognise that overriding all the particular qualities discussed above and inherent in all that I have said is the crucial importance of commitment and congruence. The change agent should be so committed to his chosen task that his enthusiasm for it is obvious and his resolve strong enough to cope with the demands made of him. This is perhaps most likely if the special interests of the change agent approximate to the felt needs of the client community.

Incongruent behaviour is acting in a manner which is false in relation to your feelings, such as insincerity, hypocrisy or repression. Aboriginal people are quick to sense incongruous behaviour and to see when a change agent is not fully aware of his feelings and reactions, or is not communicating the feelings of which he is aware. Thus, while there is a need to encourage Aboriginal expression, and strong expression at that, it is not necessary for a change agent to fawn to and pamper aggressive Aborigines. The respect I mentioned above must be mutual. If you continue to smile while someone knocks you on the head far beyond any reasonable limit of tolerance, and fail to express the annoyance you must obviously feel you will lose the other person's respect, and you will lose congruence. During my time in Bourke I was not above giving my tongue and my emotions full reign on the very few occasions which called for it. Those occasions are well remembered by the Aborigines concerned, with affection and good humour, almost as if I had at last begun to talk their language. In other words, a successful change agent must always 'be himself'.

I would hazard a guess that when the principles of change-agentry are better understood, the one skill or quality which will be stressed above all others is that a change agent must always 'be himself' when dealing with his clients. Any sham or insincerity, any mask of concern hopefully covering a basic indifference or hostility, will soon be seen through and destroy his effectiveness. He can learn all the rules and all the tricks, but if his actions are not congruent with the way he really feels, they will fall flat. A 'right feeling' between a change agent and his clients is more powerful than all the techniques which can be learnt; when the right feeling is there, many right things seem to happen.

Chapter 13
The psychiatrist as a change agent

Although I worked as a general practitioner to the Bourke Aboriginal community I was also qualified as a psychiatrist. Indeed it had been envisaged by the Director of the Human Ecology of the Arid Zone Project and his board of advisers from the New South Wales Institute of Psychiatry that my involvement in the project would be a purely psychiatric one (Cawte, 1968). In the introduction to this book I have discussed how and why I came to change my contribution to the Human Ecology of the Arid Zone Project from the narrow field of a social-psychiatric intervention to a broader application of social medicine.

Nevertheless, I did offer a psychiatric service to both Aborigines and whites in the area and since my involvement with Aborigines was not obvious to whites in the first six months that I lived in Bourke, their early reactions to me were based mainly on my role as a psychiatrist.

My intervention as a psychiatrist was based on the theories of the American psychiatrist, Dr Alexander Leighton and the Australian psychiatrist, Professor John Cawte. Leighton and his co-workers in Canada showed that social and cultural disintegration were of major importance in the development and perpetuation of psychiatric symptoms (Leighton, 1963). They also postulated that psychiatric disturbance in more than a minority of members could contribute to the social disintegration of a community and suggested that a doctor could promote cultural change towards integration by using his medical skills to reduce the prevalence of psychiatric symptoms in people from these disintegrated societies (Leighton, 1965).

Extrapolating and modifying this north American experience to the Australian scene Professor Cawte suggested that a 'psychiatric ecologist' could be of assistance in promoting integrated Aboriginal communities by treating those members who are socially malfunctioning or psychiatrically disturbed (Cawte, 1968; 1972). The techniques that I used in the practice of community psychiatry, especially when working with other 'helping agents' such as school teachers, were based loosely on the writings of Gerald Caplan, Professor of Psychiatry at Harvard University, in his book *The principles of preventive psychiatry*, 1964.

It should by now be apparent to the reader that I believe the greatest benefits to the health of man have arisen not so much from an ability to treat his individual illnesses as from a general improvement in his social and economic environment. Social and community psychiatry involve both preventing and treating psychiatric disorder by concerning itself not only with individuals but also with the factors in their environment which affect mental health and social functioning.

This chapter describes my special role as a community psychiatrist in the field and, in particular, how this role tended to be rejected by the white community at the outset, only to become accepted as the expectation of the community about psychiatry and me as a psychiatrist changed.

The general attitude of the people towards outsiders

The relationship between stranger contact and aggressiveness has been widely observed and is the subject of a review by the psychiatrist Hamburg (1971). The Bourke population in general confirmed this observation though there were many exceptions in the attitudes of individuals. There was a widespread vague distrust of newcomers unless they had an ascribed role such as a bank employee or a schoolmaster. No matter who they were, a definite delineation existed between 'locals' and 'blow-ins' with a period of over two decades needed to blur the distinction. Many of the local population exhibited a defensiveness which took the form of aggressive jokes at a newcomer's expense, a marked over-reaction to any real or imagined criticism of the rural life, and an often unreasoned resistance to any attempt to alter the *status quo*. The mildest of 'deviant behaviour' such as long hair and unorthodox dress was poorly tolerated, even when exhibited by those members of the community with ascribed status such as the clergy, general practitioners and schoolteachers.

In the eyes of many, experience was valued above learning and the ability to use one's hands commanded greater respect than the ability to use one's head. University 'experts' fell into the latter category and the following extract from an otherwise unusually liberally minded letter to the editor of the local weekly newspaper is illustrative of this attitude:

To my mind, before the final tragedy of extermination takes place at the hands of commercial exploitation, the Federal Government should make kangaroos a Commonwealth possession and assign good, ordinary, observant bushmen (not high-falutin professors of such and such a University) with no strings of commercialism attached to them to camp out all the year round on different station properties in different areas and quietly observe the habits, eating, breeding, migratory, numbers, etc. of the kangaroos.

(The *Western Herald*, 16 March 1973)

This anti-academic stance was probably related to the consciousness of their relative lack of formal education by most of the rural populace. In addition to the widespread distrust of 'outsiders' and 'academics' the local population proved to have a highly developed distrust of 'psychiatry'.

Attitudes to the mentally ill

A recent survey in Melbourne showed that despite a comprehensive mental health education programme which had been functioning for fifteen years, there existed in the community a great deal of misinformation, erroneous belief and prejudice against psychiatric institutions and the mentally ill (Graves *et al.*, 1971a and b). Bourke had never had any health education about mental illness. Attitudes to psychiatry in this area were several decades behind those reported in the Melbourne studies. Mental illness was still seen in terms of forcible restraint by the police, certification and incarceration. The reaction of the community to mentally ill people who became actively disturbed was to demand their hasty extrusion to the regional 'lunatic asylum' over almost 500 km away. The less disturbed mentally ill were tolerated but shunned. Many relatives of the mentally ill did not accept a diagnosis of psychiatric disorder easily, since they equated it with an inherited tendency to feeble-mindedness. This was especially true of those families who had achieved the status of local aristocracy by virtue of their predecessors having settled in the area several generations previously. They preferred to believe that the illness was due to some physical cause such as organic phosphorus poisoning from using sheep dip. Second and sometimes third opinions from specialists in capital cities were necessary before the need for psychiatric treatment was accepted. The myth of the rugged, individualistic pioneer dies hard in the west. Mental illness was regarded as being responsive to will

258

power and accepting psychiatric help was seen as a shameful admission of weakness, which was expressed by the frequent opening statement by a new patient of 'I never thought I'd have to stoop to this'.

The ambivalence of patients to receiving psychiatric care was expressed by broken appointments and, on occasion, by public ridicule of me as their therapist. There was a tendency to drop out of treatment early in an illness episode. If the patient later sought further treatment he would often excuse his failure to re-attend earlier by saying that he felt he had been getting better by his own efforts anyway.

Most patients did not like to be seen in the hospital foyer waiting for a psychiatric appointment and went to great lengths to avoid this. In the United States of America, a psychotherapist working in a small community off the coast of Massachusetts found that he needed two doors to his consulting centre—a front door and an anonymous side door (Mazer, 1970). In Bourke this situation also applied to home visits. A husband who requested an urgent house call spent more time telling me how his front door was jammed and explaining how to park in his back lane, than he did in telling me that his wife was destroying their house. Even patients who were referred to me for a physician's opinion felt that they were being tarred with a psychiatric brush.

Community attitudes towards myself as a psychiatrist

The most common irrational stereotypes of psychiatrists are that they are mind-readers, that they can define all your dirty or anti-social thoughts in which they have particular interest . . . (Caplan, 1964:202–203)

These stereotypes obviously existed in Bourke and accounted for some extraordinary exhibitions of irrational behaviour. Nearly all the guest speakers that I heard at various functions of the Rotary, Rotaract and Apex Clubs of Bourke were greeted with uncritical respect. On the few occasions when their views were challenged by one or two of the audience, it was clear that there was an accepted limit at which further criticism constituted bad manners and the offending member was always brought back into line by his peers. In my first year in Bourke I was conscious that I had so threatened the majority feeling that this unwritten rule, limiting a display of poor manners, did not apply to me.

Two months after I arrived in Bourke I addressed a service organisation to explain my project. The president replied that 'We've had psychologists, sociologists, anthropologists and a whole lot of other bloody "ists" up here all trying to find out if we're mad. I can't pick the difference between you and I'm blowed if I'm going to pay tax to support the likes of you'. He concluded with the statement that none of us 'knew our arses from our elbows'. A second member then arose and stated that I had 'conned him' by not telling him I was a headshrinker and warned me at the risk of a bloody nose to forget every word he had ever spoken to me before the meeting began.

In the early months of my residence in the area, I was conscious of the lack of ease of many people whom I engaged in social conversation and their conscious efforts to avoid allowing their gaze to meet with mine. Even after living in Bourke for two years my entry into a pub which I did not usually visit produced an instantaneous silence, followed by the defensive jest of 'Shut up boys! Here comes the headshrinker. He's going to analyse every word you say. The government's sent him up to see if we're all mad.'

Most of the local people did not realise that a psychiatrist was a qualified doctor who would be able to offer a medical service. In my first year in the area most white people addressed me as 'mister', with only a few obviously doing so to make the point that I was not in their view a 'proper doctor'. I was frequently asked if I was allowed to write a prescription and even the Clerk of Petty Sessions queried my right to issue a death certificate.

Helping agencies

One of the functions of a community psychiatrist is to assist other helping agencies in coping with psychiatric disorders in their community. The psychiatrist may help by direct or indirect consultation with a client, or by helping to plan for facilities which may be of benefit to the mental health of that community. The injection of a new role into the set patterns of a community needs to be accepted before it can make a contribution to the function of that community.

Teachers

The visits of the Education Department's Student Counsellor from Dubbo were valued by the headmasters in the area and my psychiatric assistance was seen by the schoolteachers as an extension of that service. Even so, one of the school principals rejected any such help. One schoolmaster, sincerely concerned about any psychological or medical difficulties in his students, was at first sceptical of the value of such a service, based on the lack of communication he had received and the lack of change in behaviour of the children he had referred to child guidance clinics in the past. Following two meetings with the teachers, it was agreed that I should spend one-and-a-half hours a week consulting with individual teachers about any children who were a worry to them. Only one teacher actively avoided making use of at least one session and about 30 per cent of teachers were regular consultees. Although the mental health consultation was ostensibly to assist the teacher in helping problem children, it was often used for helping with the teachers' own problems.

Many of the teachers were strained to the limit, especially those with a large proportion of Aboriginal children in their classes. Some took the view that their charges were ineducable and others that they personally were inadequate and untrained for such a task. In time, some teachers from the private school began to seek advice. I had little doubt that my liaison with teachers was fruitful.

Clergy

The clergy in this rural area were adept at discovering members of their community who were disturbed. All were grateful for help with congregants who exhibited psychiatric or acting out behaviour. The clergy, in turn, helped to keep a watch on patients with a psychiatric disorder who lived in isolated areas. Three of them assisted me in the therapy of several families, a situation in which I function better with such support. They also helped in an abortive attempt to resurrect Alcoholics Anonymous, and on some occasions by tempering the views of some of their congregants whose actions were obstructive to Aboriginal community development. At no stage did any of the clergy indicate that, as a therapist, I was trespassing on their territory. Indeed, two stated that they had developed greater insight into their counselling role from our collaborative experience. A psychiatrist in a rural area is culturally isolated and I found the relationship with some of the clergy to be an adequate substitute for the usual intra-professional contact to which I had become accustomed in a large city.

Police

In this small town, the thirteen policemen formed a beleaguered garrison against what they regarded as outside discrimination. Those policemen with more liberal views were fearful of the total isolation which could result if they were ostracised by both their colleagues and the townspeople. Because of the frequent turnover of senior staff, informal leadership was exercised by the officer with the longest period of local service. His views of psychiatry and myself as a psychiatrist were very strongly antipathetic and were adopted as the norm by the majority of police. No amount of direction from a sympathetic police inspector was of any avail in reversing these attitudes. My identification with and assistance to the Aboriginal community, especially with bail and the gaoling of children, was regarded as a challenge to the very ethic of the keepers of the law and added to the distrust in which I was held. It was a sad observation that at that point in time, working with Aborigines and with the police seemed to be mutually exclusive. Although I was rung 'off the record' by four different policemen for advice, and had policemen and their families as patients, and social and sporting acquaintances, I was never able to enter into any dialogue with the police body as a whole.

The Court

The attitudes of the police to me also extended to the courts. My offers of help were passively rejected in that the court continued to send Aboriginal children to remand centres for psychological assessment, despite my offer to fulfil this role. To send a child 800 km for an assessment by a psychiatrist, often with little if any knowledge of the cultural patterns and social background of the child, is a futile exercise which, combined with the lack of personal contact between psychiatrist and magistrate, does not help the magistrate in his sentence-making process. My lack of success in either being able to provide this information or advice, or in preventing the unnecessary distress that the legal separation process caused Aboriginal children and their parents, was a source of great concern to me.

Voluntary service organisations

The voluntary service organisations in the town were usually helpful in providing a forum in which I could present my views. A number of the members were liberal and fair-minded people whose opinions were respected in the town. They ensured that I usually obtained a fair hearing, especially when I was trying to dispel misconceptions about my role. Both the Rotary and the Apex Clubs assisted me on two occasions with finance and manpower.

General practitioners

There were five general practitioners in the rural area in which I worked and two in the town of Bourke. As a psychiatrist, I posed no threat to their medical status, and because of their work load, they were happy to have help in managing psychiatrically ill and inadequate patients. Partly for the same reason, and partly due to more pressing interests, all but one practitioner were unwilling to accept 'a client-centred case consultation'[1] (Caplan, 1964:214), except in regard to medication. They saw the role of the resident psychiatrist as a psychiatric houseman who would take over the total care of their more demanding patients. This has been described as the 'psychiatric dumping syndrome' (Malone, 1970:15).

I felt that to comply with the expectancies of my medical colleagues was to constrict my community role. The result was that they tended to by-pass my services altogether. Being very much at their mercy, I found that in order to function as a psychiatric doctor in the area I had to accept all those patients regarded by their practitioners as being in need of individualised psychiatric therapy.

Another difficulty of being a psychiatrist in a small community was that of knowing what to do when I recognised incipient or overt psychiatric distress in a person who had never been a patient of mine. An embarrassing situation twice arose when my observations about such people to the person's doctor were seen as interfering with another doctor's patients. Fortunately this response was not common.

Nursing staff

My relationship as a psychiatrist with nursing staff in the district hospitals was no different from that I had been used to in large general teaching hospitals. Those who had psychiatric nursing experience were co-operative and handled disturbed patients with ease. Those who lacked this experience tended to react with fear and anxiety and demand the transfer of the patient to the regional mental hospital. At the same time, nearly all the senior nursing staff displayed an interest in psychiatric conditions and when made aware of the special importance of confidentiality in this form of medicine, responded accordingly. The nursing staff were frequently instrumental in persuading distressed or

---

1. This consists of helping a doctor to treat his patient through discussion with the doctor but without actually seeing his patient.

disturbed acquaintances to seek psychiatric help. The Bush Nursing Staff in outlying areas obviously welcomed the opportunity to receive advice by 'phone which helped them to deal adequately with even major psychiatric emergencies.

Some difficulties with helping agents

A major difficulty encountered in working with many potential 'helping agents' was their apathy. This was most marked in those who were captive in the area, for example, teachers and policemen. These people often identified poorly with the local community. Their prime aim was to see out their two or three years without undue stress and most definitely without being labelled as a 'stirrer', a 'radical' or a 'communist' by becoming involved with people regarded as suspect because of their liberal views.

Another difficulty was the mobility of the service population which made the practice of community psychiatry like a game of snakes and ladders. Just as some mutual personal regard developed and action was imminent, the particular officer concerned was tranferred to another town and the community psychiatrist slid back to square one.

The lack of psychiatric anonymity

In a large city the psychiatrist is unlikely to come into frequent social contact with his patients, whereas this is not so in a small town. I may have treated a patient and then found myself sitting next to him an hour later at a Rotary Club function. Although, in theory, this could lead to a confusion of roles, in practice this was never a problem. The middle-class patients usually addressed me by my first name in any situation, the grazier and the working-class person demarcated my role themselves by addressing me as 'Doctor' in the professional and by my given name in the social situation.

Except on two occasions, patients seemed to have no fears over the confidentiality of their disclosures. This was surprising since relatives, friends and adversaries of the patient would stop me on the street to offer information which they thought would help me to 'solve the case'. After a while, I anticipated such occurrences and sought the patient's permission to discuss his problems or prognosis with other key figures in his life. This was seldom refused. Headmasters, bank managers and other men of standing in the community reacted adversely to being totally excluded from the concerns and possible prognosis of their subordinates. Co-operating with them was always more beneficial to the patient.

The American psychiatrist, Mazer (1970), working on a small island off the coast of Massachusetts, commented that his therapeutic successes and failures were on public view. Like him, I have often received credit for successes which I hardly deserved. One example of this was the cure of an alcoholic lady who ceased to drink following the exhortations of an evangelistic lay preacher while she was under my care in hospital.

The process of acceptance

The mental health professional must recognize that his position in a small community is based much more on his acceptance as a person than on his acceptance of a professional. (Tranel, 1970:427)

The beginnings of my acceptance as a person occurred through playing sport. One of the local aristocracy, a superior player having an off day, defeated me in the final of a tennis tournament supported by such advice as, 'Don't let him psyche you', 'He's hypnotising you. Change ends on the opposite sides to him.' The regional radio station reported that the local player defeated Dr M. Kamien, the Sydney psychiatrist. Perhaps because the local people had affronted their own sense of fair play, or because to play tennis was to be a normal human being, I began to become acceptable. Two years later we met again with the same result, except that by this time my opponent was the emotional underdog.

The second stage of acceptance came when I was seen to be offering a service at the convenience of the client and that many of them became asymptomatic or at least able to function. I was also seen to be a doctor who could cope as a general practitioner when no other doctor was available.

For reasons still obscure to me, many of the *dramatis personae* of the town considered that I had influence in the higher echelons of the state and the federal health services. Although this was exaggerated, I did agitate on behalf of such organisations as the Bush Nursing Association and the Isolated Children's Parents' Association. I had thus identified myself as being on the side of the community and had become a community asset. This change in attitude towards me was expressed by such compliments as, 'You don't seem to be like a psychiatrist', and by the withdrawal of the eponyms, 'headshrinker', 'nut-cracker', 'nut-doctor' and 'intellectual idiot'. The final proof of acceptance occurred at a Federal Conference of the Isolated Children's Parents' Association which was attended by over 600 delegates and two Federal Cabinet Ministers. The chairman, dissatisfied with the trend of the debate, without prior warning prevailed upon me to 'put some sanity back into the proceedings'. At the meeting, while describing the difficulties of these isolated families, I mentioned that in one rural area 40% of the white females had consulted me because of emotional distress. Eleven women promptly rose to their feet or raised their hands and said, 'Me'. Even allowing for the optimal emotional atmosphere, this occasion could be regarded as the acceptance of psychiatry in the Shire of Bourke.

Fear of psychiatry and the psychiatrist had diminished in the space of two-and-a-half years. Several very disturbed people who had hidden their troubles for years from all but their close relatives finally thought it safe enough to seek psychiatric help. Suggestions to admit patients to either the regional mental hospital or a university unit were accepted as little different from transfer for a physical disease. I am still credited by some people with Mandrake-like powers of instant hypnotism. However, instead of people fearing these imagined powers they asked for them to be harnessed in their fight against such conditions as smoking and obesity. It cannot be claimed that it has yet become a status symbol to have attended a psychiatrist, but few still regarded it as a shameful sign of weakness and several publicly acknowledged their psychiatric patient role at farewell functions to me. Six months after my departure, the Bourke branch of the Australian Labor Party passed a resolution to petition the Minister for Health to improve local facilities for the mentally ill in the western region of New South Wales (The *Western Herald*, 18 January 1974).

The conceptual basis and theory of community psychiatry has been described by Caplan (1964). Applying his criteria, I could only be described as a naive community psychiatrist with a set of faulty techniques. I find the approach of *How to win friends and influence people* (Carnegie, 1936) incongruent and distasteful and so did not cultivate a group of people who could interpret my role to the community. In truth, I was not sure what my role would be. I do not enjoy hanging around pubs, the major place of social intercourse in this area, nor entertaining people simply because they are influential. I think my role definition in the community was blurred because I also functioned as a physician and as a general practitioner and community developer to the Aboriginal population in the town, and this desire to be all medical things to all men was seen as a status threat by my colleagues.

Despite the stereotypes I have painted in my description of attitudes in the town, there existed a number of people who could only be described as fair-minded. It was their perception of the irrationality of the degree of rejection which I at first encountered which eventually began to reverse the tide of opinion in the area. This change was greatly assisted by my being seen to be both a relatively normal person who did normal things and by becoming known for assisting people both black and white in my professional capacity. In retrospect, I believe that a community psychiatrist (like any change agent) is likely to be less acceptable in the long term if his behaviour is incongruent to his normal nature, so that he is perceived to be playing a role, than if he remains congruous and is seen to exhibit similar behaviour to most other people.

Community psychiatry has not been found to be an easy discipline by those who have practised it at grass roots level. The ability to tolerate ambiguity, confusion and frustration is a necessary quality in those who wish to try (Panzetta, 1971; Mazer, 1970; Tranel, 1970). In rural Australia, the community psychiatrist needs to be able to cope with the hostility and rejection which arise from the anxiety and threat that mental illness, and by association those who deal with it, still arouses in the community. If the psychiatrist can ride out the initial storms without incurring the everlasting wrath of the Neptunes in that community, they will gradually open their ranks and the practice of community psychiatry will become possible, rewarding and increasingly useful in the process of social change.

Chapter 14

Nurturing leadership— the changing views and fluctuating feelings of emergent Aboriginal leaders

The development of leadership is one of the factors needed to change a disintegrated Aboriginal community into one that is able to function both socially and politically. Those who emerge and/or are elected as leaders have a difficult task that is fraught with anxiety. In Bourke the Aboriginal leaders found that the support of their 'constituents' was spasmodic and that even finding out what their 'constituents' wanted was often a confusing exercise. The leaders had to learn to tolerate and resolve feelings of ambivalence to each other, to me as a change agent, to other white 'helpers' and to the lack of definition in their job. They had to cope with accusations by their peers that they were being manipulated by whites and were thus betraying their fellow Aborigines. At the same time they had to overcome their uncertainty and reticence in negotiating with influential white people such as the shire clerk, the building inspector, the school headmasters and the matron and chief executive officer of the district hospital. Complaining to the police about incidents of alleged police discrimination and heavy handedness against Aborigines required even greater courage.

When the first field officers who had been elected in February 1972 began to work at the beginning of April, I spent each Monday lunch hour with them. They either discussed their problems or brought tape-recordings of thoughts that had occurred to them during the week and we listened to these and deliberated over them. The exact reproduction of these tapes would add greatly to the length of this book. Also much of the content is fairly repetitive and so, with their permission, I have taken the liberty of reproducing extracts of some of these tapes, verbatim, to illustrate some of the changing attitudes and feelings of developing Aboriginal leaders. In addition these comments present a brief picture of some of the events and changes which occurred through other eyes beside my own.

268

To the best of my knowledge, these two Aborigines were the first full-time, democratically elected Aboriginal leaders in New South Wales whose election was a purely Aboriginal affair without white influence or interference. I hope that in the future their comments and insights will be read and discussed by other emergent Aboriginal leaders as a basis for understanding their similar ambivalences and anxieties in their new and vital role. I would further hope (probably a forlorn hope), that white people whose executive actions affect Aborigines would also read this one chapter. It may act as an eye-opener to those who view Aborigines as non-thinking, non-persons.

The two elected field officers: who they were

Mr Wally Byers

"I was very small. My life was not very promising. We lived in West Dubbo. Dad was in the Army and away a lot, so I can remember real plain when our family broke up. We went away with Mum and our stepfather to Wellington. There we lived in a little pump house in one of the gardens where Mum started to drink and go on; it wasn't all that good. She ended up in Sydney with a crook chest, and died not long after, so that left us with our relations which was not real good for they did not worry very much about our welfare. If they had been a little more harder on me I would not have got to go around and get into trouble. I left Peak Hill not long after that and we started to hitch hike about and started to get in as much drink as I could.

I came to Bourke and went to work on *Windbar* for three years as a gardener. I guess when I went to *Windbar* was when I first started to understand people, and talk up for what was really mine, like we were watching the boss fellow kill a roo one day and a fair few of the boys were all standing around. I happened to walk over to where the big boss was killing the roo and I said to him: 'This is a bloke who knows how to kill a roo'. He looked at me and he said: 'Bullshit, don't go that far'. It was all right, I never said nothing. A few weeks later, one of the big heads came down to inspect the station we were working on. I happened to be cleaning the boss's car at the time, and he walked over to us, and he said: 'This is Wally here; he does a good job, keeping the cars and everything trim'. I turned around to the boss fellow then, and I said to him: 'Oh, look, bullshit, don't go that far'. From the expression he had on his face, I learned words can hurt just as much as getting in a scrap. After that lot, we got to understand each other, we knew where we stood with each other, which was very good, I reckon, for after that whenever he went away anywhere, he'd always bring home something or fetch me back something. He sort of put a lot of trust on me after that, I reckon this is only from speaking up for your rights.

I left the station and came to Bourke and met Patsy.[1] I used to still drink and be locked up every weekend. The police told me I was another E.O. (the name of the man most affected by drink in Bourke), which was not very nice. I said to myself: 'Wally, old boy, you have to wake up to yourself'. So, I got a job on the meat works, and everything was going fine. I used to get drunk every so often, but not as often as before. I think my really changing came at the meat works. Working one night, I took a load of bones down to the boilers. There were three or four blokes down there, and they were trying to get a leg of reject bullock which was down in the boiler. I went to give them a hand to release it. We had a double headed hook, and I happened to be unfortunate to get the hook in my hand, and went over the boiler. If nobody had been there, I would have gone down for sure. It sure is funny how many thoughts can go through your head when death is only a few seconds away. It was not so bad when the hook was in the back of my hand, I was saying to the men, hang on to me, but when it got to the palm of my hand, I was praying to God for them to let me go. It seemed like it was unreal. After that, I guess I was more for helping other people. You could say that was the changing point in my life.

After that, I got on the shire collecting garbage and put in about nine years. When we were going around the run, it was great to hear so many kids say: 'Here comes Uncle Wal'. Not just the Reserve, but all over town. Then Max Kamien came along, and wanted us to do something to help the dark people; that is when I thought that I might be of some real help, and the people thought so too.''

Pastor Bill Reid

''I just want to state some of my earlier memories. But I just can't pin point just where they began or how far it was that they were apart. The earliest memory that I have is of my father coming home from work. He'd been working on a station and we walked down the flat to meet him down from the mission house, and when I got there, he had a billy

1. Now his wife.

an full of grubs. Grubs were my favourite dish, and I was quite pleased to be allowed to carry the can, knowing that I would get a good feed.

I don't remember much about my father. I was only four when he died; a horse had kicked him in the stomach. I don't know what happened, but I had a stepfather; I don't know when my mother got married again, but this other man had come to live with us, and I eventually learnt that he was my stepfather. He was quite a good man. He didn't hurt us in any way. He didn't flog us or anything like that, and provided for us fairly well, as well as can be expected in those days.

My grandfather was a great favourite of mine. He was fairer than my father but he knew everything about the old laws of the Gamilaroi. He used to tell me about them. He was blind for as long as I knew him and he lived in the Aboriginal way in a low camp around a fire.

I had a feeling that my brother was more favoured than what I was. They seemed more proud of Fred than of me. Maybe they had good reasons to because he was working for his living, he was a good horserider and he was a fairly smart boy, whereas I was only small, and going to school. I felt people protected me rather than letting me go out like they did Fred. Fred could look after himself and I was not able to do that; they were frightened of me getting hurt.

We used to work on a station, where my stepfather was employed. These station people used to treat us as one of the family, used to take my sister for a holiday to Sydney and pay her fifteen shillings a week. It was a pretty good pay at the time for a girl, and she was on wages all the time. My brother was also employed there; he used to do station work there, and was on a wage, although he was only 14 or 15 years of age. I was not being schooled during the time that I was there. When I reached school age, we had to leave the station and we came to Pilliga mission. It was a good place, except for the manager, who professed to be a Christian. But there was not a qualified teacher for the school and they couldn't teach anyone above third class. However, I learnt to put in taps, running the water along the mission station, digging toilet holes, running telephone wires, fencing, gardening, anything that required manual work. The manager's wife used to teach the girls to keep her place spic and span. None of us had much of an education at school.

One of the things that hurts me now is the fact that if any man spoke up at the mission, he was blackballed or disqualified from coming within a radius of five miles of the mission. The town was only three miles away, and even if he was seen in town he was locked up. The man had to either leave the district or sneak up at times to see his family. This may have served to cause me to be what I am today in taking a stand for my people and trying to help them in the way that I am at present.

I would like to mention some special likes and dislikes that I have had. I am referring to things that may have caused these dislikes such as stories that my mother had told me, especially one of a tribe being rounded up, put into a yard and surrounded by white men, and when these people wanted to leave the yard they were rushed on by the elders of the tribe, telling them to keep quiet, and that the white man was going to bring them flour and tobacco. However, the white men returned with shear blades tied on sticks and began running them out the gates, and as they ran past, stabbing them with the shear blades, pulling the young babies out of their mothers' arms and hitting them on the ground. I used to feel real hatred for the white people when I heard tales like this, and there are quite a few tales that I could relate pertaining to this kind of treatment. This could have caused a feeling of hatred in later life for white people, mistrust over people who shouldn't have been mistrusted because maybe they were trying to do something good.

I didn't like the idea of [black] people who worked on stations being separated from white people when they came to eating, some of them even eating outside on the wood heap. I don't know if a lot of people do this, but nowadays it is not so common, but at the times I am talking about, it was quite a common occurrence to be treated in this manner. In those days our boys and girls couldn't get a full education. After they were 14, they were apprenticed at a mission station at a miserable fee. All they had was clothing and food and 1/6 a week for the work they did. This would add up to £40 or £50 by the time they reached the age of 18. They were supposed to put it in the bank; this was to set them up in later life.

When I was 13, I went to work ring-barking [trees] around Wee Waa. I went droving when I was 16. I hadn't seen much of Australia apart from western New South Wales, so I decided to go to Dubbo when I was 18. I got in with Bill Ferguson[1] and was elected secretary of the newly

1. Bill Ferguson was one of the first Aborigines in Australia to fight for Aboriginal rights. His struggles are described in the book *Vote Ferguson for Aboriginal Freedom* by J. Horner. Australian and New Zealand Book Company, Sydney, 1974.

ormed Aborigines Progressive Association. We went on a tour of northern New South Wales in an old Essex ute with a slogan slung across the back: 'Citizenship for Aborigines'. We didn't have any money and had to play gum leaves and sing to get some money for petrol and food. We lived on pumpkin, potatoes and stale bread. I couldn't write too good so Bill Ferguson would write the letters and I would copy up to a hundred of them by hand. I was a sort of human cyclostyling machine. We broke up in Tenterfield. I've done lots of things since. I went boxing in Jimmy Sharman's tents. That's why my brain gets addled sometimes. I've run my own fencing team and wood yard but it didn't work out. I came to Bourke in about 1940. The wages were good there. They paid you the same as the white guys. In Wee Waa they only paid a half [of white wages]. I joined the shire in 1965 and stayed there till I became a field officer."

Initial reactions of the two elected field officers

The field officers took up their duties at the beginning of April 1972. Their initial reaction was one of excitement and increased self-esteem.

I think the Aboriginal people are quite keen on the field officers, or they wouldn't have elected us in the first place. I'm only just too proud to be working with them and getting the co-operation of some of them behind me. It makes me feel that underneath they feel they have something to work for and that they understand me a little better and that I will help. I think both of us will get more co-operation from the people by letting them get out and do something for themselves. I think this idea of field officers will be successful, because we are both real keen about the idea. (Quoted from an interview with the field officers by Radio-station 2SM Sydney, 3 April 1972.)

This feeling of elation was quickly followed by a realisation that the new job was difficult, the hours of work irregular and that there were new strains and complications involving a field officer's family and provoking jealousy and insecurity from his wife.

My first three weeks as a field officer are quite difficult. It is hard to understand the work and also the people. I am not sure of myself, for I am used to working for someone else. Even my wife makes it difficult for me. I wanted to go to school the other night but when she knew another woman was going along she wouldn't let me. If she would only try and understand. If I can't get through to my wife it's even harder to get through to someone else.

The other day we called a meeting at a bad time and the people would not move from the bingo to go and see about houses which were for their own good. I got very annoyed and lost my temper.

I'm most interested in finding out what most Murries want and how much time they are prepared to put into it. They will have to change for their families' sakes but I

273

would not like to see them lose their own old ways. If they could understand what they want before they shifted into things like houses, we could arrange things to help them to be more contented and to be happy.

As I said before, the work for the Aborigines is hard. Without a strong committee which is not frightened to speak up when you try to make a decision and tell you you are wrong, you can make all kinds of mistakes. Perhaps things will work themselves out after a while, but they could get worse. That remains to be seen. The dark people are always trying to understand but they are like myself. They will make decisions which they think are right. Then they turn out to be wrong. It's everyone on the committee's problem to try to get a better understanding of things and help each other. Max [the change agent] should be a member of our committee because I don't think it's right for him to be left out of it. We are not strong enough yet and we still need help. For instance, at the rate we are going we will be bankrupt in six months if we don't wake up to ourselves.

The other field officer reported that:

The first week of my appointment as a field officer entailed having the names of as many as are eligible to vote submitted for inclusion on the State Electoral Roll. The need for this action was explained as 'giving them a voice with the Member of this area'. I was not surprised to hear that those of our people who had been previously approached by whites on the matter of voting were also told that it was not necessary for an Aborigine to be on the Electoral Roll.

My letters to Mr Ian Mitchell requesting a grant for adult education have eventually resulted in $740 being made available to us. A meeting was arranged with several teachers in regards to classes and the subjects being taught. The response was rather surprising for quite a number came forward in the hope of learning to read and write, or to better the education they already had. The subjects that are going to be taught include typing, English, maths, arts and crafts, reading, writing and mechanics. It was also decided that a secondhand Toyota minibus be purchased by the Association and that this be used in the general service of our people. When the bus arrived we learnt it was necessary to have an endorsement of our licenses to certify our ability after a driving test to be able to drive the vehicle. The failure to pass our tests on the first and second opportunity means that we had to practise a lot, especially in changing gears, before we finally had our licenses endorsed. We spent a lot of time organising a barbecue for the take-over ceremony of the bus. I had an interesting meeting with Mrs Frost and Father Glynn from the Australian Freedom From Hunger Campaign and they informed me that they were very happy with the election of Wally and me as field officers.

We have lost a great deal of time and had some setbacks with the Shire Council. This brings me to the conclusion that our movements must be clear and precise. When our plans are presented for approval by the Council we should be perfectly clear in every aspect pertaining to the project in mind. We must also plan on the rental payments to recoup the outlay by the Building Society. The negotiations with the Council [about building the first house] have resulted in the plans being set aside as being sub-standard. This is disappointing in that so much time has been taken up with this kind of run-around. Our architect will be at the next Council meeting to explain and if necessary, make modifications to the building plans.

This week I have covered 400 miles [c. 650 km] in my own car and doing work for the A.A.A. All things considered I think it's good to see such an admixture of young and old getting together in an attempt to bring about a change in our present condition.

The duties of a field officer

An example of a fairly typical week in the life of a field officer is taken verbatim from Bill Reid's report for the week ending 30 July 1972:

Monday　After talking to Max and having lunch I returned to the Department of Main Roads to talk with the yard boss about getting equipment to be used in consolidating the soil for the building project. I eventually caught up with the yard boss who promised to be available for the job. I then learned that John Luckens [one of the white helpers on the building project] had previously made arrangements with another contractor to finish the soil. I then went to Wood Bros. about the timber and learned that it was all there. After work there was a good roll-up for the clean-up effort around the houses and this speaks of promise if the interest can be kept alive. On Tuesday the Shire Clerk asked to see me and he told me we had forfeited our clean-up deposit for the use of the oval because of neglecting to clean up the mess made by the crowd during the sports. I then went to Mr Armstrong [a lawyer] and received verification of the lease and building application which I had signed. I then wrote to Canberra about the building grant since we had had no word from them as yet. I went to the train to meet the architect but he failed to put in an appearance probably because of the threatened train strike.

The bus run is a real time consumer taking up most of the mornings and a good part of the afternoons. I can't see that there is much being accomplished in the run from the Reserve to the Convent School as the children only come to the centre and walk the rest of the way to school.

The Shire Clerk came up and told me that drastic action was to be taken in regards to unclean premises, not only in Aboriginal houses but with white people too. He asked me to inform our people and to seek their co-operation in placing their rubbish in one place and then the Council would come and remove it especially any old cars that need to be taken away.

I feel that I need an office away from home and that would be a great advantage to us in getting more work done. There are far too many interruptions in the course of a day to allow for any great efficiency in our work, untrained as we are for this type of work. On Wednesday, Professor Hollows[1] visited and we went to Enngonia to assist him in getting people for the eye testing. Wally assisted him in interviewing the people.

We had a general meeting Wednesday night and that went well. We dealt with several matters which included bus service payments, the medical benefit fund, the housing society and the choosing of the building workers, who will be used to take over the training of others who may desire to learn this trade. The names of twelve applicants were submitted for consideration, the choosing of these workers was left to John Ferguson, Gladys Ebsworth, John Luckens, Bernie Coates and myself. On the Thursday I was approached by P. M. [a 44 year old Aboriginal woman] to obtain a loan of enough

1. Associate Professor of Ophthalmology, University of New South Wales.

money to pay for the fare to Sydney, her son being in trouble and having to be taken to court for some reason or another. On Friday I typed a circular and delivered it to the people in the area due for a clean-up campaign that we hoped to conduct in the area with the co-operation of the Council. On Friday I later read a letter of protest to the housing commission on behalf of a Mrs L. O., requesting that her request to have a broken stove replaced with an electric stove be honoured. Her former requests had been ignored and she had been forced to cook on an open fire in the yard for the last nine months.

Some difficulties reported by the Aboriginal field officers

Lack of white skills

A major problem for the field officers was their lack of skill in the areas of literacy, accounting and in understanding the white business and legal system. It was a measure of the intelligence, motivation and persistence of these two main leaders that one learnt to type with fluency and the other who was functionally illiterate in 1972 was able to write an eight foolscap page letter to me in 1974.

By 1976 many Aborigines including the field officers, had insights into the white man's systems without being able to fully manipulate them. However in 1972 the lack of even minimal white skills caused the Aboriginal leaders great anxiety and put them at a severe disadvantage when negotiating with white people or with governmental agencies. Examples of such anxieties are expressed in the following statements.

I have been endeavouring to work out a table for the hospital benefit fund. The problem that I find hard to work out is how to enter them all into the books as I would want the books to be done in such a manner as to be clearly understood by anyone with little understanding of bookwork.

I had a go at running another meeting which was no good. If I didn't have to read any papers it would be a lot easier for me to talk and get people into conversation and try to find out what they really want.

Contact with white authority figures

The Aboriginal field officers like other Bourke Aborigines introjected the role of the second class citizen. Their new position placed them in the situation of having to shed this role and act as spokesmen seeking a fair deal for other Aborigines.

The police were by far the most difficult people they had to approach and this required a certain type of inner courage. Later they lost their initial diffidence with policemen and learnt that the relationship with them did not necessarily have to be all in the one direction.

One of my biggest problems is just talking to Gubs. I get all shook up going to see people like Harvey [a policeman] and I know I shouldn't—he's just another bloke.

When we were at Enngonia we got a bad report from some women who had been locked up all day without any food. I went to see the Welfare Officer to enquire into the truth of this matter. I then went to the police and enquired into the reason why one of our boys was refused rations. The officer in charge gave me no reason and said that I should ask the person why he was sacked from the shire. It is a worrying thing to be placed in this situation for I become confused and unsure of myself. However, I approached the Welfare Officer to see what could be done in regard to getting rations for the wife and children.

While I was visiting the Reserve I was approached by a woman who explained her son had been picked up by the police for being drunk. I was asked if I would approach the police and see if anything could be done on behalf of this person because he was not drunk. I said I would go to the police station with the woman. I went to the police and explained the circumstances of the case as they were stated to me. I asked for a blood test to be performed. The constable referred me to the sergeant who after hearing me declined to submit the lad to a blood test on the grounds that two hours had elapsed since his arrest. His mother failed to put in an appearance. The next day I approached the police station in regards to getting an appointment with the inspector of police. This came about from the meeting [of the A.A.A.] where it was brought to the notice of all present that some juveniles had been put in gaol. On endeavouring to contact those who stated that they would be available to go to the police station with me only Wally was available as the others said that they had to go to work or else they had gone out into the bush.

Standing out like a sore finger and causing a good deal of discussion among our people is what took place on Saturday in the blitz on blacks by the police. There were about twenty arrests; some of these were not necessary. It seems to me that too many were arrested on Saturday. It looks as if the police have just set their mind on a blitz on blacks. I was on the Reserve with Margaret Laurie [Liaison Officer of the Department of Aboriginal Affairs in Canberra] talking to different people when a police wagon came down at O.G's place. He was asleep lying on the ground alongside the wall of his place. A policeman walked over, placed his foot on O. and shook him with his foot and kept calling him to wake up. I was under the impression that he was waking him up to arrest him so I walked over and spoke to him. I said 'The man is all right, he is not doing any harm, his is asleep at his own place'. I was told to attend to my own business and that the young constable would attend to his. He said he wanted to talk to O. so I said 'Go ahead'. He asked O. if he had seen a yellow Bic pen [a 15-cent ball point pen]. I don't know if this was an excuse or if he had intended to arrest O. He got back into his wagon and drove off but before he drove off he said, 'I'll be quite inside the law to arrest this man as this is a public place, the area is not fenced and I could have locked this man up if I wished'.

277

I have contacted Mr Renshaw, M.L.A. and Mr Waddy's office [Minister for Child Welfare and Social Welfare] regarding the meaning of the 1969 Aborigines' Act. They have placed my complaint in the hands of the Crown Solicitor and Mr Waddy has promised to act on this solicitor's advice. [No further communication on this matter was ever received.]

Self-doubts

Feeling their way in a strange new world at the same time that they were finding themselves in a new role-relationship with other Aborigines often gave rise to feelings of self-doubt in the field officers.

What makes me mad is the Gubs. They are a funny lot. The Murries get a grant of $32,000 and then the Gubs come and tell the Murries it is good to shift off the Reserve and join in a self-help project with everyone living happy ever after. But they don't tell the Murries the bad side of these things which are the side they should tell them. A house at $7,500 will take the Murries a hell of a long time to pay back, where, if the government would give a grant of $32,000 to the Reserve that would be really common sense. For they could make small houses and there would be enough of them to make the Reserve a better place to live. They could plant some trees and make lawns and really get things looking up. I am sure the Murries on the Reserve don't want to shift away so why do we [field officers] have to be the ones who have to judge what is best for them when we can see how much harder we make it for them. If we [field officers] don't fit into white society, why should we try to make the other Murries think that they will fit in. We should tell them it is not easy when you have to pay rates, maintenance and electric light bills. Do you think that that would make them happy then? These are the things that I would like to know. But when they shift up into a big house it will cause the Murries much unhappiness when the wife wants to live like 'Mrs Jones' and the husband feels his pocket cannot take it. That's when they will really start to argue. I guess I'm getting paid for spoiling things. I am what I am but I don't think I could be dishonest to the Murrie. You might call us the spoilers [the field officers] because we think we know what the Murries want but we don't, because it's only the Murries who can tell you. I've been talking to some of the Murries down on the Reserve again and I come up with this little lot. They say that with so much change going on down there it is getting better all the time so they are feeling that with so many changes it is better to stop where they are. At least they don't have many worries yet but they could have when they move up to town.

John Luckens comes up to me and says 'Can we have a meeting tonight, we have to discuss the proposition that Dr Coombs made?' and I say 'O.K.' and when I get there I discover that this is just to get a group where there was the builders plus Max saying that I am always wrong and that I should come around to their way of thinking. But if they would come half way to my way of thinking I would be satisfied. Mannie said that Archie said that I was dishonest and then John Luckens says it is bad when your own colour starts to criticise. Max says that's not important, what is, is do you want all the rest of the people to have a house? I am not working to get a house, I am just working to see that other people get a house. Then Max says T.O. [a woman] can't have a house and G.T. [a man] can't have a house and that really shat me off for as I said before, where there is life there is hope. So it is only natural that I want out. But after speaking it out with Max I have decided that these people need me to give them a lot more encouragement yet. I am sure we will soon sit down and have a long talk as soon as we shape up again. It is funny when you come to think about it, for once the Murries had nothing going, then they get a grant of $32,000 and they are squabbling over houses and they are at each other's throats. They think someone is getting more opportunities than the next Murries and it seems the way they are it gets more complicated all the time. They think that when they get a house their troubles are over, but it is only the beginning.

Wally seems to be very unsure of himself seeming to be ever ready to take it out on Max or any other white person who happens to say anything. This is now making me unsure too as I'm at a point where I'm beginning to wonder if I may be missing something that is clear to Wally but lost on me.

Fear of rejection by their constituents

A further cause for self-doubt and erosion of self-confidence arose from their ambivalent feelings to their new role. Most binding decisions in the Bourke Aboriginal community were evolved by a process of consensus. The new role of field officer tended to change this decision making process in that many Aborigines now relied on 'the field officers' to make the decisions. The field officers on the other hand were then responsible for decisions which had formerly been determined by a group. Their new position of authority resulted in considerable insecurity either from the fear of misusing that authority or from being rejected by their friends because of their new relationship with them.

The thing I don't like is to tell Murries one thing and have to go back and tell them another thing. Murries are a trusting people. If you say something they believe it and then if it doesn't work out they get disappointed and forget about it. It's like when Max says to get a lot of people together to go to Armidale to that workshop to which we want to go. So I get a lot of people and then Max says to go back and tell them there isn't enough money to take them all. It makes me feel no good. It makes me feel like a Gub to promise the Murries somethimg and then change it.

I don't like knocking anyone back. If I do knock them back then it plays on my mind.

It is about time that we got through to the Murries that to gain a little more than we have they have to give a little bit in return. This is very hard for me to do, to tell other Murries to start paying for things because they are all used to getting things for nothing and it is not so easy to change these things. Like when I'm supposed to tell people who haven't paid they can't get on the bus. Or when three or four little white kids hop on to the bus I haven't the heart to tell them 'No'. If I have to do things like that it gives me a bad conscience and it really bothers me.

279

I don't feel that there is much the A.A.A. can do now with the employment situation as it is. We [the field officers] feel self-conscious about approaching our people in regard to money matters because we are just turned out. Because of the worries which people have about money they must feel inadequate to cope with the situation as it is without us adding to their hardships.

Confusion about what Aborigines want

One of the difficulties I faced as a change agent was finding out what Bourke Aborigines really did want. This was no less of a difficulty for the field officers and at first was a source of confusion and uncertainty for them, especially when they had to commit themselves to a decision.

The Murries are at a stage where they don't know what they want. They come up with a new answer every time. Like when we pulled a name out of a hat [for the houses] Peter . . .'s name came out and it was rejected, then they had another go at the hat and came up with Mannie . . . so that was O.K. The same with bingo, no more complaints until the general meeting then some people say it's not right and a week later they say it is right. We don't know what is right and it seems that some of them do not know what they are talking about.

Ambivalence about the job

The job of the field officers is not easy and in Bourke their feelings about their job ranged from optimism to total pessimism depending on their most recent successes or failures. In the early days their most common emotion about their job and the emotion they had to learn to handle was that of ambivalence.

Well I am continuing to work for the Murries. We are getting them to move a little at a time. It is certainly hard to make them realise that they themselves are stronger than any field officer and that until they realise it our job is uphill. With so many things going for them they only have to pull together and really try to understand one another and work together because without the voice of the people we are nothing. If we could only get them interested and hold their interest, that is half the battle. Murries are real hard to understand and easy to get discouraged, you only have to make a mistake or two and get too far away from them and too involved with whites. One person with a few Gubs is easily swayed to see things Gubs way which is usually the wrong way because when a Murrie sees you too much with the whites he never tells you the truth and thinks you want to do everything without the other Murries.

Are we just as bad as the old handout system in catering to Murries' whims without some mention of the need to pay for these services? We have been elected to the position of field officers by the people because they believe that we have the ability to do something that could help them with their problems. Certainly we have met with government bodies and have been instrumental in setting up grants for housing, sport, benefits, etc. But I'm beginning to realise now that we've missed the main issue, which is the building up of our people to the point of independence. I am sure that we are failing to do this and that we are only helping to delay any tendency that they may have towards a forward step in this direction. The real problem that surrounds our people is that of a lack of confidence in their ability to do some particular thing for themselves. Our job is to cater for this need rather than to do something for them which they are quite capable of doing without our help. Our people need to be able to cope with the little things like keeping the bus service going before taking on big steps of going into houses and paying rent.

I have changed to the handout system too. I remember when I first came to Bourke. All I knew was working hard for something that I wanted, but all that is changed. When I saw a place in Bourke for a job as a field officer I started to think like a Gub. I said to myself, here is your chance to get a cushy job. And by working on the mistakes made by others I seem to know people pretty well. The others who could have been field officers used to knock people who could have put them in as field officers whereas I made sure I had them on my side. So when it all boils down I have moved in on another man's mistakes because I have a certain feeling about people. But I am paying for that mistake now. No matter how good we are there will always be someone better. It is really my conscience that bothers me. I have the feeling I am getting paid for sitting down and that is certainly not the bloke I knew. I can remember when I got my first car. Some people used to say it is funny that you should have a car for we have been around here for all our lives and not got a car and you an outsider can get a car. You can understand people who are straightforward with you and who you know are a little jealous. It is different now when they say you have a car the black power bought for you.

I feel that we are failing to fulfil the real purpose of our job by not being continually with our people searching and observing while drawing them out about their likes and dislikes and problems. If we did this we could arrive at a closer answer to the things that we should be really concerned about and get closer to our people to get the true meaning of what we should really be doing.

Pessimism

At times ambivalence gave way to black pessimism. At these times the change agent needed to point to the positive things which a field officer had accomplished. This eventually tended to restore perspective to the field officers' life and job view.

I get very discouraged with the Murries at times. Like yesterday afternoon. I went to the Reserve, there was a bit of dust blowing and a slight rain. The boys said it looked too much like rain to go to football training. Johnny Mumbler [the Aboriginal coach] went down to the oval three times. He must have been discouraged too for he had told us we will need a lot more training. I really got uptight about it. I was mad at the Murries. When I went to the meeting that night I took it out on Max. It's just that I put too much faith in the Murries when they aren't ready yet.

281

Every day seems harder for me. I seem to lose a lot of faith in the Murries. There is a lot of things going for them but they don't seem interested. It is certainly hard to get them to join any of the things we have going for them. I think the Welfare Board and the government have a lot to do with spoiling the dark people. They gave them so much and asked the Murries for so little in return for the handouts. It's like I've always said it's the white man's fault. I know I am most times wrong but there is an old saying 'A good Murrie can work if you don't feed him. For once you feed him he will go to sleep'.

Relationships with Aborigines

In general the field officers had a deep understanding of the democratic process and as described earlier in this chapter tried hard to find out what their fellow Aborigines wanted in order to fulfil their expressed needs. However, the Aboriginal leaders had few models on which to pattern their behaviour and it was not surprising that one of the phases through which they inevitably passed, especially when excessively frustrated by the non-cooperation of their constituents, was a copy of the authoritarian behaviour that they had observed and to which they had been subjected by white authority figures in the past.

My general feelings at this juncture are that in order to make any headway with our people we must keep after them. That is if we make any statement in regards to a particular rule by which they are to abide, then should they fail to observe same they should be acquainted of the fact. I am of the opinion that they should be made to realise that it would be so much easier for all to keep to a strict schedule or a least to be on reasonable time.

We had a meeting to discuss the forming of the building society which seems to me to be getting a little confusing in that the rules are all there for us to see but the thing to work out is how we are going to make it work in our community. How are we to get our people to face up to their responsibilities in the upkeep of payments of rent when we can't get them to contribute to such things as the funeral fund, medical fund, bus and ambulance which would only cost them $6 a month.

I am not at all happy with the building boys, they can't seem to grasp the idea that the thing that they are doing is more than just a job. I have tried to explain to them that they should be proud of doing something for their people. We are trying to prove that we can be trusted to carry out our responsibilities and that we can succeed where the old style of welfare has failed.

More Murries should join in and not just Bill and myself. We go on doing a lot on our own. As for the committee, I'm getting sick of running around for them. They really should be a working mob instead of just sitting back and giving orders.

What makes me wild is that when we have a meeting of committee members, or just a meeting, we make a motion that should be carried out, which isn't. If we can't carry them out why make them. Like, the bus was supposed to be off the road last weekend but I see it still going around.

When Bill and myself try to talk to some loud-mouthed Murrie and tell him to talk to other Murries and so make our job a bit easier, they say 'he (the field officer) gets $90 a week'. So what the hell do you expect Bill and myself to feel if they won't wipe their backside and join in and try to do something.

Relationships between Aboriginal leaders

The relationship between the two main Aboriginal leaders was like most human interactions, one of fluctuating feelings ranging from admiration and solidarity to rejection, criticism and competition.

A meeting with Pastor Roberts seems to have made a big change in Bill. He seems different, he seems to have a lot of confidence in himself. The day after that meeting with Pastor Roberts I saw Bill speak up to the building inspector in a way I was glad to see him doing, and not only that, he came with me to the Clerk of Petty Sessions and he spoke up there too. If we went round together we could accomplish a lot by doing things like that, we could really start pushing other people like the police and make a big noise. But that puts me in the position of doubt because if we don't have the backing of the Murries we could really make a shambles of things for ourselves.

I've been thinking about the situation between the Murries, Bill and myself. I really don't think we have much communication with each other. For if we really want to understand each other we have to pull together and learn to work together. It's not just at a meeting but every day to let everybody know what is going on. Bill and myself haven't the faintest idea of what each of us are doing since we don't do things together. When I see Bill going around with a book and a pen I naturally think it is much easier for him and yet he never asks me to go. So I think everything is O.K. Then we have a meeting and I find out that he goes around and tells the Murries that he will call on pay-day and he doesn't. If he would take me with him I could give him a hand and make sure one or both of us could make sure that these things were done.

Bill has some good ideas but we never give him much of a go. Every time he suggests something we knock it. But Bill gives in too easily. He won't stand on his dig [dignity] for what he thinks. When people put more work on to him he just takes it instead of refusing some of them. I know how he feels, that he owes them something which is wrong, the more you do for them the more they want you to do. I thought that one of our main jobs was to get the dark people to help themselves and not Bill and myself to do everything. I proposed that the blokes on the building should talk more to the other Murries and tell them how they are the ones who could be better off, that would be more sensible than going and telling the Gubs that they could supply the town with organic bricks.

Then there is Bill who is a very funny man. He seems to go all out to help people who can help themselves but he does not worry too much about the real no-hopers. Where there is life there is hope. For we are no better than they are. That is why I guess I reckon that we should keep on moving around the Murries and prodding them. The way I see it we could have 100 big Gubs like Dr Coombs come up and still until we get to the seedy lot we will always have problems with the dark people.

I am a little bit worried about Wally and his decision at the last meeting to hand in his resignation as president of the Association. This could present a big problem and I feel it would be better if Wally were to withdraw his resignation until at least the year is out and we have the re-election of officers. I myself at times feel like putting in my resignation also as I feel the association work is taking up too much of my time, more really than the job of field officer which I am being paid for and was elected to by the people. I feel sure that Wally must feel the same way. The position that we are in at present is that we work at home, especially myself doing writing and things like that with constant interruption so that we are not able to concentrate and do justice to our job.

Relationships of Aboriginal leaders to white helpers

The leaders and the change agent

The ambivalence which the Aboriginal leaders exhibited to each other was of minor proportions when compared with that which they exhibited towards me as a white change agent. Working towards a less ambivalent, more mutually honest relationship with a white change agent is a necessary first step in enabling an Aboriginal leader to develop some of the interpersonal skills he will need in negotiating with white power figures in his town, state and country.

Max said it would be good to front some of the big Gubs and not ask them for anything, just say how good it is of the money they have given and what we have done with it and the big Gubs will be very pleased with us so that they make a big thing of it when they get back to Sydney. The only thing I didn't like was the way that Max said that our builders should be paid to build the hall [a community hall for black and white youth] when he knows the white builders will probably be voluntary. That does not solve anything. For if our builders get paid, they won't have many Murries to come along with them and help so a lot of the whites will say the Murries don't want to be equal. If I got as many Murries as I could and John Maroulis [an active white member of the Apex Club] got as many whites as he could and they were all willing to build this hall, then they will all feel equal and feel that they are part of the building of the hall. That Max is really a strange man. He has a mind like a lot of the Murries, he changes it overnight. He sits down and judges people before he gets some sort of feeling of them. One minute he is saying to go to the Gubs and tell them how good it is and the next minute he is saying don't let the Gubs stand on you, show them who is the boss. I think we should all be equal, Max could tell me I'm wrong again.

We have certainly come a long way since Kamien came to town. He has done so much in such a short time to make the Murries realise that they can do much for themselves by trying to accomplish what really is their legal rights.

After talking to Max I came to the conclusion that he is worried about his being a good doctor in medicine so he can sit back and see the big improvement in the Murries and say 'Look what I have done, it is great. My experiment on the dark people of Bourke has worked, I am famous.'

It seems I have been very wrong about certain people, one man in particular, Dr Max Kamien. For only now I have come to realise what a great job he has been doing for the dark people of Bourke. It is funny when you think of it because we were both on with helping the Murries, I in my way and he in his. I have criticised him a lot not realising that without Max it would have been impossible for Bill and myself to be what we are or to gain so much ground in bettering the people of Bourke. I have got a lot more confidence in myself through Max and I am sure quite a few other Murries have too. My only disappointment is that I now have a feeling that once Max goes there will be no more doctors to follow up Max's work. But that is the white man's way. I am sure that the A.A.A. will realise how difficult it is without a man who can make a bit of noise like Max.

The other day Max says to me 'You are always saying things about doing things for the kids but you don't do much about it'. It is advice like this that makes my job easier. Now I am kept busy because I went and got some boxing gloves and a cricket set and boy, do we have some kids over at our house. It is good to see them enjoying themselves. I also started water polo and it is marvellous to see so many interested in it. We are also going to go to other towns to get some stiffer opposition.

I thought I would muck up the TV programme ['Four Corners' programme] the other day but everything went O.K. I wasn't game to do it but that is where it is always good to have someone like Max to give me advice and confidence and let me know that I am doing O.K.

I had a long talk with Dr Hollows [Professor Hollows] and I was telling him it was going to be a shame when Dr Kamien goes, but he said that if the A.A.A. had a long talk amongst themselves it should not take a lot to get someone to take Max's place. For down in Sydney around Redfern they have doctors like Max. I told him if someone like Max came he would also have to be an adviser as well as a doctor and go and treat the Murries like human beings instead of some kind of trash. At that rate he would get the confidence of these people and the mothers would bring the little ones along before they got that bad but if he was like some doctors we have had then all of Max's work will be wasted. He would not have to be a really big doctor like Max. It could be someone with a good understanding of people or even a practitioner or a student doctor.

These feelings of ambivalence also applied to other Aborigines who were influential with their people.

285

A former male leader who had also been employed as a health aide in the latter half of 1971 stated that:

'When you [Max Kamien] came along and talked to me [in November 1970] I decided I'd do something for my people. I've got the brains for it, you said so yourself. But everything I did you reckoned was no good. Trouble was the job [health aide] was beyond me. You shouldn't have picked me for it. I know what I'm doing. I do things my way. You always reckoned that wasn't any good. Well I've tried to help all those bastards [other Aborigines] and they don't want to be helped. Now you've laid off but you've got all the Murries doing the shit for you. Well I'm shat to death. I don't change for anyone. I'm shooting through where I can go back to being P.I. [his name] without everyone getting on my back. Anyway, [shaking my hand] you're the best mate I got.'

The leaders and other whites besides the change agent

Relationships with whites were influenced by a long legacy of Aboriginal mistrust. It was necessary to help Aboriginal leaders strike a balance between a gullible belief in the musings and half-promises of whites and a paralysing suspiciousness of all white motives and actions. It was a measure of the maturity and fair mindedness of the Aboriginal leaders that they were able to overcome many of their antipathies to those whites with whom they had to work and negotiate.

It was good to get away for a while [to Wilcannia] to see someone else from a different town and to see for myself the conditions the Murries live under there. They are far from the proper conditions. From my point of view those Murries are certainly a hard lot living for so long in those conditions. It's a great shame to see so many young men that get caught so deep in alcohol. Where they go wrong it's hard to say. The longer I continue to work for the Murries, the more I'm beginning to dislike Gubs in a way, for if it was not for them and their alcohol Australia would be a better place for the Murries. I keep telling myself not to write things like this but I can't help it. The more Murries I see headed for destruction the more I feel sorry for them. Yet I know that they remind me of myself and what I was headed for and how I've changed. That change could be for the best, I really don't know. It's not for me to judge other people whether they be black or white.

Bill Lucas [the architect] came to Bourke and had several discussions with the people and told us his hopes for the building project and the part that he is playing in it himself. I am amazed at the amount of trouble he has gone to, also the many items that he has donated through his negotiations with a number of manufacturers. I feel sorry when he is questioned on various things relating to our project and when, after a lengthy explanation by him he is still being misunderstood. Thank God that Bill is such an understanding person and generally gets through to the Murries eventually.

When Dr Coombs came we all had a discussion with the Shire President and the Shire Clerk and this resulted in a new line of thought where we could work in together (Murries and Gubs) on many various kinds of things that could benefit both communities. I'm not impressed to a great extent by the attitudes of these prominent members of our community as being sympathetic to our cause. I think that they are after such financial help as can be got from the Department of Aboriginal Affairs to raise their standing in their community. But with the employment position as it is we must get along with them in the hopes of getting a grant to finance such projects to alleviate Aboriginal unemployment.

At the last meeting John Luckens mentioned that it was not necessary for those who were going to serve on the building society to have any education. I strongly disagree with that. This is too important a position for any person to hold unless they are clear on all points pertaining to what it involves.

The Aboriginal Advancement Association seems to becoming recognised as being useful to the community [black and white] for we've been invited to attend several white meetings. Whether the invitations are to serve the purpose of assisting our cause, or whether they are to assist their cause with a view to making a profit from us remains to be seen.

The meeting of Thursday evening on the Reserve was quite good. Wally raised the subject with Bernie and John that the white people could not be trusted and I think Bernie and John were very much hurt by this allegation. They did mention that they were hurt and I can see their point of view. I opened my big mouth too and told Wally not to apologise because that is bad for Wally, he is always apologising and I don't think he should apologise unless he is really and truly in the wrong, not to seem sorry for something he should not be sorry about.

The Murries of Enngonia claimed that they couldn't get a job on the relief when there are three white men on it and one of them is a station owner. They said what hope has a Murrie of getting a job out bush if they are putting station owners on relief. I went to see the Shire Clerk and asked if he knew anything about the relief at Enngonia. He said there was relief money out there but he didn't get many complaints from there. I said there were 20 men out there out of work and what was he going to do about it, or did he want me to bring them all into town. He said 'Now, hang on Wally, I had to stand down 45 men this morning. How about the A.A.A. writing down to Mitchell or Waddy and see what they think about more relief money for Enngonia'. Then he said he didn't like the three Gubs out there being on relief but they were only getting four days a week. It is just like a Gub to make out that everything is O.K. and always trying to smooth things over.

The stop-start tactics of the Australian Government have done little to increase the confidence of Aborigines in the word of the white man. This report is taken from the Widjeri Co-Operative Ltd, *Newsletter*, August 1976.

This is how I see things in Bourke with the cutbacks. It is really a shame to see so much muck-up by the Government Department especially when you see the Minister and Public Service saying that it is time Aboriginal people run their own affairs.

It is a shame to see the Government cut back now when the people are just starting to learn how to do things for themselves. For a long while, it has been a battle to get the right people to make this Housing Company to work right. I would like to see somebody try setting this Housing Company up again from scratch, just so they will know how much time and worry it takes.

You see the cutbacks the Government talks about is something they don't know about, because if they knew they would have to go through some of the setbacks we have had here.

It is quite easy for them to sit in the office down in Canberra saying blacks are wasteful, what you must remember they take blokes off jobs as labourers, and say we are going to make field officers out of you and you are going to do wonders for the Aboriginal people here.

What they don't tell you is that you are being used for some sort of 'scrap [*sic*] goat' for the Public Service. They just sit in their warm little offices saying you are doing a bad job, so we will have an enquiry into what you are doing. What I am trying to say is that if the Government does make these cutbacks on the Bourke Aboriginals, then all the work that people like myself have been doing, has been wasted.

As you can see, we have a carpenter which is white and understanding. Also two Aboriginals who are young boys that are really going well and it wouldn't be very long before they are doing a lot of work themselves. So what do you do with young boys like these you get going just right then tell them that 'sorry mate, moneys run short'. It will be the same with people like myself that has worked about nine years on the Shire, and to give it up just to help Aboriginal people. Then along comes some white Government man saying we are going to cut back on funds.

With the cutbacks you will be only putting five people out of work, but by doing so, you are going to cause a great big muck-up to this Housing Company. We have blokes on Special Works, the rents to collect from people is a battle, that is without everyday problems about the people's welfare.

You see it is really going to be worth watching just to see how much these people think that we have just been wasting our time here. While all this is taking place does the Government think it can leave people the way they are when they're really trying so hard with so little education.

If you think that we are going to stay and start from scratch, like all the other times before when I should say we are only Aboriginal people that are used to being made fools of.

Wally Byers

The positive aspects of being a field officer

Although I have concentrated on the difficulties faced by the field officers this presents only one side of their experience. Both field officers developed new skills and insights into themselves, their jobs and the wider Australian society. This resulted in an increasing number of successes with accompanying periods of optimism and even elation.

Learning to exercise power

Synonymous with learning leadership is learning to exercise power. This may be through personal charisma, persuasion, through social action or through the use of what finance they had obtained from the Department of Aboriginal Affairs. For a people as powerless as the Aborigines in Australia this is of the utmost importance. However, for the leader who is in a power situation for the first time in his life, this is one of his most exhilarating and also one of his most anxious moments; a time when non-interfering emotional support is quietly welcomed.

We had a stop-work meeting to support the National Aborigines' Day and to make it a public holiday. If we get it, it would mean more people would be entitled to it. So we went out to get some whites to make out a petition that would really make the government help the Murries. I am sure there would be a lot of white supporters in Bourke especially if they would get a holiday themselves.

I had a talk with the Shire Clerk and he said he would not hold it against us for standing up for what we think is right. Anyway it has got to the stage that we will have to make a stand and go out to the whites and tell them that they will have to go a long way to understand the way the Murrie thinks. For when a Murrie does things on the spur of the moment, a white man will think about it for a while. But when a Murrie makes up his mind that's it.

So I think we have upset the whites this time but I hate to think what will happen if they don't start any of the Murries that went out on Friday to support their day. [That is, give them back their jobs on Monday.] It's not as if we were asking for the world. All we were asking for was to have a day that we could say is our own day, but if they try to begrudge the Murries one day then it will really stir up the Murries and will cause a big stir in Bourke that's for sure. I think the Murries have been very easy going and you could not blame them for being upset. If the white people would try to be a little bit more understanding they would see that the Murries are only standing up for their rights.

National Aborigines' Day caused a slight stir in our local area as the stop-work by Aborigines in support of the moratorium march [on land rights for Aborigines] would draw attention to the fact that the Murries are beginning to stand behind their own organisation despite the fact that there was a cry of 'Who will feed my family if I lose my job?' There was a good roll-up to the park meeting where the reason for the meeting was explained and I assured all those present of the fact that the association would continue to work for their benefit but emphasising the fact that the association could only be as strong as its supporters made it. The petition was signed by every adult present requesting the land right claims by Aborigines be respected, that more financial support be available to them for starting their own enterprises, and their request was made too that the Prime Minister's electoral policy for Aborigines be made available to us. I then sent a telegram of support to the moratorium marchers in Brisbane which they wrote back was a peaceful event.

289

Insight

The growth of insight into the workings of the majority society and the effective levers necessary to initiate change helped them to carry out their jobs more effectively.

There were two white students visited Bourke and they were concerned about the political views of our people. They said our people should be brought into an awareness of politics by the methods devised by the black power organisation which in all probability were also instituted by prejudiced whites. It is quite possible that I am wrong in surmising this and that the only reason that the A.A.A. has made such rapid progress is that the government doesn't want a repercussion of Canberra and other places where there has been a disturbance [referring to the Aboriginal tent embassy].[1] However, I am more inclined to think that our success hinges on our negotiations with those in higher places and through being able to have direct contact through the services of a very knowledgeable adviser Dr Kamien, and by our direct approach to delegations of ministers and through representations to our local member.

Their new learning also gave them an understanding of the difficulties of other Aboriginal leaders and enabled them to offer first hand assistance when this was indicated.

I spoke to T. M. [a field officer from Armidale]. He seems to be worried about something or other and is quite unsure of himself. It could be that he is suffering the first-stage symptoms of being a field officer and learning that it is like putting a jig-saw puzzle together except that the pattern keeps changing. I am finding that the solution to one person's problem doesn't necessarily apply to that of another individual with the same problem.

Two field officers from another country town were also assisted by the Bourke field officers. They remarked: 'Wally has helped me to understand how an Aboriginal helper feels. Bill Reid has helped me to understand myself which is the first lesson in understanding people.'

Optimism

Without some feeling of optimism the job of a field officer would be intolerable. Although the periods of despondency tended to over-shadow those of optimism the latter occurred sufficiently often to make the job rewarding and worthwhile.

We have just had some good news about the houses. The Council had agreed to let us go ahead with one house to start with. There is one Gub doctor that we have to be

1. This was the setting up of a 'tent embassy' on the lawns of Parliament House, Canberra to protest against the refusal by the McMahon Government to grant Aboriginal land rights. The embassy remained from 26.2.72 until its forcible removal by over 60 Commonwealth Police on 19.7.72.

thankful for getting that through the Council, and also getting a grant for the Murries to do it.

I spent the rest of my time back in Bourke helping Sister Hamlyn to arrange the measles vaccination, so I'll be busy for a few more days. I really think the Murries are going to move and really get things going now. I have been going around doing some interviews with people too, and I have recorded some of them to try to find out what they really think. Bill Elwood, age 22, told me that all the blackfellows have been wanting is someone to lead them on and that now they've got Bill and me they're ready to move.

There was a meeting of the A.A.A. and one of the subjects which we discussed was increasing the builder's wages. We had a vote and the A.A.A. said they were in no position to increase the wages. The boys were cranky and said to me that they get all the knocks and no-one appreciates what they were doing. I pointed out that it is the same for Bill and myself. That if there weren't blokes like us to keep on we would never get nowhere because there is times that I wish I had never taken on this job; but when you look around at some of the little ones you know that one day you have maybe made it a lot easier for them.

The continuing process of change

After my departure from Bourke the Aboriginal leaders continued to develop and to work for their own people. A measure of their progress can be gauged from the following communications from Mr Wally Byers and the other from Mrs Pat Cameron, a sympathetic white helper from Bourke.

Bourke, 21 November 1974

Dear Max and family,
Just a few lines to let you know that Patsy and the kids and myself are all well and hoping you and your family are the same. Well mate, things have changed down here a lot in $2\frac{1}{2}$ years. We don't seem to have made much headway in some ways, but in other ways, yes. You seem to get things going then they seem to backfire and I remember you saying one time to me that when you put yourself on the line for the Murries you start to forget your own commitments to your family. Well Max, that is how it is with me. Now, where do I go from here. It is really the white man's system which mucks things up and makes things so unbearable as you know from the time you were here with us.

Some of the highest gubs to the smallest gubs have visited us and they fetch some educated Murries along to make out that they know what Murries want. Then they go back to Canberra and say they have solved the problems of the Murries.

Well mate, I have really stuck my neck out this time for the Murries and I am starting to get a little worried about it. We have started to take up house buying and that is really hard for someone like me because I don't understand the education part much. Well mate, we went to Canberra to get money for buying houses and it turned out O.K., that is until we got back to Bourke. We thought it was time to tell the Murries that we were getting more houses. They came to the meeting and there was a big crowd there. I open the meeting, we start to talk about the houses and how the rent was to be paid. Then someone said something about the bingo that Bill had stopped and things started to warm up. Alf L. and Bill Reid started to have a row about the bingo and Alf said that I was just a loudmouth so I told him he could have my job and I walked out of the meeting. Alf followed me out to say something. That's when I got the shock of my life. Patsy told Alf off. She said 'You blokes are all the same you like to use people like Wally. Because you're afraid to stick out your necks. But you are quick to take over when all the hard work is done.' To tell you the truth it took me a while to get her into the car. So I have to tell you about that.

Wally Byers

27 March 1975

A day in the life of a field officer, 1975

Dear Max,

I thought you might possibly be interested in a day in Wally's life recently.

Thursday, p.m.   Met Joe Croft—member of the D.A.A. looking after this area. Had a 'yarn' with him. Rang me and arranged the meeting at our place as there were no lights in his office. Notified all the committee of time, place and matters to be discussed. Did the same for the Brewarrina Committee. Rang John Ward[1] and told him about the new doctor not coming, told him we wanted a doctor and that eventually we would like to employ him but Wally would like to have better control of the office and moneys he administers before taking on the total responsibility for a medical service. He accepted John Ward's suggestion of the Co-op. employing a doctor for two months (or similar limited period) white trying to fill the position. He did other things at office and home of which I don't know.

Brought Joe Croft to the meeting of the Widjeri Co-op. at 8.00 p.m. where there was a full attendance of the committee, who were all 100% sober. The people from Brewarrina were also there. Wally spoke strongly and lucidly about the need for a secretary and also asked for money immediately to keep the building programme going. Joe Croft agreed. Then Peter Tobin[2] rang about a child in Forbes who had to be in Court in Bourke at 10.00 a.m. next day [Forbes is 500 kilometres from Bourke]. Wally agreed to leave after the meeting and collect the child after having first made sure that the legal aid service would pay the Co-op. for the use of its car.

Friday 10.00 a.m.   Wally spent the morning talking with Joe Croft and interviewing Jenny Campbell[3] and she agreed to give office training and assistance to Kenny Elwood[4] as he requires it for about two hours a day.

1. Director Aboriginal Health Services, New South Wales Health Commission.
2. Lawyer in the New South Wales Aboriginal Legal Aid Service.
3. White applicant for part time secretary.
4. Aboriginal secretary of the Widjeri Co-operative Society.

2.00 p.m.   Came up to hospital to repay the $50 I lent him for the Forbes trip and he was then going to the pre-school to pay the wages of the Aboriginal assistant there.

As he left the hospital a taxi driver approached him about $400 an Aborigine owed when he took a taxi to Dubbo to see his wife who was dying. Wally asked the hospital not to allow the taxi drivers to get in and demand money off the wife and he went off to see the taxi drivers to see if he could arrange a compromise.

6.00 p.m.   I took Patsy some ointment for the child's finger and had a 'yarn' with Wally during which he organised me and Patsy into a Mothers' Meeting next Tuesday (he watches the soccer that night—so it's a good night) and told us to try to make some contact with the teachers again as the mothers and kids need this.

That's just 24 hours as I know it. Obviously other things happened, and maybe it's not typical. But it's not a bad day's work for a powerless illiterate Aborigine is it? And I thought possibly might be some measure of change.

Pat Cameron

Chapter 15
The development, decline and re-organisation of a self-help housing project

Initiating change in an Aboriginal community is not an easy task. Supporting the change process after it has begun is even harder. The internal difficulties and deficiencies inherent in the very nature of a disintegrated community are major obstacles to continued change. The road blocks, deviations, misdirections, misunderstandings, and at times the sheer malevolent bastardry, bred from racial prejudice, of those whites with power to hinder Aboriginal initiatives can so bewilder and frustrate the Aborigines that it is little wonder that they give up and fail to complete a given endeavour.

This chapter describes an attempt by Aborigines in Bourke to build their own houses. Many of the facts mentioned here are scattered throughout this book. I have consolidated them into this particular chapter in the hope that a review of the Bourke housing project will provide insight for other people, black and white, who are or will be involved in solving the problems of Aboriginal housing elsewhere. It will not convert those prejudiced against Aborigines. It may, however, provide insights for those sympathetic to Aboriginal progress but whose actions have inadvertently hindered it.

The problem

In June 1971, the 730 Aboriginal people of Bourke lived in 92 dwellings, an average of 7.9 people per dwelling unit, compared to the figure of 3.8 people per dwelling for the town's white population. The physical and mental health hazards of overcrowding in the Aborigines' houses were compounded by the almost invariably poor quality of the houses, especially on the Bourke Aboriginal Reserve where 229 people lived in 31 shanties, lacking electricity, inside water supply or sewerage.

Most Bourke Aborigines were ashamed of their living conditions, which contributed to their low self-esteem and a survey conducted in 1971 showed that more than half the Aboriginal families wanted better housing and were prepared to work for it. The accuracy of this general sentiment was borne out by the residential mobility of the Bourke Aboriginal families: 47 families changed their places of residence in 1971–1972.

Very few privately-owned houses in Bourke were offered for rental to Aborigines and those that were available were generally decrepit and not worth the exorbitant rents asked for them. The Aborigines' main source of rental housing was the N.S.W. State Housing Commission, which provided specially designed houses for Aborigines at subsidised rents as well as letting some of its ordinary houses to them. However, both types were in short supply, with a long waiting list of would-be tenants. Aborigines who rented houses in the town were not readily accepted by white neighbours and often felt insecure in their tenure and expressed feelings of minor harassment. Their own people, too, often criticised them as being flash[1] for moving off the Reserve. Several families had suffered the indignity of being evicted for being unable to keep up the rent. All these factors were more fully described in chapter 8.

Clearly then, there was a need for better, low-cost housing for Bourke Aborigines and they themselves felt that need. What follows is an account of how, in July 1972 after many initial setbacks, a self-help building project got under way and why, when the project came to a sudden halt two-and-a-half years later, only three houses had been built, with two others almost completed.

Matters to be discussed below are: (1) whether the building project should be regarded as a success or failure in itself; (2) its effect on the Aborigines' desire for better housing; (3) what the Bourke Aborigines learnt from the project and (4) whether or not the project contributed in any way to the community solidarity of Bourke Aborigines.

Relevant factors affecting the problem

1. There was no real Aboriginal community in Bourke and there was little positive community feeling to mould people together in a common endeavour. The community existed only in a negative sense of awareness of white criticism and white rejection. The only organisation of Aborigines was the United Aboriginal Mission Church, which had fewer than twenty members, and they organised an Aboriginal girls' basketball team. The functional Aboriginal social unit was the

---

1. Vernacular for pretentious.

extended family and the opinion leaders and sources of authority within these families were the grandmothers.

2. In the past white governmental agencies had been seen as authoritarian, arbitrary and paternal. The resultant attitude in Aboriginal people was one of demanding-dependency, helplessness and apathy. Since they saw themselves as powerless against the actions of these agencies, they tended to flee from difficulties and frustrations rather than fight them.

3. The Aborigines' previous experience of housing had not been very successful. All had relatives or neighbours who had returned to the Reserve after falling behind in rent or having had arguments with officers of the old Aboriginal Welfare Board, who controlled the housing. Aware that they were not wanted by white people in the town, Aborigines who left the Reserve were jeered at by those who did not, for allegedly starving their children in order to pay rent. Some of those who had shifted off the Reserve had been unable to make a success of it because too many of their relatives had moved in with them.

4. For most Bourke Aborigines, employment in the area was irregular and income uncertain, which led to difficulties in maintaining rent payments.

5. Although the Bourke Reserve had an area of only 26 acres and was regarded by white law as a public place, it had become emotionally invested as an area of security to Bourke Aborigines, who saw it as their land, the one place where no rents or rates existed and where any Aborigine could always find food, shelter and friendship.

6. The Aborigines were poorly educated. Only two men and two women amongst the Bourke people were capable of handling basic correspondence dealing with legal or business matters. The Aboriginal people also lacked the organisational skill, business acumen or legal knowledge to cope with such a venture as a co-operative housing society and the sums of money involved were more than they had ever known.

7. Only one Aboriginal man in Bourke had ever had any experience with the construction of buildings.

The course of events

In November 1970 I joined a small gathering of Aboriginal people who had decided to meet to discuss ways and means of improving the circumstances of Aborigines in Bourke (*see* chapter 2). I was asked to explain the workings of the Commonwealth Capital Grants Scheme for Aborigines. Although the scheme was intended to enable Aboriginal people to set up their own business enterprises, three of the Aborigines at that meeting immediately saw it as a possible means of obtaining houses. At subsequent meetings of what was to become the A.A.A., the question of housing was brought up again and again, sometimes in the positive sense of seeking ways to build or improve houses, but more often in the negative sense of simply expressing grievances about the Aborigines' present housing conditions. Nevertheless a consensus of what the people attending these meetings felt they needed soon became clear. They wanted cheap houses (and as they put it, 'nothing flash') to be built quickly in large numbers. They wanted these to be constructed in indestructible cement brick, have large verandahs, fireplaces and adequate airflow. I was asked to find out if there were any architects interested in designing low-cost housing for Aborigines, but my approaches to eight different Sydney architects and two schools of architecture proved fruitless.

In April 1971, Dr Ned Iceton invited me to attend an Aboriginal Human Relations Workshop at the University of New England with three Aboriginal men from Bourke. This event provided the impetus for the A.A.A. in Bourke to become a functioning reality and discussions about housing began again at A.A.A. meetings. A major problem was to find out what Aboriginal people really did want and then to make allowances for changes which might take place in their felt needs if their later experiences expanded their horizons. For instance, a woman who has only seen a wood stove is unlikely to want any other kind. However, after having the experience of using an electric stove she may decide that that is a more convenient method of cooking.

Two main methods were used to attempt to obtain valid information on which to act. The first was the human relations workshop method (*see* chapter 2, page 77). In the sense that it was used, the human relations group provided an opportunity for a form of personal growth and confidence and also provided both Aborigines and the white people assisting them with insights into each other's behaviour. It helped Aboriginal people to express what they really did want and partly avoided the pitfall of white people assuming that they knew what was wanted. The second method of information-gathering was by discussion between the elected Aboriginal field officers and Aboriginal individuals or families. It must be stressed that this form of consultation was necessarily a slow process in order to allow the Aborigines and their leaders plenty of time to try to crystallise their ideas. After some consensus of opinion had been reached it became necessary to enlist support from government agencies who, it was hoped, would provide the financial assistance that was needed.

The Secretary of the Bourke A.A.A. made contact with the New South Wales Director of Aboriginal Welfare, Mr I. Mitchell, to see what help he could give to begin a housing project. The Director's response was encouraging, and he subsequently visited Bourke for three days in June 1971, accompanied by his parliamentary master, the Minister for Child Welfare and Social Welfare, Mr J. Waddy. After three visits to the Shire Clerk and five trunk calls to the minister's office, the A.A.A.'s spokesman obtained a half-hour of the minister's time to discuss their proposal on housing. I was also granted a ten-minute audience which by chance took place prior to that with the A.A.A. The meeting between the A.A.A. representatives and the minister went badly and the A.A.A. then accused me of 'white-anting' them and spoiling their chances of getting housing. They felt that I had given the minister an opportunity to formulate some difficult questions. However, a month later a message was received from the Director of Aboriginal Welfare expressing some guarded interest in the housing proposal, but stating the he believed that the tensile strength of most of the soil in Bourke was unsuitable for the concrete base on which the proposed houses were to be built.

In August 1971, a group of Abschol students from the University of New South Wales came to discuss the health needs of Aboriginal people with respect to housing. Abschol saw this as a project in which they could possibly become involved. At the first meeting between them and a large number of Aboriginal people I was surprised to learn that what the Aboriginal people really wanted was a communal hall first and housing second. The leader of the Abschol delegation, Mr Stephen Joseph (a metallurgist) then designed a corrugated iron hall. He took his plan back to Sydney to show a friend who was a private architect. He was so horrified by it that he arrived in Bourke two days later together with two architects and two architectural students from the University of New South Wales. They spent a full 24 hours talking with different groups of Aboriginal people. Few of the

Aboriginal people followed the architects' allusions to Greek and Roman architecture, but they formed a good relationship with the Sydney people. The architects offered to draw up plans and make wooden models to aid the Aboriginal people's understanding of the proposed design.

The Bourke Shire building inspector was involved in the original planning and together with a Department of Main Roads engineer he devised a method for building on a concrete base which he thought would not move on either red or black soil. The Shire Clerk was also involved in the proposed housing project, but he developed an unreasonable fear that any housing for Aborigines was going to be sub-standard and that this would reflect poorly upon his town.

In December 1971, eight Aboriginal men elected by the A.A.A. went to Sydney where they lived with the architect and his team and discussed their ideas of what sort of houses they would like to live in and the best way to build them. They were unable to renew contact with the N.S.W. Minister who had visited Bourke (Mr Waddy) and in frustration and anger decided that they would go to Canberra instead. They arrived back in Bourke with renewed hope and with some wooden models to be used in discussions with other Aboriginal people. The A.A.A. then made an application to lease two blocks of land on which to build either a community hall or a model house. This was followed by a marked increase in interest in the building project by Bourke Aborigines.

In January 1972, a mixed N.S.W. and Commonwealth Parliamentary delegation visited Bourke and was approached by spokesmen from the A.A.A., who showed their wooden models of proposed houses and received an attentive hearing, which was a great boost to their morale. Following this the A.A.A. officially informed the Bourke Shire Council through its building inspector, of the Aborigines' proposed building plans. At the suggestion of the Office of Aboriginal Affairs in Canberra, moves were begun to form a co-operative society in the name of the A.A.A. to undertake the building programme.

In March 1972, two of the members of the architectural team that had first visited Bourke went to live there. One held a B.Sc. in architecture and the other had experience in commerce and landscape gardening. Both were interested in experimenting with 'alternative life-styles' (so much so that the white residents of Bourke referred to them as 'hippies'). The two men brought ideas for another prototype house to put to the Shire Council, but since the plans for it were incomplete, the Council deferred discussing them for a month.

In April 1972, the Shire Council exercised its powers 'under the Interim Development Order No. 1, and disapproved of the proposed development on account of: (a) the character of the proposed development on the adjoining land and in the locality; (b) the existing and future amenity of the neighbourhood; and (c) the circumstances of the case'. It was clear that the Shire Council did not understand the aims of the Aboriginal building project and had become suspicious of it. Since they were unable to turn down the house as being unsuitable in design, they had done so on a town planning qualification. It was learned later that at the meeting, the housing inspector (who had been involved in the planning of the house) had described the prototype house as a 'split-level humpy' and this had stuck in the minds of the shire councillors more than any other fact. It was also possible that there was some outside comment from the N.S.W. Housing Commission (N.S.W.H.C.) against the project. Several shire councillors were also angry at the policy of the N.S.W.H.C. of putting Aboriginal people alongside white people in the town, and they mistakenly thought this practice was due to my supposed influence with authorities in Sydney. However, after some of the councillors gained a better understanding of the proposed plans, they obtained a rescission of the previous motion.

In May 1972, the Shire Council agreed to allow the A.A.A. to build a prototype house on leased land. However, it was stipulated that if the completed structure was not approved by the building inspector for use as a house it might have to become a community centre, and if it was not suitable even for that, then it might have to be taken down. This unexpected new opposition by the Shire Council caused the members of the A.A.A. to further doubt their own ability and the worth of the project, but this loss of morale was only temporary and was restored after a visit from the architect.

There was, however, one other set-back before the project got under way: it had been intended to build the houses with panels made from re-cycled organic waste material, but just as work was about to start it was discovered that the panels were not yet being mass produced and would therefore be far too expensive. This revelation came at a time when quite a few people on the Bourke Reserve were becoming excited about the possibility of getting housing and the climate was psychologically ripe to begin a self-help project. The set-back was

Plate 30 Prototype house for the Bourke Aboriginal Advancement Association (details of structure are described in *Architecture in Australia*, 62(3):9, June 1973).

taken very hard by the Aboriginal leaders, who felt that their credibility with their own people had been shattered and that they had been wrong to put their trust in any white man.

Nevertheless, a substitute building material was found and preparations were made to start building. Although it had been stipulated that the Aboriginal builders and their two white helpers were to be accountable to the A.A.A. (and all paid the same wages), the building team of six Aboriginal men was in fact selected by the two resident white helpers, with the participation of only three members of the A.A.A. The criteria used in selecting the six builders were that they were 'worthy' candidates, not too old to learn, were from the Reserve, had young families and did not have permanent jobs.

Building of the first house was started in August 1972. Although there were the usual delays that seem to occur in any building project, the house was completed in December 1972 (*see* Plate 30).

The six builders were obviously proud of their work, but the rest of the Aboriginal population did not share their sense of triumph. Almost immediately there were complaints about the cost of the house— $18 000 for an 18-square structure—and about some of the planning and workmanship (eg. sliding doors which were difficult or impossible to move). The A.A.A. had lengthy debates on whether to ask a politician, a town dignitary or a full-blood Aborigine to officiate at a ceremony to mark the completion of the first house, but in the end no decision was reached and no ceremony was held. This deprived the building team of an opportunity to bask in the glory of what was for unskilled workmen a creditable performance. (It was also a missed opportunity to get community involvement in the building project.) In fact, most Aborigines regarded the completed house with derogation or disinterest. They did not identify with it as a community project. It did not seem to have much meaning for them.

One of the Aboriginal field officers who was most influential with those who had elected him expressed the opinion that because only six men were building the houses, it did not really constitute a community project and that unless all the people joined in, none would be interested in it. His considerable anxiety about the cost and effectiveness of the houses affected Aboriginal opinion, especially on the Bourke Reserve. The general lack of interest caused a loss of morale amongst the six men doing the building work. They became less interested in the project and began to treat it as just another job for which they earned money, and began to express dissatisfaction with their wages and workers' compensation cover.

When the second and third houses were nearing completion, the building team decided without any discussion with other Aboriginal people that allocation of the houses should be limited to people living on the Reserve, but that the names of all the Reserve dwellers should be eligible for a draw out of a hat for the houses. Contrary to the thinking and practice of the N.S.W. Housing Commission, the builders did not consider that houses should go to the most 'deserving' (ie. people who signified that they wanted a house and were prepared to put money or labour into it). Everybody on the Reserve should be given a chance, they said, and allocation should be purely a matter of luck. They expressed the opinion that if the most down-and-out Reserve dweller should win the right to move into one of the houses, he and his family might change their style of life.

The ballot was conducted within two days of the builders' decision. People on the Reserve put their names into a hat, not quite understanding what the ballot was about. The first of the three names drawn turned out to be that of a man whose name had been entered by his mother, with whom he was temporarily living in a house in the town, although he had lived on the Reserve until six weeks before the draw. He was declared ineligible and another name drawn, but after acrimonious debate the first man was reinstated at the head of the list. This meant that the fourth person drawn, one of the builders, would not be given a house. He took this very badly and expressed extreme disappointment. The three ballot winners were required to put $5 to $10 a week into a building fund, but two of them either failed to do so, or put in some money and then withdrew it.

The second and third houses were still incomplete when all the available money ran out. The building team left Bourke to work in Sydney and the two white helpers went on holiday. While the white men were away, a censure motion against them was passed by the A.A.A. However, they returned at the same time that more money arrived from Canberra, the censure motion was rescinded and instead they were voted authority to hire and fire employees, a power which had previously been the sole prerogative of the A.A.A.

Meanwhile, the first completed house had been approved by the building inspector and was being used temporarily as a community centre by the A.A.A. to enable Aborigines to use and comment about its qualities as a dwelling. A television set was installed and a growing number of people began to use the building and to associate with it. An Aboriginal family from the Reserve moved into the second house when it was completed and exhibited a marked change of attitude. They began to take a great deal of pride in their house and in their personal appearance. They seemed anxious to show whites that 'We live in a house as good as yours and we are as good as you'. Many other Aborigines began to see housing as possible and desirable for themselves, especially a house controlled by their peers, available at fair and economical rent, equipped with an electric stove and hot water system which they could easily learn to use.

A second housing movement had also begun as a result of the views of one of the field officers and consultation between the Commonwealth Department of Aboriginal Affairs and a delegation concerned with Aboriginal housing from the Royal Australian Institute of Architects. This was that the people living on the Reserve who wanted to upgrade their dwellings should be able to do so through a grant of $1000 which would be repaid at about $2 a week. This created enthusiasm amongst people on the Reserve and plans were submitted to begin such a project. However, a change of attitude in Canberra meant that the project had to be abandoned for lack of finance.

In November 1973, the building co-operative suggested by the Office of Aboriginal Affairs 23 months previously, was finally registered under the name of the Widjeri Co-operative. Its administration centred around the two white members of the original architect's team who had been living in Bourke for over 20 months. They saw the co-operative as a continuation of the A.A.A. with the advantage of it now being a legally incorporated body. They also tried to make the co-operative into a body with a 'strong' decision-making executive. A meeting of about 25 Aborigines and a few whites elected a board of ten directors. One of those elected was an Aboriginal carpenter from another area of New South Wales who had just arrived in Bourke in search of a job. He was put in charge of completing the fourth and fifth houses. By force of personality he gained the support of the majority of the younger Aborigines on the board of directors and so took control of the co-operative. Those elected leaders of the A.A.A. who were also on the board of directors of the co-operative were repeatedly out-voted and resigned. The two whites who had started the buildings were also forced to resign for the same reason.

Thus the elected board of the co-operative became isolated from the majority of Aboriginal people and was left without either their support or their control. Mistakes went unnoticed or unchecked. The 'people' had been excluded and general discussion of issues had ceased.

Although six members of the board of management of the Widjeri Co-operative had attended a ten-day course in Sydney on how to run a co-operative, the intricacies of administering such a venture overtaxed their present capabilities. The control of the building programme became chaotic. With up to twenty people being employed on completing the fourth and fifth houses, the extra wages made a considerable dent in the finances of the co-operative.

However, just when the Aboriginal carpenter was beginning to learn from his mistakes and had turned to both the leaders of the A.A.A. and one of the white helpers for advice, this opportunity for the Aborigines to correct their own errors was pre-empted by an officer of the Department of Aboriginal Affairs who visited Bourke for one day in April 1974. There are several conflicting versions of the events of this visit, but two things were agreed upon by my informants: there was little discussion with Aboriginal people (about twelve attended a meeting); and the Aborigines were led to understand that 'Canberra' had ordered them to stop building. The Aboriginal people understood that the dicta laid down from Canberra were that the A.A.A. had to regain power over the Widjeri Co-operative, that the Aboriginal carpenter had to resign and that the houses had to be finished by contract. The Aboriginal carpenter was invited to tender for that contract but he was openly criticised by the man from Canberra and left Bourke that evening. A month later the Bourke Aborigines were angry, confused or apathetic. Most felt that the Aboriginal carpenter had been harshly dealt with, that although he had not had any previous experience of management he was just at the point of having learnt from his mistakes, and that, had the Aboriginal community been left alone, they would have solved their various problems over the next few months by themselves. This view was shared by the two now uninvolved white helpers in spite of the fact that it was the Aboriginal carpenter who was the cause of their resignation from the project in the first place.

In 1974 the Widjeri Co-operative had also purchased two old houses and renovated them a little and this was regarded by the inhabitants of those houses and others as being a much cheaper, better and easier way of providing houses for Aboriginal people.

Analysis

It is a cardinal rule of community development that the people of the client community should participate in the planning of technological projects intended to benefit them. As has been described above, the initial impetus for a co-operative housing project arose from many hours of discussion at meetings of Bourke Aborigines in the hope of reaching a consensus of community opinion, but this process of involvement was undone by some rushed decisions made by the small number of whites and Aborigines directly involved in the building work. The six builders were not chosen by the people, the method of allocating the houses was decided without discussion and the directors of the Widjeri Co-operative were appointed by only a handful of people at a hurriedly called meeting.

The ideal of the widest possible participation in decisions affecting the group is especially appropriate in Aboriginal communities such as the one at Bourke. The Widjeri Co-operative was set up in such a way as to 'get action' through quick decisions, which is the white man's style of administration, whereas the Aboriginal style is to hold prolonged discussions over several weeks, or even months, until a consensus is reached. The fact that the white style of decision-making was followed so often in the Bourke housing project prevented many Aborigines

305

from expressing opinions and alienated many who had originally supported the idea.

The events outlined above also show how carefully the self-confidence of emergent leaders within the client community must be nurtured and how easily events quite beyond their control can destroy that confidence, not to mention their trust in those trying to help them. The Aboriginal people who negotiated with politicians and architects in Sydney returned to Bourke with a sense of accomplishment and they began influencing their peers in discussions centred around the models of proposed houses. However, when the plans agreed upon in this way had to be changed because of cost and unavailability of the chosen building material, these emergent leaders lost face with their peers, became confused and lost confidence in themselves. Half of them saw the changes in plan as yet more proof of the untrustworthiness of the white man and turned against the entire project.

The confidence of those Aborigines who became closely involved in the project was not helped, either, by the considerable criticism from white authority figures (such as the shire building inspector and one clergyman) and even from white oriented Aborigines. This criticism sowed seeds of doubt in the minds of the A.A.A.'s two elected field officers. The one who felt he represented the people living on the Reserve became concerned that the building project might not benefit his 'constituents', but his views were rejected by the building team and he was excluded from their deliberations. He then became one of the project's loudest critics.

The building inspector and others, including Aborigines, also undermined the confidence of the six Aborigines involved in the construction by criticising their work as unskilled and inefficient. This constant criticism, and at times ridicule, aggravated the lack of morale amongst the builders especially since they did not receive sufficient emotional or physical support from the Bourke Aboriginal community as a whole. Even in their moment of triumph at the completion of the first house, the building team did not receive what they might have felt was due praise. The builders' initial altruism faded, they began to look upon the project as just another job, and they expressed their feelings in complaints over wages and conditions.

The lack of community support for the builders was probably due to the fact that there was no real sense of community amongst the Bourke Aborigines, no collective voice to be expressed at meetings of the

A.A.A. and to guide the field officers and builders. In reality, the effective social unit was the extended family and had planning and building taken place more in accordance with that reality, it probably would have been more successful. It is significant that by May 1974, two of the three houses built by the Aborigines in Bourke and one of the two houses purchased and renovated by them were occupied by members of a single family.

The general lack of interest amongst the bulk of the Aboriginal population of Bourke was also due to the length of time taken for the project to produce a house and the long odds against any given family acquiring a house through the scheme. The arbitrary method of allocating houses did nothing to make them seem any less remote to most families, although interest in the houses increased noticeably after the first family moved into one and happily pointed out to their friends and invited guests, both white and black, its apparent superiority to houses provided by the Housing Commission.

As has been described above, the completion of the first house brought to a head the problems caused by the builders' insecurity, the criticism of their work and lack of support for their efforts. It was at this crucial moment that a classic piece of arbitrary bureaucratic bungling dealt another blow to the project itself, and even more importantly, prevented the Bourke Aborigines from gaining an important benefit from the project in terms of community development. Although the originally elected leaders of the A.A.A. were rapidly developing organisational skills, the administration of the building co-operative proved to be still beyond their managerial ability. The new elite, the younger men of the building team who had been appointed as virtual directors of the building co-operative, split with the older A.A.A. leaders and repeatedly out-voted them. Both resigned in frustration. The financial affairs of the co-operative soon became chaotic. This was the crucial moment.

Despite the factionalism and confusion, it seemed possible that the Aboriginal people, in time, might well have been able themselves to bring order out of the chaos, which would have been a great step forward and would in itself have justified the housing project as an instrument of community development. Instead, the dead hand of Canberra intervened, in the form of an official from the Department of Aboriginal Affairs who visited Bourke for one day, adopted a managerial approach, consulted with only ten or twelve Aborigines at

307

a meeting which did not include the most influential A.A.A. field officer. This brief intervention by one man had a devastating effect on the housing project itself and its community developmental function: the immediate resignation and departure of the Aboriginal carpenter who had come to be in charge of the building team, a feeling in the community that he had been badly treated and the suspension of all the activities of the Aborigines' building co-operative for a period of eight months. Even worse, the Aborigines saw their attempts at house building as yet another of their failures and many white people in the town could not resist reinforcing that point of view.

Final judgement of the Bourke Aboriginal housing project should take into consideration the degree of consumer satisfaction provided by the houses, compared with other available forms of housing, the cost, the effect on those Aborigines still without houses and the effect of the project on the development of the Aboriginal community in Bourke. At first the occupants of the co-operative houses expressed a high degree of satisfaction, finding them more suited to their needs than any other type of housing available in Bourke, although this early satisfaction was later diminished when the houses did not stand up well to normal wear and tear and when leaking roofs were allowed to remain unrepaired.

In terms of a proposed low cost project, the construction of three houses, with two others unfinished, and the purchase and renovation of two old existing houses for $78 000 in two years, is hardly a success story. However, the co-operative remains and the Aboriginal leaders place some store in its being the first legally-incorporated body the Bourke Aborigines have ever had. As a result of the project, there are now six Aborigines with almost enough building skill to get jobs on any building site and who can continue renovating and maintaining houses bought by the co-operative. The project succeeded in focusing the attention of the Bourke Aborigines on their housing conditions and by 1974, 70 per cent of those who were living on the Reserve in 1970 had moved into a variety of houses in the town. Two floods in three years have further motivated the desire to leave the Reserve and nearly all the people still there have expressed a desire to move when they can find houses.

Although at first the business child of the Bourke Aboriginal people, the Widjeri Co-operative overwhelmed its parent body, the A.A.A., simply because it had the money. The A.A.A. has yet to reassert its authority even though it has been incorporated in the co-operative. However, the people concerned do seem to have learnt something from their experiences. There is little doubt that Bourke's Aboriginal leaders have acquired new skills with which to cope with the dominant white society and are better able to make an appraisal of political realities and possibilities in their efforts to improve the lot of their people. For instance, in November 1974 two of the leaders took it upon themselves to resolve the co-operative's financial problems after months of frustrating inaction by their auditors and the Department of Aboriginal Affairs. The two Bourke men found the money for deposits to buy four more houses, went uninvited to Canberra to explain their problems and then initiated further meetings in Bourke for the Aboriginal people to discuss their housing problems (*see* chapter 14). They also helped find a white contractor to work with two of the original Aboriginal builders to complete the two unfinished houses.

This system has continued with an employed and sympathetic white carpenter training two or three young Aborigines at the same time as they build houses. In the last two years (1975 and 1976) a further ten houses have been built or renovated in the town and ten have been constructed on the Bourke Reserve.

There is currently a new initiative to purchase prefabricated houses as a means of reducing the time it takes to provide a house for those in need. Thus, although the original building project may, from the point of view of a building contractor, be considered as something of a failure, it has been of discernible benefit in terms of problem solving and community development, as well as doing something to improve the standard of housing of the Bourke Aborigines.

Conclusion: the lessons to be learnt

1. The widest possible community involvement must be sought and sustained. The objectives established and the time taken to achieve them must be realistic. It is better for a majority of people to simultaneously obtain a basic living unit which can be extended in the future than for only a few families to be housed in any one year.

2. The project must give the greatest possible number of people the hope that they may benefit from it. Aboriginal people, like whites, will want their chances of moving from a reserve into a house (once they decide to do so) to be greater and quicker than that which has so far

applied with regard to the houses built and bought by the Widjeri Co-operative.

3. All white people involved, from local well-wishers and paid helpers to government officers visiting from far-off seats of power, should restrict themselves to offering advice and opinions which the Aborigines can heed or reject as they wish. This also applies to Aboriginal authority figures from outside the particular community concerned, although perhaps to a lesser extent. A managerial approach by advisers retards the Aborigines' development of administrative skills, reduces their self-confidence and fosters in them an attitude of dependence rather than independence. Furthermore, decisions imposed upon the community may well be based on misconceptions or inadequate information and prove far more harmful than any naive false steps which the Aborigines may take if left alone to make their own decisions in their own way. The two white architects who helped the Bourke Aborigines plan their houses had an idealised view of the communal life they believed the Aborigines led and which, they thought, given proper housing in an adequate ecological setting, would provide a model life style for those white people in search of 'alternatives'. This led the planners to tend to superimpose their own ideals on to the real desires of the Aboriginal people.

In a situation such as exists in Bourke, the answer to the housing problem seems to be to purchase and renovate more existing houses, including Housing Commission homes, rather than build new ones. All Aboriginal housing should be administered through a co-operative such as now exists in Bourke and modifications and maintenance should be carried out by Aboriginal people employed by the co-operative.

If there are Aborigines with the skill to administer the co-operative, so much the better, but if not a carefully selected white person should be employed for the purpose. However, he would need clearly to understand that he was filling a temporary need, a technical adviser training Aborigines to take over his job. He should be employed by, and therefore answerable to, the particular Aboriginal community, in the same way that Aboriginal people in Sydney and Perth now employ doctors in their Aboriginal Medical Services.

Chapter 16
Epilogue

Life is short, the art is long, the problems pressing. Even the most empirical approach is justified in medical research if it offers any hope of yielding results of practical usefulness.

Dubos, 1959:159

This project was based on the value judgement that a planned and thoughtful effort to improve the health of Bourke Aborigines through intervening in their life circumstances was better than doing nothing and leaving the Aborigines to themselves and to chance. This project was also based on the view that although Australian doctors have done much for individual Aborigines they have (given their potential to influence society) done less than they might in helping Aborigines achieve social equality and justice without which they cannot attain a high standard of physical, mental and social well being.

The present study was designed to test ways in which a doctor who used the theory and practice of planned social change, could consult and combine with Aboriginal people to help them to attain not only their health needs, but also their other felt needs. Although the concept of the doctor as an agent of social change is not new, it did represent a fairly radical departure from the traditional role played by doctors in Australian society.

This type of medical intervention appears to have possibilities in that it resulted in real solutions to the immediate health problems of Bourke Aborigines and encouraged them towards an active and ongoing consumer demand for health care which has persisted for three years after my departure.

Even so, it is not easy to evaluate my part in the Human Ecology of the Arid Zone Project. Indeed I had not intended to do so. I had hoped that the medical aspects of my work would be assessed by the doctor who succeeded me in the Bourke programme and that a person of appropriate sociological and psychological training and experience would evaluate the effects of the programme of community development. In neither case has this occurred. Since my departure from Bourke in 1973, the Aborigines have been dependent upon the ordinary medical services provided in the main by only one general practitioner and he does not have the time to organise further epidemiological studies.

Evaluation of the successes and failures of my intervention in Bourke is difficult for three reasons. The first is that I did not have a control population in another town with which I could compare, except in anecdotal terms, the effects of planned change with that of unplanned change. The second reason is that I am forced to make a self-assessment of my value as a change agent. This is notoriously unreliable since I naturally have a bias towards seeing my intervention as a success. The third reason is that it is very hard to decide whether the short-term changes now apparent will prove to be merely trivial or really significant in the longer term. Given these three qualifying factors I shall try to evaluate this project in terms of whether or not my objectives stated on pages 3 and 4 were achieved. That is, did the health of the Aboriginal people of Bourke improve? Has there been any improvement in their social circumstances? What other signs are there that change has occurred?

Change in medical status

Much of this book has described the effort involved in trying to bring about a better level of health in the Aboriginal people of Bourke. This included trying to prevent disease and discomfort through the provision of immunisation clinics run in the Aboriginal Community Centre, a family planning service and a community and infant health clinic on the Bourke Reserve. I also made an effort to improve the nutrition of Aboriginal people by fortifying their bread with vitamins and small amounts of iron and by concentrating attention on improving the quality of the diet of infants and young children.

Because my prime concern was with the Aboriginal population of Bourke, I was able to provide a more comprehensive general practitioner service for those who were already ill than had been available from doctors who also had to look after the white population. In 1968 the number of Aboriginal consultations made with a very popular general practitioner was 1332 (Coolican, 1973). In the first half of 1971 before I was fully accepted by the Bourke Aborigines, the number of official consultations (ie. people who came to my clinics or to the hospital to see me) was 537. The number who consulted 'unofficially' was many more and a conservative estimate of my total consultations with Aborigines was over 3000 per year. This does not include those people I saw as part of my research or preventive medical activities. In addition, I was able to improve the access of Aborigines to other medical services. This increased the Aboriginal proportion of the total consultations to the specialists visiting Bourke from 1.7% in 1971 to 19.8% in 1972. Also the epidemiological data I provided to the other health workers in Bourke resulted in them paying greater attention to treating previously neglected disorders in children such as ear disease, infestations of the gut and iron deficiency anaemia. An increased emphasis was also put on the domiciliary care of children through the provision of a community health nurse and two Aboriginal health aides.

So far I have described an increase in the quantity of health care that became available. This by itself is meaningless and a more realistic investigation is to measure the results of this increased effort.

The effect of increased effort

Infant mortality

Between 1967 and 1971 there were 18 infant deaths out of 224 births, an infant mortality rate of 88 per 1000. From 1972 to 1976 there were seven deaths from 133 live births, an infant mortality rate of 53 per 1000. Given the small numbers, this is not a major improvement. However, in 1967 to 1971 twelve of the infants who died were older than one month. Ten of these deaths were due to the gastroenteritis-pneumonia complex and one was due to whooping cough. In theory then ten deaths were preventable had medical care been sought or given at an earlier stage of their illness, and one death was probably preventable had the child been immunised. Between 1972 and 1976 the causes of death of the five children who died after the age of one month were largely non-preventable. Two children both well nourished died unexpectedly from inhaling vomit after having been admitted to the district hospital with mild upper respiratory tract infections, one child choked on a broad bean, another was born with a severe neurological abnormality, and the only child to die from the pneumonia-gastroenteritis complex was brought to the Bourke Hospital in a moribund condition from a town 300 km away which lacked a resident doctor. In the last two years (1975 and 1976) there have been only two infant deaths in Bourke and neither could have been prevented by even the most sophisticated paediatric care.

Morbidity

In the first year that I was in Bourke approximately 10% of infants admitted to the Bourke District Hospital with gastroenteritis were so ill and dehydrated that they had to be rehydrated by intravenous fluids. This was also reported to be the case prior to 1970 (Coolican, 1973:73). In the 56 month period from August 1971 to March 1977, there was a marked decrease in the severity of all sickness episodes. Apart from one newborn infant who died from staphylococcal septicaemia and the child who died from gastroenteritis, no child has required intravenous therapy during that time despite an epidemic of a severe form of dysentery which occurred during a heat wave at the end of 1972. It was my policy to admit children to hospital for any minor complaint which could conceivably have become worse and also to give intensive therapy to such conditions such as chronic suppurative middle ear disease, anaemia and intestinal parasites. Despite this there was a gradual reduction in hospital admission rates which has continued after my departure from Bourke (see Table 30).

This reduction in the hospitalisation rate of children was also a reflection of the diminished birth rate resulting from the ready and continuing acceptance of family planning (see Table 31). Another factor which diminished the severity of disease episodes, especially measles, was that all children were fully immunised by 1973.

In 1973, Aboriginal mothers claimed that their children were no longer sick and this impression was shared by the nursing staff of the by then almost empty children's ward of the district hospital.

A one-in-eight random sample of children examined in 1971 was re-

Table 30 Hospital admissions of Bourke Aboriginal children aged 0-9 years

Year	Admissions	Days average stay per admission	% Proportion of total hospital admissions
1970	419	7.2	18.2
1971	480	7.8	25.5
1972	372	6.6	19.7
1973	335	6.6	16.8
1974*	146	5.5	13.1

*to 31 August 1974

Table 31 Birth rates for Bourke Aborigines: 1964–1974

Year	Number of births	Birth rate/1000
1964–1971	340 (42.5/year)	71
1972	26	35
1973	19	35
1974	25	32

examined in 1974 and this shows the basis for the impression that there had been improvement (*see* Table 32). The results quoted are not conclusive but they indicate that the severity of some disease processes had diminished and that the prevalence of trachoma, running ears and iron deficiency anaemia was much reduced. Not all the objective evidence confirmed the mothers' subjective judgement about the improvement in their children's health. There was no improvement in height and weight, upper respiratory tract infections were still present in half the children and scabies and roundworm had increased, although this was probably as the result of floods early in 1974 which had led to evacuation of people from the Reserve to overcrowded conditions in tents and houses.

Dr Barry Duffy of the Department of Paediatrics in the Prince of Wales Hospital, Sydney, has conducted a longitudinal survey of the growth and development of a cohort of Aboriginal children in Bourke since 1970. It is his impression, too, that by 1975 the health of these children had improved in that they appear to be better nourished and have less iron deficiency anaemia. He found no such improvement in

Table 32 Morbidity in children aged 0-14 years in 1971 and 1974

Disease number = 45	Percentage positive	
	1971	1974
Trachoma	36	13
Angula stomatitis (fissures at angles of mouth)	13	0
Enlarged liver > 2 cm	11	2
Running ear	27	7
Upper respiratory tract infection	49	51
< 10th percentile height	53	56
< 10th percentile weight	40	51
Iron deficiency anaemia	18	7
Scabies	0	20
Roundworm	1	3
Bed-wetting	30	4

315

Aboriginal children from Brewarrina, a town about 100 km from Bourke, in which no such medical or social intervention has occurred (Duffy, 1975, pers. comm.).

It is difficult to pinpoint the causes of the improved health of the Aboriginal children. Improved living conditions may have had an effect, but the main reasons were probably an increased awareness of health factors on the part of the parents with a consequently greater consumer demand for health care, coupled with a better cultural understanding of and subsequently better communication with Aborigines on the part of the health personnel. A major factor in supporting this change has been the acceptance by Aborigines of the two community health nurses whom they helped to choose (firstly Sister Marj. Payton and currently Sister Diane Gaynor). This enabled sick children to be seen earlier than had previously been the case. Another major influence on the children's health was the success of the family planning programme which enabled mothers to space their children and so give more attention to each child in turn.

In terms of my stated aim to initiate and support programmes to improve the health conditions of the Aboriginal people of Bourke, I think it reasonable to claim that the type of medical intervention offered was adequate in lessening the severity of disease as well as being culturally acceptable to Bourke Aborigines. It also succeeded in setting up patterns of continued consumer demand for health care and improved the co-ordination of the local health services offered to the Aborigines. However, it could not be said that the programme was adequate for eradicating disease.

The evaluation of social change

The major long-term aim of this project was to encourage the development of a functioning Aboriginal community (that is a community in which leaders had emerged and in which a significant proportion of the population participated in decision-making) in the hope that such organisation would reduce the degree of disintegration and powerlessness evident in this Aboriginal community in 1970.

As I have mentioned, in 1970, the only organisation within the Bourke Aboriginal community centred around the United Aboriginal Mission Church, which involved only 20 people. This group sponsored a girls' basketball team and organised an annual talent show to commemorate National Aborigines' Day. By 1972 there was an obviously increased effort at organisation within the community. The Bourke A.A.A. had been formed and held monthly meetings; there were weekly meetings of four different human relations groups; a housing co-operative had been established and there were various social and sporting organisations active within the community.

The effect of all this endeavour was the development of a better functioning Aboriginal community. The A.A.A. became a political organisation to which Aborigines could put their ideas or their grievances and through which they could ask for action to be taken. This Association reduced the apathy of many people and diminished the degree of fragmentation of the community. Leaders were spawned who became the spokesmen for the Bourke Aborigines and their voices were heard in places where Aborigines had never been heard before. This new found assertiveness led to a collective confidence in Bourke Aborigines. More began to participate in the affairs of the Aboriginal community and they contributed ideas and methods for solving problems.

Both a recognised leadership and a political organisation attracted financial support from the Commonwealth Department of Aboriginal Affairs and this gave the A.A.A. and their leaders buying power in Bourke, which in turn led to many whites recognising the legitimacy of the Association. White organisations began to negotiate with it and to work through it. However, it was not as strong as it might have been because its members could not always rely on each other to carry out individual undertakings. This was due in part to a lack of previous experience of self discipline and group discipline and to ignorance of the skills needed to complete many of these tasks. It was like a football team in which some members could not be relied on to kick the ball while others would sometimes kick it away from their own goal. Such behaviour did not make for a properly functioning team. Nevertheless there was a team where there had not been one before and it had enough members who it was hoped would develop enough skills and apply enough social pressure to encourage everyone to kick the same way.

The increasing coherence of the Aboriginal community resulted in changes of attitude and behaviour of many of its members. The attitude of despair which they had expressed by accepting their ascribed status as 'the lowest of the low' gave way to a belief in the possibility of change and to an assertion that they were as good as the next man.

317

Perhaps one manifestation of this was the increase in Aborigines registered on the electoral roll from 37 in 1970 to 144 in 1974 (Electoral Roll, 1974). Since only three were prosecuted for not voting in the 1974 federal elections it is also safe to assume that they exercised their right to vote.

Many of those who attended human relations groups had developed an increased capacity to trust their fellow man, to express themselves verbally and to exercise increased self control. They were more desirous and better able to participate in the making of decisions concerning their future. There were enough Aborigines involved in the affairs of their community to provide emotional support for each other, to make it safe to enter into competition with whites and to participate in some of the affairs of the white society.

The posture of psychological withdrawal with the face hidden behind and guarded by the hand which was so common in 1970, was replaced by a more upright stance and increased eye to eye contact by 1972. Partly due to the increased dignity of their parents, Aboriginal children (especially those who had the opportunity to attend the Bourke pre-school) stopped hiding from white people and clinging to their parents in the presence of a white stranger. Their teachers commented on their increased confidence and participation in all aspects of school life and those teachers who encouraged Aboriginal students were surprised by the pride that these students displayed in their Aboriginal ancestry.

It is obvious that Aborigines wanted change, that change occurred and that at its peak, it involved at least a third of the Aborigines in Bourke. The important question is whether this change is significant or trivial and whether it has resulted in internalised or superficial changes in some Aborigines. It is too early to give a definite answer and only a further report in five or ten years time will enable definite conclusions to be reached. However, an idea of the direction in which further change may be expected can be postulated by reviewing the factors which favour further change and also those factors which are detrimental to further change.

Factors favouring further change

There is a core of Aboriginal people who are aware that there is a new climate regarding the place of Aborigines in society. These people feel that there is a reasonable hope for change and they are motivated to work for this change. Out of their new role they have evolved self respect, dignity and at times even feelings of potency. They attempt to show more involvement in the affairs of their people and less avoidance of potentially difficult tasks or threatening situations. Their attitudes are less fatalistic and their behaviour to whites less hostile.

They have developed a form of problem-solving behaviour and even when their skills are limited they know where and how to ask for help when they need it. Their ability to arrange meetings and to consult about problems is a new form of group behaviour; that is, it appears to be a new group norm. These people have a developing competence in managing their own affairs and are becoming more sophisticated in their dealings with the white man. Their children too have benefited from this improved social climate and some are pursuing opportunities and skills denied to their parents. Another factor favouring further change is that, up till now, the negative side effects of change have been few: one potential Aboriginal leader suffered a loss of 'face' when he was unable to cope with this role and was rejected by his own people; the hopes that many people had of obtaining low cost housing were not fully realised; and there was a degree of white backlash but this was relatively mild and was limited to rumour and 'sick humour' and had little effect if any upon the Aboriginal people.

Factors detrimental to further change

These factors are at the personal, the organisational and at the economic level. At the personal level not enough people have yet developed those basic skills in reading, writing and book work to translate into action many of the possible solutions to their problems, without calling on white help. Even some of the community leaders who had taken the trouble to improve their literacy skills still exhibit considerable anxiety over book work.

At the organisational level the hindrance to real change has been subtle, unintentional, but nevertheless crucial. The original body set up by the Bourke Aborigines was the A.A.A. Through it Aborigines had the chance of expressing their views and many were able to take part in negotiating directly with local or central government people whose actions affected or could affect them. A measure of its success as a forum for discussion was that at its peak up to one-third of all Bourke Aborigines over the age of fifteen years were attending its meetings. The field officers were then paid officers whose job was to provide information and help in carrying out the decisions agreed to at the A.A.A. meetings. The formation of a co-operative withdrew power from the larger informal A.A.A. and resulted in its collapse. This threw more of the onus for decision making on to the small executive of the co-operative and many Aborigines felt disenfranchised and lost interest.

At the same time requests from Canberra or from local government were transmitted to the field officers and the officers of the Widjeri Co-operative. Unwittingly they became more representatives of government than of those who had elected them. The co-operative in fact became to a considerable degree an arm of the Department of Aboriginal Affairs, more concerned with implementing broad, non-local policies than in representing the views of Bourke Aborigines.

My current feeling is that unless the Widjeri Co-operative makes an active effort to reinvolve 'the people' it will lose its potential for reinforcing those deeper more lasting changes which had begun to occur in the individual and collective psyches of Bourke Aborigines.

An even greater cause for the withering of the potential developed by the Bourke Aborigines is their lack of economic opportunity. During the last few months that I was in Bourke and on my visits since, I have been aware of this increasingly large, economic shadow overlying the whole basis of my social and medical intervention. I was not able, nor has any other agency yet been able to improve the economic opportunities for Aborigines in Bourke. Without such opportunity I have the uneasy feeling that community development is a form of phoney war akin to firing rubber bullets at secondary targets, while the primary target (the lack of economic opportunity) goes ignored and unscathed.

Conclusion

In summary then, I think I can safely say that change for the better has occurred and that, judging by the state of the Aboriginal communities in surrounding towns, this change would not have occurred without the direct intervention of myself as a change agent. A change agent can only be said to have been truly successful in his work when his client community no longer needs his services, because it has resolved its problems or can cope with those that remain without his assistance. He must neither overstay his welcome, nor depart too soon leaving his client community feeling unsafe and insecure without the technical knowledge and emotional support he provided. Unfortunately, this latter condition was not fulfilled when I left Bourke. Although there is in 1977 an Aboriginal political body in Bourke, there are leaders, there is increased knowledge and power and lessons have been learnt from both successes and failures, the Bourke Aborigines still need help in fulfilling their hopes of advancement. The success of the enterprise is that they no longer need help in working out just what it is they want. The pity is that when I left I was not replaced by another doctor change agent or indeed any other kind of change agent. Nevertheless, I do not think it rash to claim that enough members of the Bourke Aboriginal community have been permanently affected for the good of themselves and their community by what has happened since 1971 to ensure that there will be further improvements. Even without the assistance of a resident doctor change agent, the Bourke Aborigines are finding ways of achieving the goals that they themselves set, in order to live in the way that they choose.

About eighteen months after I started on this work, I began to look upon myself as the forerunner of a new type of doctor much needed in Australia. I envisaged a growing number of future doctors taking up the challenge of extending their roles into the field of community development in order to benefit the communities in which they worked. These doctors would experiment upon and refine my crude model so that the practice of the doctor change agent would become increasingly scientific. Some of my medical colleagues were sceptical about my vision because they could not see too many of the present products of Australian medical schools taking up such a challenge. Unfortunately, their criticism has proven to be realistic and this situation will not begin to change until the teaching and socialisation process of medical students results in more socially aware and socially active doctors.

Nevertheless, all health and welfare workers who have even a peripheral involvement with Aborigines should understand the principles behind the practices which I have described. Without them they are unlikely to be able to adapt their expertise so that it is of use in reducing the ill health and social misery of Australian Aborigines.

Another criticism of this work is that it is unscientific because it has resulted from my 'special talents' and is therefore not easily reproducible by other workers in the same field. I would agree that much that happens in the diverse and all-encompassing field of community development is a function of the 'singer and not the song' and I discussed this at length in chapter 12. In the sense that each of the singers cannot be easily reduced to a common denominator, the end result of such an intervention is not reproducible and it may be that the results obtained were due to a lucky mix of a particular Aboriginal group gelling with my particular personality. However, I dispute that the song is not scientific. This work is an early Australian exploration into the relatively new field of change agentry. Although it deals with an Australian Aboriginal community, it describes and analyses those strategies and tactics which can be used to stimulate change in other needy communities. Future workers will develop and refine this model so that gradually a series of generalisations about such work will emerge.

The critical shortage that Australia faces in trying to solve the problems of Aborigines is not a lack of money or of will. It is a lack of knowledge. Allocating funds to government agencies, doctors, architects, lawyers or teachers and telling them to improve the health, housing, education or legal discrimination against Aborigines will not help if they do not know how to go about it. A variety of pilot programmes to improve the social and health conditions of Aborigines needs to be instituted and critically evaluated so that basically successful formulae can be applied to help other groups. It is only in this way that we can make any real and significant contribution to helping Aboriginal people achieve what they see as their felt needs and ensure that our continued intervention in the lives of Aborigines will not be as arbitrary and as disruptive as it has been in the past.

Appendix

Wally Byers' views on change in Bourke up to the end of 1974

For the last two and a half years it is one of the most heartbreaking jobs that I have ever had and the most difficult. For all the time that I have worked for the Murries I have seen all types of people come and go but we are still not much changed and the Murries are not all that advanced. We have had student doctors to professor doctors. We have had Murries, ministers and politicians. You name it, we have had it. And everybody thinks they know what the Murries want.

Just take myself for instance. As I had not much schooling I get a lot of people telling me what is right for the Murries. So I tell the Murries over and over again things like 'Do you want a house? We will get you a house.' And I do these things because some big white gub tells us to do these things. But that is as far as it goes, because the same big white gub then tells you that you cannot do that. Then there are some more gubs who tell you this is the way the Murries should live but they never do much about it. When all things are boiled down you cannot blame the Murries for taking things as they come and not wanting to try to better themselves.

The only thing I am sorry about is that Bill and myself did not have at least six months training for this job and that may have made things a bit different. But getting back to the time I started in Bourke.

I was going past Bill Reid's church one night and there was a meeting going on. That is when I first met Dr Max Kamien. That was when things started to happen in Bourke. For Bill and myself, we talked a lot to this Dr Kamien and eventually we decided to go to Canberra and Sydney to get money for two field officers and a minibus for three years. We came back to Bourke and we talked to the Murries about an election in which Murries would have to elect two people as field officers. There were about seven or eight people including myself. When all the votes were counted I was one and Bill Reid was the other and that is how I got the job.

Looking back at the change now I know that it mightn't look much. But this big white Dr Max Kamien had done so much to help the dark people. Some say he was just doing his job to get a degree. Well even so the government should take a look at some of his reports and would see for themselves how the infant mortality rate had dropped and it is still much better since he went because we had such a doctor like Max that made black people feel like human beings. I, myself, did not know that there were so many people with problems till Max Kamien, Bill Reid, Noel Gillon and myself went to a workshop in Armidale. That was when I seen people for the first time, Murries with problems and heartaches. For it was a shame to see how the white man's system makes a lot of dark people's problems worse for they try to fit into the white system when they have not been taught. Human workshops work for some people, even whites, because you see white people for what they are and you know that there are some whites that are alright.

Better get on with things in Bourke. We went to Sydney to see about some money to build some houses. We had met a man from Sydney before we went down there named Bill Lucas. He had two white students named Bernie Coates and John Luckens. We were to see him and then go on to Canberra which we did, and not long after we got some money from Canberra. Along with some heartaches the A.A.A. had been formed. But Bill Lucas, John Luckens and Bernie Coates and six Murries from Bourke tried to build cheaper housing for the Murries. They called them prefabricated or something like that. But seeing how the boys did not have the right idea about building, it took much longer and more money than the average house. So that was a setback, but we got more money from Canberra and finished the first house which we used for a centre. We got two more houses when the people started to get fed up with things because at this rate it would be years before most people got a home and we had about 37 families down on the Reserve. We had already made a muck of balloting the first houses because some town people put in their names in the ballot box and a lot were not satisfied with the result.

Things started to look up again and the Murries started to get back a little encouragement. Then we decided to form a Widjeri Co-op which a lot of Murries did not understand. They had gotten used to the A.A.A. But we went ahead anyway and formed the Widjeri Co-op. The Co-op was working alright and looked like getting more houses started and the others finished, then along comes a Murrie called Mick Telly and he knows a lot more about building than John and Bernie. So that's alright because he is a Murrie and could easily get a building licence. He done a lot on the two houses that were just getting started when he came. So the Bourke Murries could see things looking up and it was only right to give him a lot more authority. But it turned out that Mick had not had a lot to do with Murries. He also had a few problems of his own. He also put more Murries on to work and that got rid of a lot of the funds. Mick couldn't work in with John and Bernie because he couldn't understand why so many Murries let these white students do most of the work that the Murries could do for themselves. But Mick started to see that Bernie, Bill and John were right in a lot of their ways about the wages and other things and I am sure he would have come good with a bit more understanding. I for one was glad to see someone like Mick come along and I give him credit where it is due. It is a shame when someone like him is made a fool of by a man like L.Y. who came up to Bourke and starts to blame one man. That is ridiculous when we are all partly to blame for the way things went. The way I see it things were all spoilt by the white men from Canberra. They know how to keep Murries down, for they only give the Murries enough to keep the Murries at each other's throats. If they would give enough things they could make work for Murries like industry or a factory or something like that. I reckon that we have so many towns that need help that the government should spend more on say, Wilcannia or Brewarrina and let some towns go the way they are for twelve months or so. Then the next year they should give Bourke or Walgett the same amount of money and at that rate things would be much better. Because when you can only help half of the Murries in one town, you cause a split in the community and when you do it is the hardest thing to get it going again. I have seen these splits in Bourke and it takes a long time to rectify.

Well, as I said before and I say again, it would take more than a crop of politicians to sort out the Bourke people. It will have to be done at a grass roots level and in case you don't know where that is, that is the Murries themselves and the conditions where they live. It is the same old story, that if you are a strong Murrie you can get ahead a lot faster than the average Murrie. I have seen that done quite a lot. You get the Murrie who thinks he is better than the next Murrie. But I say that a bloke like that is not worth very much anyhow. I have been taught to give as far back as I can remember. I was also taught that if you could not do some things good for someone why do the wrong thing by him. So if you have thoughts like these I'm sure you should be a great help to Murries or anybody for that matter. All my work for the Murries is not regretted. There is a great lot of Murries that I have come to respect.

A great lot has happened here in Bourke and I don't know where it will end. For I have seen Murries have money handed out to them by the government people, unsure of what it was for. They have tried to better things themselves without much supervision from Canberra. For the only time Canberra wanted to get involved is when things start to go wrong. Like when we had a few Murries trying to make the special work grants work. It was not easy for them for the simple reason that it was easy-come and easy-go and when you get a bloke like Mick Telly or John Dillon that are easy-going and easy to get on with and always trying to help the needy Murries it is only natural that they end up getting the worst end of the criticism. The special works did not work because of John Dillon, or the houses did not work because of Mick Telly. The whole lot of the blame had to be put on everyone in Bourke and Canberra for the simple reason that you cannot expect people whether they be black or white to make things work without some compassion and understanding to each other.

After two and a half years of working for the Murries and representing them, I find it hard to tell them that it is time for them to make a change. I say to them 'Now look, if we want to fit into the white man's system you have to start to pay your way. It is the only way. So we form up the co-operative again and we start to charge 15 cents a mile for the bus and the car.' The people agree to that. And I have to be one of the people that tell them about this and you really start to find out how much they dislike you for what you are doing. I had a bloke come down from Walgett saying to me that I was robbing the Murries by making them pay 15 cents a mile. Then try to explain to him that it was the only way to keep the vehicles on the road. Not like legal aid, they get a new car when they like it. He says that he works most of the time and don't get paid. But it still falls back on what I say again and again. That if the government are going to go around making things like legal services, why don't they do it properly instead of half building it up then slamming it. I reckon it stinks because they don't have enough money. The people that fight the case for the Murries have to run around looking for bail money. Legal aid should have some sort of bail fund. But if they put money into things like this then it may work and that might hurt the white system to see things going right. So you can see that working for Murries is not so rosy. There are many other people, Murries and whites who think they can solve the problems of the Murries. But what we must remember is that it is only when you get the Murries to help that things will happen. And that takes a hell of a long time to get the Murries to help themselves. So no matter how hard we try it will take a long time.

But things have really changed here in Bourke and the Murries are really starting to tell you what they want. When I first started the Murries were afraid to talk up for what they wanted. But now if you start to talk you always have somebody telling you that you are wrong and that is a good sign.

One of our biggest setbacks is that we don't have an office or a place to hold our meetings.

So that is about all I want to say for now. We have ten Murries on the Shire, and they look like they will get permanent jobs. We have one white Sister [Mrs Marj. Payton] that understands the Murries and she also has two Murrie assistants, one up town and one down on the Reserve. The Reserve gets the afternoon service and our end of town gets the morning service. We have a pre-school up town where black and white go and we have another pre-school of our own where the small kiddies go. We hope to have a centre where all the other Murries can go for things like meetings and night school. We also have some sports that we play. So you see as bad as things look we have come a long way in a very short time and I am sure that things will be much better. When I came to Bourke about 20 years ago I lived on reserves myself and we had to cart water from the river and use toilets that were holes in the ground. So you see there are big changes. Even down on the Reserve they have water taps not far away and pan toilets and a gravel road and some flood lights and a wash-house that the white sister uses. So most times it does pay to look at some of the things that have worked. With the help of the Co-op things could go a lot further than they have so you see things have improved since I came to Bourke. This is how Wally Byers, part-Aboriginal, sees the Bourke people with their everyday problems. So I only hope that somebody gets some satisfaction out of reading all this.

Signed,

Walter Charles Byers

References

Adair, J. and K. W. Deuschle 1970 *The people's health. Medicine and anthropology in a Navajo community.* New York: Appleton-Century-Crofts.

Arthur, R. 1902 *The treatment of middle-ear suppuration.* Intercolonial Medical Congress of Australasia. Sixth Session.

Australian Institute of Anatomy 1957 *Standard height-weight tables for Australians approved by the Nutrition Committee of the National Health and Medical Research Council, Canberra.* Canberra: Commonwealth Government Printer.

Australian Morbidity Index 1971 Vol. 1. January–March 1971; vol. 2. April–June 1971. Sydney: Health Research Services of Australia Pty Ltd.

Batten, T. R. 1965 *The human factor in community work.* London: Oxford University Press.

Beckett, J. 1958 Marginal men: a study of two halfcaste Aborigines. *Oceania*, 29:91.

Beckett, J. 1964 Aborigines, alcohol and assimilation. In *Aborigines now: New perspective in the study of Aboriginal communities,* M. Reay (ed.), pp. 32-47. Sydney: Angus and Robertson.

Beckett, J. 1967 Marriage, circumcision and avoidance among the Maljangaba of northwest New South Wales. *Mankind,* 6(10):456.

Bennett, P. H., Burch, T. A. and M. Miller 1971 Diabetes mellitus in American (Pima) Indians. *Lancet,* 2:125.

Bennis, W. G., Benne, K. D. and R. Chin 1970 *The planning of change,* 2nd ed. London: Holt, Rinehart and Winston.

Berelson, B. 1969 *National Family Planning Programmes: Where we stand in fertility and family planning: a world view,* S. J. Behrmans *et al.* (eds), p. 341. Ann Arbor: University of Michigan Press.

Berg, O. 1971 Personal view. *British Medical Journal,* 1:286.

Bertuch, G. and J. Leeton 1971 The effect of publicity on oral contraceptive practice. *Medical Journal of Australia,* 2:1067.

Bird, G. C., Giles, P. F. H., Martin, J. D., Stenhouse, N. S. and E. D. Waters 1970 A gynaecological cancer survey in a rural community: Busselton, Western Australia. *Medical Journal of Australia,* 1:1039.

Black, L. 1942 *Cylcons, the mystery stones of the Darling River Valley: Part 2, being a continuation of a series on the customs of the Aborigines of the Darling River Valley and of central New South Wales.* Privately printed by Mr L. Black, 'Mokanger', Leeton, N.S.W.

Black, L. 1950 *Stone arrangements: Being a continuation of a series on the customs of the Aborigines of the Darling River Valley and of central New South Wales.* Privately printed by Paterson Brokensha Pty Ltd, Perth.

Bowlby, J. 1951 *Maternal care and mental health.* World Health Organization Monograph Series, No. 2.

Bridges, B. 1970 The beginnings of medical care for Aborigines in eastern Australia (N.S.W.). *Medical Journal of Australia*, 2:879.

Briscoe, G. 1974 New models for Aboriginal health services. The Aboriginal Medical Service in Sydney. Report for Nutritional Seminar at Monash University 15-17 May 1972. In *Better health for Aborigines?* Hetzel, B. S., Dobbin, M., Lippmann, L. and E. Eggleston (eds), pp. 166-70. St. Lucia: University of Queensland Press.

Brody, E. B. 1966 Cultural exclusion, character and illness. *American Journal of Psychiatry*, 122:852.

Brown, T. 1972 *Dental decay in Aborigines.* Research Seminar: Aboriginal Health Services. Centre for Research into Aboriginal Affairs, Monash University.

Burden, J. K. 1971a *A report on the acceptability of contraception to Australian women in areas north and west of Port Augusta.* Adelaide: University of Adelaide.

Burden, J. K. 1971b *A report on the acceptability of contraception to Australian women in the north west region of South Australia.* Adelaide: University of Adelaide.

Burgess, P. 1971 Black nuns in a black shanty town. The day Sister Celine stood guard over the grog. *Daily Mirror*, 14 January 1971.

Calley, M. J. C. 1956 Economic life of mixed-blood communities in northern New South Wales. *Oceania*, 26:200.

Calley, M. J. C. 1957 Race relations on the north coast of New South Wales. *Oceania*, 27(3):190.

Capell, A. 1963 *Linguistic survey of Australia.* Canberra: Australian Institute of Aboriginal Studies.

Caplan, G. 1964 *Principles of preventive psychiatry.* London: Tavistock Publications.

Carnegie, D. 1936 *How to win friends and influence people.* Sydney: Angus and Robertson.

Carstairs, G. M. 1957 *The twice-born: A study of a community of high-caste Hindus.* London: Hogarth.

Cartwright, A. 1970 *Parents and family planning services.* London: Routledge and Kegan Paul.

Cawte, J. E. 1968 The human ecology of the arid zone. *Australian and New Zealand Journal of Psychiatry*, 2:2.

Cawte, J. E. 1969 Psychological adjustment to cultural change: the case of the Australian Aborigines. *Australian and New Zealand Journal of Psychiatry*, 3:343.

Cawte, J. E. 1972 *Cruel, poor and brutal nations. The assessment of mental health in an Australian Aboriginal community by short-stay psychiatric field-team methods.* Honolulu: The University Press of Hawaii.

Cawte, J. E. 1973 Social medicine in central Australia. The opportunities of Pitjantjara Aborigines. *Medical Journal of Australia*, 1:221.

329

Cawte, J. E. 1974 *Medicine is the law: Studies in psychiatric anthropology of Australian tribal societies.* Adelaide: Rigby.

Cawte, J. E., Bianchi, G. N. and L. G. Kiloh 1968 Personal discomfort in Australian Aborigines. *Australian and New Zealand Journal of Psychiatry*, 2:69.

Chase, S. 1965 *The proper study of mankind. An inquiry into the science of human relations.* London: Phoenix House.

Clark, K. B. 1965 *Dark ghetto: Dilemmas of social power.* London: Victor Gollancz.

Collins, E. and G. Turner 1973 A suggestion for reducing the incidence of habitual analgesic consumption. [Letter to the Editor] *Medical Journal of Australia*, 1:863.

Commonwealth Bureau of Census and Statistics 1971 Canberra, A.C.T.

Coolican, R. E. 1973 *Australian rural practice.* Australian Medical Association. Mervyn Archdall Medical Monograph No. 9. Sydney: Australian Medical Publishing Co.

Coolican, R. E. 1974 The role of the general practitioner in the health team. Report of a National Seminar on Health Services for Aborigines at Monash University 15-17 May 1972. In *Better health for Aborigines?* Hetzel, B. S., Dobbin, M., Lippmann, L. and E. Eggleston (eds), pp. 127-32. St Lucia: University of Queensland Press.

Cullen, K. J. 1972 Mass health examinations in the Busselton population, 1966 to 1970. *Medical Journal of Australia*, 2:714.

Cullen, K. J. and T. Woodings 1975 Alcohol, tobacco and analgesics—Busselton, 1972. *Medical Journal of Australia*, 2:211.

Curr, E. M. 1886 *The Australian race: Its origin, languages, customs, place of landing in Australia and the routes by which it spread itself over that continent.* Melbourne: Government Printer.

Diem, K. 1962 *Documenta Geigy scientific tables*, 6th ed. Basle: Ciba Geigy.

Department of Child Welfare and Social Welfare 1969 *The Aborigines Act, 1969.* Canberra: Government Printer.

Deutsch, M. 1971 Conflicts: productive and destructive. In *Social intervention, a behavioural science approach*, Hornstein, H. A., Bunker, B. B., Burke, W. W., Gindes, M. and R. J. Lewicki (eds), pp. 566-76. New York: The Free Press.

Douglas, A. 1973 The team: doctor, nurse and social worker. *Hospital and Health Care and Administration*, 3:3.

Dubos, R. 1959 *Mirage of health. Utopias, progress and biological change.* London: George Allen and Unwin.

Dunbar, G. K. 1943 Notes on the Ngemba tribe of the Central Darling River, Western New South Wales. *Mankind*, 3(5):140; (6):172.

Electoral Roll 1974 State Electoral District of Castlereagh. Commonwealth of Australia. State of New South Wales. New South Wales: Government Printer.

Ellis, C. J. 1972 *Family planning among Pitjantjara women. A communication problem.* University of Adelaide: 8.

330

Fawcett, J. T. 1970 *Psychology and population—behavioural research issues in fertility and family planning.* New York: The Population Council.

Fink, R. A. 1957 The caste barrier—an obstacle to the assimilation of part-Aborigines in north west New South Wales. *Oceania,* 28(2):100.

FitzPatrick, J. 1971 States Grants (Aboriginal Advancement) Bill. Canberra; Hansard, 4047.

Freire, P. 1972 *Pedagogy of the oppressed.* London: Sheed and Ward.

Frith, N. C., Hausfeld, R. G. and P. M. Moodie 1974 *The Coasttown project.* Action Research in Aboriginal Community Health. Australian Department of Health, School of Public Health and Tropical Medicine, University of Sydney, Service Publication No. 11. Canberra: Australian Government Publishing Service.

Gale, F. 1964 *A study of assimilation: Part-Aborigines in South Australia.* Adelaide: Library Board of South Australia.

Gale, F. 1966 Aborigines and the normal social welfare channels. *Australian Journal of Social Work,* 19(2):5.

Gandevia, B. 1967 The prevalence of signs of chronic respiratory disease in Pintubi and Walbiri Aborigines at Papunya, Central Australia, and Warburton, Western Australia. *Medical Journal of Australia,* 2:237.

Gillies, M. A. and A. P. Skyring 1972 The pattern and prevalence of Aspirin ingestion as determined by interview of 2,921 inhabitants of Sydney. *Medical Journal of Australia,* 1:974.

Goodenough, W. H. 1963 *Co-operation in change: An anthropological approach to community development.* New York: Russell Sage Foundation.

Gough, I. R., Josephson, M. M., Justins, D. M., Lodge, J. F. and N. F. Senior 1970 Aspirations of Aboriginal children. *Australian Psychologist,* 5(3):267.

Graves, G. D., Krupinski, J., Stoller, A. and A. Harcourt 1971a A survey of community attitudes towards mental illness. Part 1: The questionnaire. *Australian and New Zealand Journal of Psychiatry,* 5:18.

Graves, G. D., Krupinski, J. and A. Stoller 1971b A survey of community attitudes towards mental illness. Part 2: The semantic differential. *Australian and New Zealand Journal of Psychiatry,* 5:29.

Groves, B. 1966 Comment on the effects of raising Aboriginal wages on Aborigines by P. G. Albrecht. In *Aborigines in the economy: employment, wages and training,* Sharp, I. G. and C. M. Tatz (eds), pp. 187-88. Melbourne: Jacaranda Press.

Guevara, E. C. 1969 *On revolutionary medicine, Venceremos! The speeches and writings of Ernesto che Guevara,* J. Gerassi (ed.). New York: Simon & Schuster.

Hamburg, D. A. 1971 Crowding, stranger contact and aggressive behaviour. In *Society, stress and disease,* L. Love (ed.). London: Oxford University Press.

Hamilton, A. 1974 The health of Aborigines—sociocultural aspects. The traditionally oriented community. Report of a National Seminar on Health Services for Aborigines at Monash University 15-17 May 1972. In *Better Health for Aborigines?*

331

Hetzel, B. S., Dobbin, M., Lippmann, L. and E. Eggleston (eds), pp. 14-28. St Lucia: University of Queensland Press.

Hart, J. T. 1971 The inverse care law. *Lancet*, 1:405.

Hausfeld, R. 1963 Dissembled culture: An essay on method. *Mankind*, 6(2):47.

Heathcote, R. L. 1965 *Back of Bourke: A study of land appraisal and settlement in semi-arid Australia*. Melbourne University Press.

Hennessy, B. L., Bruen, W. J. and J. Cullen 1973 Canberra Mental Health Survey. Preliminary Results. *Medical Journal of Australia*, 1:721.

Hippocrates 460–375 BC *The genuine works of Hippocrates*. Translated by F. Adams Vol. 2. London: The Sydenham Society.

Hoffer, E. 1964 *The ordeal of change*. London: Sidgwick and Jackson.

Hurst, J. A. 1970 Birth Control—The views of women. *Medical Journal of Australia*, 2:835.

Hutton, H. J. 1971 A Black community looks at family planning. In *Advances in planned parenthood*, Vol. VI. Sobrero, A. J. and R. M. Harvey (eds). Amsterdam: Excerpta Medica.

Jones, D. L., Hemphill, W. and E. S. A. Meyers 1973 *Height, weight and other physical characteristics of New South Wales children*. Part 1. Children Aged Five Years and Over. New South Wales Department of Health. New South Wales: Government Printer.

Jones, E. G., Macdonald, I. and L. Breslow 1958 A study of epidemiological factors in carcinoma of the uterine cervix. *American Journal of Obstetrics and Gynecology*, 76:1.

Jones, M. A. 1972 Housing and Poverty in Australia. Carlton: Melbourne University Press.

Jose, D. G. and J. S. Welch 1970 Growth Retardation, Anaemia and Infection, with Malabsorption and Infestation of the Bowel. The Syndrome of Protein-Calorie Malnutrition in Australian Aboriginal Children. *Medical Journal of Australia*, 1:349.

Kamien, M. 1975a Ear disease and hearing in Aboriginal and white children in two schools in rural New South Wales. *Medical Journal of Australia, Supplement*, 1:33.

Kamien, M. 1975b Family planning in a part-Aboriginal community 1970–1973. *Medical Journal of Australia, Supplement*, 1:21.

Kamien, M. 1976a The physical health of Aboriginal children in Bourke, New South Wales. *Medical Journal of Australia, Special Supplement*, 1:33.

Kamien, M. 1976b The physical health of Aboriginal adults in Bourke, New South Wales. *Medical Journal of Australia, Special Supplement*, 1:38.

Kamien, M. 1976c Behaviour disorders in Bourke Aboriginal children. *Medical Journal of Australia, Special Supplement*, 2:6.

Kamien, M. 1976d Psychiatric disorders in Bourke Aboriginal adults. *Medical Journal of Australia, Special Supplement*, 2:11.

Kamien, M. and J. A. Bissett 1974 The future of the district hospital in rural Australia. *National Hospital*, 18:21.

Kamien, M. and P. Cameron 1974 An analysis of white and Aboriginal children under 5 years admitted to the Bourke District Hospital from September 1971 to August 1972. *Australian Paediatrics Journal*, 10:343.

Kamien, M., Woodhill, J. M., Nobile, S., Cameron, P. and P. Rosevear 1975 Nutrition in the Australian Aborigines: Effects of the fortification of white flour. *Australian and New Zealand Journal of Medicine*, 5:123.

Kerrigan, W. [1880s] Brewarrina in the sixty's. *Brewarrina News*, 3 December 1971.

Kessel, N. and H. Walton 1971 *Alcoholism*. Middlesex: Penguin Books.

King, M. 1966 *Medical care in developing countries: A primer on the medicine of poverty and a symposium from Makerere*. Nairobi: Oxford University Press.

Krupinski, J., Stoller, A., Baikie, A. G. and J. E. Graves 1970 *A community health survey of the rural town of Heyfield, Victoria, Australia*. Melbourne: Mental Health Authority, Special Publications.

Lancaster, H. O. 1956a Infant mortality in Australia. *Medical Journal of Australia*, 2:100.

Lancaster, H. O. 1956b The mortality of childhood in Australia. Part I. Early Childhood. *Medical Journal of Australia*, 2:889.

Lancaster, H. O. 1957a The mortality of childhood in Australia. Part II. The school ages. *Medical Journal of Australia*, 1:415.

Lancaster, H. O. 1957b The mortality in Australia of young adults. *Medical Journal of Australia*, 2:821.

Lammi, A. T. and V. A. Lovric 1973 Assessment of iron deficiency in children without anaemia. *Medical Journal of Australia*, 2:541.

Lancet 1970 Recurrent Bacteriuria. [Editorial], *Lancet*, 2:554.

Last, J. M. 1970 Organisation of medical care. In *Medical practice and the community*, Brown, R. G. and H. M. Whyte (eds). Canberra: Australian National University Press.

Leighton, A. H. 1963 Chapter XIII: The Frame of Reference. Comment and Review. In *The character of danger. Psychiatric Symptoms in Selected Communities*, Vol. III. The Stirling County Study of Psychiatric Disorders and Sociocultural Environment. Leighton, D. C., Harding, J. S., Macklin, D. B., Macmillan, A. M. and A. H. Leighton (eds). New York: Basic Books.

Leighton, A. H. 1965 Cultural change and psychiatric disorder. In *Transcultural Psychiatry*, de Reuck, A. V. S. and R. Porter (eds). London: T. & A. Churchill.

Lickiss, J. N. 1970 Health problems of Sydney Aboriginal children. *Medical Journal of Australia*, 2:995.

Lickiss, J. N. 1971 Social deviance in Aboriginal boys. *Medical Journal of Australia*, 2:460.

Lippitt, R., Watson, J. and B. Westley 1958 *The dynamics of planned change. A comparative study of principles and techniques*. New York: Harcourt Brace and World.

Lippmann, L. 1970 *To achieve our country—Australia and the Aborigines*. Melbourne: F. W. Christie Publishing.

333

Long, J. P. M. 1970 *Aboriginal settlements. A survey of institutional communities in eastern Australia.* Canberra: Australian National University Press.

Lovejoy, F. H. 1970 How to play the housing game in New South Wales. Rules for Aboriginal players. [Roneoed sheet] Department of Economic Statistics. Armidale: University of New England.

Maddison, D. and B. Raphael 1971 Social and psychological consequences of chronic disease in Childhood. *Medical Journal of Australia*, 2:1265.

Malone, C. H. 1970 Children. In *The practice of community mental health*, H. Grunebaum (ed.). Boston: Little, Brown & Co.

Martin, F. M., Brotherston, J. H. F. and S. P. W. Chave 1957 Incidence of neurosis in a new housing estate. *British Journal of Preventative Social Medicine*, 11:196.

Mazer, M. 1970 The therapist in the community. In *The practice of community mental health*, H. Grunebaum (ed.). Boston: Little, Brown & Co.

Mead, M. 1965 Adult Roles. In *Transcultural psychiatry*, de Reuck, A. V. S. and R. Porter (eds). London: J. & A. Churchill.

Medical Research Council 1957 Working party for research in general practice. Acute otitis media in general practice: Report of a survey. *Lancet*, 2:510.

Merton, R. K. 1957 *Social theory and social structure.* New York: The Free Press.

Mitchell, I. S. 1968 Epilogue to a referendum. *Australian Journal of Social Issues*, 3(4):9.

Mitchell, T. L. 1839 *Three expeditions into the interior of eastern Australia: with descriptions of the recently explored region of Australia felix, and of the present colony of New South Wales*, 2nd Ed. London: T. & W. Boon. Vol. 1. Reproduced by Australian Facsimile Editions No. 18. Adelaide: Libraries Board of South Australia, 1965.

Moodie, P. M. 1973 *Aboriginal health.* Canberra: Australian National University Press.

Moodie. P. M. 1974 The part-Aboriginal community. Report of a National Seminar on Health Services for Aborigines at Monash University 15–17 May 1972. In *Better health for Aborigines?* Hetzel, B. S., Dobbin, M., Lippmann, L. and E. Eggleston (eds), pp. 88–96. St Lucia: University of Queensland Press.

Murphy, J. M. and A. H. Leighton 1965 *Approaches to cross-cultural psychiatry.* New York: Cornell University Press.

McDermott, W., Deuschle, K. W. and C. R. Barnett 1972 Health care experiment at many farms—a technological misfit of health care and disease pattern existed in the Navajo community. *Science*, 175:23.

McPherson, P. 1972 The role of the public health nurse. Centre for Research into Aboriginal Affairs, Monash University. Research Seminar—Aboriginal Health Services 14–17 May 1972.

National Health Act. 1953 Section 7. Pharmaceutical Benefits. Canberra: Commonwealth Government Printer.

Neel, J. V., Fajans, S. A., Conn, J. W. and R. T. Davidson 1965 In *Diabetes mellitus— genetics and the epidemiology of chronic diseases*, Neel, J. R., Shaw, M. W. and W. J. Schull (eds). Washington: Public Health Service Publication No. 1163.

New South Wales Department of Health 1972 Personal health services within metropolitan regions. Report of an Advisory Committee.

New South Wales Teachers' Federation. 1972 Survey of Aboriginal children in N.S.W. secondary schools, 1971. [Roneoed] Sydney: N.S.W. Teachers' Federation.

Nobile, S. and J. M. Woodhill 1973 A survey of the vitamin content of some 2,000 foods as they are consumed by selected groups of the Australian population. *Food Technology of Australia*, 25:1.

Nurcombe, B. 1970 Deprivation: An essay in definition with special consideration of the Australian Aboriginal. *Medical Journal of Australia*, 2:87.

Nurcombe, B., de Lacey, P., Moffitt, P. and L. Taylor 1973 The question of Aboriginal intelligence: The first years of the Bourke pre-school experiment. *Medical Journal of Australia*, 2:625.

Oates, W. J. and L. F. Oates 1970 *A revised linguistic survey of Australia*. Canberra: Australian Institute of Aboriginal Studies.

Official Year Book of the Commonwealth of Australia. 1968 Year Book No. 54, 1968. Commonwealth Bureau of Census and Statistics. Canberra, Australia.

Panzetta, A. F. 1971 *Community mental health: Myth and reality*. Philadelphia: Lea and Febiger.

Peabody, G. L. 1971 Power, alinsky and other thoughts. In *Social intervention: A behavioural science approach*, Hornstein, H. A., Bunker, B. B., Burke, W. W., Gindes, M. and R. J. Lewicki (eds). New York: The Free Press.

Pearn, J. H. and H. Pavlin 1971 Material impression in a modern Australian community. *Medical Journal of Australia*, 2:1123.

Rankin, J. G. and P. Wilkinson 1971 *Alcohol and tobacco consumption in the health of a metropolis*, Krupinski, J. and A. Stoller (eds). Sydney: Heinemann Educational Australia.

Rogers, C. R. 1969 *Freedom to learn*. Columbus, Ohio: Charles E. Merrill Publishing Company.

Roghmann, K. J., Haggerty, R. J. and R. Lorenz 1971 Anticipated and actual effects of medicaid on the medical care pattern of children. *New England Journal of Medicine*, 285:1053.

Rowley, C. D. 1966 Some questions of causation in relation to Aboriginal Affairs. In *Aborigines in the economy: Employment, wages and training*, Sharp, I. G. and C. M. Tatz (eds), pp. 345–69. Melbourne: Jacaranda Press.

Russell, J. K. 1972 Planning family planning. *Lancet*, 1:310.

Saint, E. G. 1970 Bacchus transported. Purporting to be an historical impression of alcoholism in Australia. *Medical Journal of Australia*, 2:548.

Seuss, Dr 1965 *The sneetches and other stories*. London: Collins.

Shepherd, M., Oppenheim, B. and S. Mitchell 1971 *Childhood behaviour and mental health*. London: University of London Press.

Spargo, R. M. 1975 Aboriginal communities in remote Australia. Health care delivery — a doctor's role. *Medical Journal of Australia, Special Supplement*, 1:1.

Sturt, C. 1833a *Two expeditions into the interior of southern Australia during the years 1828, 1829, 1830 and 1831*. Smith, Elder and Co., London, Vol. 1. Reproduced by

335

Australiana Facsimile Editions No. 4. Adelaide: Public Library of South Australia, 1963.

Sturt, C. 1833b *Two expeditions into the interior of southern Australia during the years 1828, 1829, 1830 and 1831.* Smith, Elder and Co., London, Vol. II. Reproduced by Australiana Facsimile Edition No. 4. Adelaide: Public Library of South Australia, 1963.

Tatz, C. M. 1970 The health status of Australian Aborigines. The need for an interdisciplinary approach. *Medical Journal of Australia*, 2:191.

Tatz, C. M. 1974 Innovation without change. Report of a National Seminar on Health services for Aborigines at Monash University 15-17 May 1972. In *Better health for Aborigines?* Hetzell, B. S., Dobbin, M., Lippmann, L. and E. Eggleston (eds), pp. 107-20. St Lucia: University of Queensland Press.

Teulon, G. N. 1886 Bourke—the Darling River. In *The Australian race . . .*, Vol. II. E. M. Curr (ed.), pp. 186–223. Melbourne: Government Printer.

Thursz, D. 1966 Social action as a professional responsibility. *Social Work*, 11(1):12.

Tonkin, S. 1970 Maori infant health. Trial of intramuscular iron to present anaemia in Maori babies. *New Zealand Medical Journal*, 71:129.

Tranel, N. 1970 Rural program development. In *The practice of community mental health*, H. Grunebaum (ed.). Boxton: Little, Brown & Co.

Wise, P. H., Edwards, F. M., Thomas, D. W., Elliot, R. B., Hatcher, L. and R. Craig 1970 Hyperglycaemia in the urbanised Aboriginal. The Davenport survey. *Medical Journal of Australia*, 2:1001.

Index

337

338

diabetes   39, 103, 225
Dixon, L.   7, 10, 16
Duffy, B.   2, 315-6

ear disease   92-4, 106, 195, 209, 315; in adults 94
education: adult   72;
    ear disease affecting   93, 94;
    level of   28, 29
Edwards, E.   7, 16
Edwards, M.   36

family planning   220-33; attitudes to 220-3, 227; communication about 229-30;
    knowledge about 221-3; provision of 223-5; religion and 228-9; social and
    psychological factors affecting 226-33; tubal ligation 222, 231-2
Family Planning Association   224, 232
Family Resettlement Scheme   58, 63, 171
Ferguson, W.   272
field officers   52, 68, 69, 298, 319, 320; election of 52, 53, 323
FitzPatrick, J.   25, 51
Frith, N.   215

gastroenteritis   167
Gaynor, D. Sr,   316
Giardia lamblia   87, 88, 208
Gillon, N.   324
'Gub'   5
gynaecological disorders   102-3, 225, 227

Hall, G.   x
Halloway, C.   246
Harrison, G.   7
Hausfeld, R.   37
headache   127, 132, 142, 143, 161
head lice   96
health education   164, 208-10, 215
health services   191-203; accessibility of 204-7; consumerism and 202, 218; co-
    ordination of 210-2, 216-9; cultural differences between providers and consumers of
    196-9, 206; delivery of 214-9; evaluation of 201-2; fee for service 215-6; fragmen-
    tation of 199-203, 211; the inverse care law 196; punctuality and 207-8
heart disease   100, 101, 105
Hollows, F.   92, 285
hospitalisation   106-7, 169-70, 193-4, 202, 314; follow up 201; from alcohol 149; from
    ear disease 94; from gastroenteritis 167; from respiratory disease 95
housing   27, 174-90, 324; ballot for 302-3, 324; and health 141-2, 178-84; opposition to
    housing project 299-300; self-help project 294-310
Human Ecology of the Arid Zone Project   2, 3, 236
Human Relations Workshop   48, 49, 55, 57, 69, 70, 77-8, 297, 324
hypertension   100

339

Iceton, N.   48, 70, 297
immunisation   63, 194, 199, 201, 210
Indian nuns   47, 48, 192
infant feeding   165; weaning 167-8
intestinal parasites   87, 88

job expectations   171-3
johnny cakes   111, 115
Jones, D.   x
Joseph, S.   xii, 298

Leighton, A.   125, 256
Lickiss, N.   136, 203
Lippmann, L.   236
Long, J. P. M.   236
Lovejoy, F.   187
Luckens, J.   xi, 55, 57, 64, 65, 66, 79, 278, 287, 324
Lucas, W.   xi, 324

McDermott, G.   7, 45
Maroulis, J.   195
Medical and Hospital Benefit Funds   194-5, 196, 205, 215
medical students   243-6, 321; knowledge of Aborigines 244
Mitchell, I.   51
Mitchell, T.   13
Moodie, P. M.   203, 213, 214
Morrall, A.   117, 123, 124
mortality: adult   84, 85;
    infant   84, 85, 313
Murphy, B.   x
'Murrie'   5
'Mystery Stones'   10

National Aborigines' Day walkout   57, 58, 61, 289
New South Wales Housing Commission   139, 140, 175, 185, 186-8, 190, 295, 300, 302;
    furniture and facilities 189
Nobile, S.   x
Nurcombe, B.   2, 36, 57
nutrition   108-17; bottle feeding 165-7; breast feeding 165-7, 181; diet 111; for-
    tification of flour 115; height and weight 108; School Milk Scheme 113, 117; 'the
    Secret Bread Tests' 117-24; vitamin deficiencies 108, 109, 110-1; weaning 167-8

O'Lantern, J.   7, 38

Payton, M. Sr   210, 316, 327
Personal Discomfort Questionnaire   141-3
petrol sniffing   135

341